GENRE AND THE PERFORMANCE
OF PUBLICS

GENRE AND THE PERFORMANCE OF PUBLICS

Edited by
MARY JO REIFF
ANIS BAWARSHI

UTAH STATE UNIVERSITY PRESS
Logan

© 2016 by the University Press of Colorado

Published by Utah State University Press
An imprint of University Press of Colorado
5589 Arapahoe Avenue, Suite 206C
Boulder, Colorado 80303

 The University Press of Colorado is a proud member of
The Association of American University Presses.

The University Press of Colorado is a cooperative publishing enterprise supported, in part, by Adams State University, Colorado State University, Fort Lewis College, Metropolitan State University of Denver, Regis University, University of Colorado, University of Northern Colorado, Utah State University, and Western State Colorado University.

The paper used in this publication meets the minimum requirements of the American National Standard for Information Sciences—Permanence of Paper for Printed Library Materials. ANSI Z39.48-1992

ISBN: 978-1-60732-442-3 (paperback)
ISBN: 978-1-60732-443-0 (e-book)

Library of Congress Cataloging-in-Publication Data
Names: Reiff, Mary Jo, editor. | Bawarshi, Anis S., editor.
Title: Genre and the performance of publics / edited by Mary Jo Reiff, Anis Bawarshi.
Description: Logan : Utah State University Press, [2016] | Includes bibliographical references and index.
Identifiers: LCCN 2016007494| ISBN 9781607324423 (pbk.) | ISBN 9781607324430 (ebook)
Subjects: LCSH: Literary form. | Rhetoric—Political aspects. | Rhetoric—Social aspects.
Classification: LCC PN45.5 .G4585 2016 | DDC 808—dc23
LC record available at http://lccn.loc.gov/2016007494

Cover photograph © VTT Studio/Shutterstock.

CONTENTS

ACKNOWLEDGMENTS

With our book's focus on the extra-textual factors (material, embodied, affective) that inform public genre performances, it seems only right to acknowledge the factors that significantly contributed to and made this book possible, beginning with the professional, expert, and extremely efficient editorial process at Utah State University Press and University Press of Colorado.

We would first like to extend our thanks to Michael Spooner for his careful attention to and feedback on our project, from the proposal to the production stage and everything in between. We are grateful for his generous guidance and support of the project. We would also like to thank the external reviewers, who provided valuable feedback that strengthened the book and clarified the contribution of each chapter. As we moved from the review stage to the production stage, we were in excellent hands with Laura Furney, managing editor, who expertly supervised the production process (coding, copyediting, typesetting, proofreading, etc.) and ensured that this process went as smoothly as possible. And for her careful copyediting, we thank Kami Day. In addition, Dan Pratt was a pleasure to work with as he guided us through the process of selecting cover art and putting together the cover layout for our book.

Most of all, we would like to thank the contributors to this collection. Our vision for the book was to explore the heterogeneous, polycontextual, and multidirectional performances of genres in public spaces, and this vision was taken up and realized through the vibrant work of our contributors whose innovative research on public genres illuminated, enriched, complicated, and transformed our understanding of the dynamic and multidimensional uptakes of public genres.

As the chapters that follow illustrate, genre performances and the formation of publics are shaped through coalitions, collective and communal actions, conversations, and collaborations—crucial connections that also informed our book. To our family and friends; colleagues in Rhetoric and Composition and Rhetorical Genre Studies; and our students, we are deeply indebted. And to each other, we are deeply grateful for the collaboration that sustains us.

GENRE AND THE PERFORMANCE
OF PUBLICS

Introduction
FROM GENRE TURN TO PUBLIC TURN
Navigating the Intersections of Public Sphere Theory, Genre Theory, and the Performance of Publics

Mary Jo Reiff and Anis Bawarshi

Over the past thirty years, scholarship in rhetorical genre studies (RGS) has contributed a great deal to our understanding of how genres mediate social activities within academic and workplace settings, providing insight into how systems of related genres coordinate ways of knowing and doing within institutional contexts as well as how individuals enact these ways of knowing and doing through available genres. From this scholarship has emerged a view of genres as both social (typified, recognizable, and consequential ways of organizing texts, activities, and social reality) and cognitive (involved phenomenologically in how we recognize, encounter, and make sense of situations) phenomena. In this way, genres help us define and make sense of recurring situations while providing typified rhetorical strategies for acting in recurrent situations.

More recently, scholars in RGS have begun to examine the inter- and intrageneric conditions (material, embodied, temporal, affective) that inform individuals' genre performances or what Anne Freadman (1994; 2002; 2012; 2014), extending the work of J. L. Austin in speech act theory, has called *uptakes*, which account for the dynamics of agency and the contingent, impromptu, multidirectional performances of genre in real time and space. Attention to genre uptakes—to the interconnections, translations, and pathways between genres—extends a core understanding in RGS of genres *as* social actions, first proposed by Carolyn Miller (1984). While the conceptualization of genres as social actions was groundbreaking and has generated a wealth of research on the role genres play in producing social actions, a focus on genres as forms or sites of social action (as social artifacts that store cultural memory and that, through their typifications, can tell us things about how individuals define recurrence and acquire social motives to act in certain ways)

DOI: 10.7330/9781607324430.c000

implies that genres *themselves* perform social actions (Freadman 2014). While genres orient us in relation to situations and provide strategies for responding to and acting in situations, and while genres "persist because they frame what they permit as that which is possible" (Dryer 2008, 506), it is only in the uptakes they routinize (but never completely determine) that genres are performed as social actions. In part because of its focus on genres as mediating tools within fairly stable activity systems such as academic and workplace settings, RGS has paid less attention to the uptakes between genres where performances of social action take place. In focusing attention on public genres and their uptakes, this collection aims to extend RGS beyond its traditional focus on relatively bounded institutional settings (workplace, professional, and academic disciplinary contexts) and into public domains where publics exist as assemblages of interconnections continuously performed and transformed in relation to one another; where networks of genres exist in less predictable or hierarchical, more heterogeneous, polycontextual ways (see Spinuzzi 2008); and where genre uptakes are more diffuse and emergent. It is within these interplays and trans-actions between genres that the performances of publics take place.

Despite Freadman's (2002; 2012) description of genre uptakes as dynamic, multidirectional, and based in selection rather than causation (involving agency rather than predetermination), a focus on institutional contexts within genre research has tended to foreground the stabilizations (even if "for now" in Schryer's [2002] well-known formulation) of genre and their trained uptakes, in which, say, a call for papers leads to a proposal, a verdict is a precursor to a sentencing, or an assignment prompt gets taken up as a student paper, which gets taken up in teacher feedback, and so forth. When studying genres within academic and professional settings, genre scholars have identified what Janet Giltrow has called "meta-genres" as well as other forms of apprenticeship that guide genre acquisition and uptakes (Giltrow 2002). As Giltrow has described, metagenres such as writing guides and professional manuals all serve to discipline genre performances within activity systems, attempting (to varying degrees) to coordinate the pathways through which genre uptakes relate to one another in the achievement of expected object-motives. But what about less clearly defined public contexts that function less as systems and more as assemblages in which object-motives are not as shared, in which the meditational means are more wide ranging and subject to transformation, in which participants are not as institutionally ranked and roles are not as clearly demarcated, and in which genre uptakes are less "disciplined" and predictable? What can genre scholarship learn from attention to such public contexts? And what can public scholarship learn from genre research? In its theoretical and methodological framework as well as its case studies, this book aims to address these questions.

Towards that end, the book brings together scholars whose work adds insight into how publics and the performances of public life are textually embodied and mediated through genre networks and whose perspectives on genre account for complex relations between rhetorical and material conditions that can enrich our understanding of genre evolution and change in all contexts. Our aim is threefold: (1) to fill a gap in rhetorical genre studies' attention to public genres, (2) to bring rhetorical genre studies into dialogue with public sphere scholarship in ways we hope will contribute to both areas of study, and (3) to enrich an understanding of public genres as dynamic performances that can contribute to research on and the teaching of public discourse.

In this introductory chapter, we explore the intersections of rhetorical genre studies and public sphere scholarship, with a focus on overlapping interests in the relationship between discursive formations and the formations of public life and an examination of the ways in which genres serve as both occasions for productive interaction/resistance and frameworks for critical analysis of publics. We will also explore a more recent focus in both areas of study on the material conditions that shape genre uptakes and the formation of publics and counterpublics. This attention to the dynamics of genre uptakes and the materiality of public performances can provide a critical framework for studying processes of public engagement and can contribute to our understanding of public performances—in ways that reveal what we stand to gain when we bring RGS and public sphere scholarship into critical dialogue.

RHETORICAL GENRE STUDIES AND PUBLIC SPHERE SCHOLARSHIP: INTERSECTIONS

In our overview of genre studies, *Genre: An Introduction to History, Theory, Research, and Pedagogy* (Bawarshi and Reiff 2010), we note the occurrence of a "genre turn" in rhetoric and composition studies, a reconceptualized view of genre as social action that was formulated approximately three decades ago and has subsequently informed research and pedagogy. Likewise, more recently, theorists such as Paula Mathieu (2005) and others have argued that the vibrant and dynamic development of public rhetoric scholarship has led, over the past decade, to a "public turn" that has expanded the field's perspectives on the complex performances of public texts and the rhetorical enactments of readers and writers within public contexts (see, for example, Ackerman and Coogan 2010; Deans 2003; Mathieu 2005; Welch 2008; Wells 1996; and Weisser 2002). However, these so-called turns—the "genre turn" and the "public turn"—seem to be moving in different directions and have not intersected, producing little cross-dialogue. Just as Frank Farmer (2013) in *After the Public Turn* notes our field's general inattentiveness to counterpublics despite the public turn, there is a similar inattentiveness to publics and counterpublics in the subfield of RGS, which has primarily focused on genre systems within more defined and delimited institutional contexts, like classrooms and workplaces. With some notable exceptions—for example, Bazerman's (1999; 1994; 2002) studies of letters, patents, or tax forms; Miller's (1980) study of environmental impact statements; Campbell and Jamieson's (1990) study of political speeches; Makmillen's (2007) study of land deeds; Dryer's (2008) study of zoning codes; Miller and Shepherd's (2009) study of blogs; and various studies of journalistic genres (Bonini 2009; Caple 2009; Ramos 2009)—few studies of genre have focused on the more dispersed, dynamic performances of public life and on genres that occasion public deliberation, mediate rhetorical and public interactions, and inform collective public action.

Furthermore, scholars of RGS (who primarily locate themselves within the field of rhetoric and composition) and public sphere scholars (who primarily locate themselves within the field of communication studies) have not been in conversation with one another despite a shared interest in the discursive dimensions and formations of publics and the mediation of public opinion. Genre scholar Charles Bazerman, in his exploration of generic sites for citizen identity and participation, calls for rhetoricians to examine how a public, through its genres, "speaks and inscribes itself into existence" and how "individuals talk and write themselves into citizens" (Bazerman 2002, 34). Similarly, public sphere scholar Gerard Hauser, through his rhetorical model of public spheres, is interested in how "the foundations of publics, public spheres, and public opinions reside in the rhetorical transactions of a society" and how "our understanding of reality is a function of how we talk and write about it" (Hauser 1999, 273). RGS scholars' view of genres "as both organizing and generating kinds of texts and social actions, in complex, dynamic relation to one another" (Bawarshi and Reiff 2010, 4)—mediating between what John Swales (1998) has called "lifeways" and "textways"—is further reflected in rhetorical approaches to public discourse. In *Citizen Critics*, public sphere scholar Rosa Eberly argues that the relationship between textual practices and social practices can be clearly seen by "analyzing the contours of public debate as reflected in the rhetorical strategies of participants' discourses" (Eberly 2000, 163). Other public sphere scholars have more explicitly acknowledged how a rhetorical approach based in genre analysis would refocus attention on the ways public discourse is embedded in its cultural settings, reflecting its history and ideology. As Stephen Lucas argues, "Rhetorical critics would seem well advised to give more intensive consideration to the interplay of generic constraints and the particular historical situations out of which rhetorical genres evolve and in which they operate. This is one step to producing a more powerful body of scholarship that moves beyond describing what rhetorical genres look like to explaining why they look that way and how they function" (Lucas 1986, 212). Both RGS and public sphere scholars seem to agree that we can gain insight into public cultures by examining the rhetorical interactions that converge around public issues and that construct publics—that is, by examining discursive artifacts such as public genres for the role they play in the performance of publics.

Public sphere scholars have noted that "a rhetorical construction of public opinion begins . . . when a pattern of sentiment—thoughts, beliefs, and commitments to which a significant and engaged segment of the populace holds attachments that are consequential for choices individuals are willing to make and actions they are prepared to support in shaping their collective future—emerges from deliberative exchanges among those within a public sphere" (Hauser 1999, 96). RGS scholars envision these patterns of thoughts and beliefs that emerge from and coordinate collective action as the typifications of situations, goals, or tasks deployed in genres, which "symbolically create social order and coordinate social actions" (Bawarshi and Reiff 2010, 74). The role genre plays in the formation and shaping of communal knowledge is suggested in Hauser's rhetorical model of the public sphere, which is defined as "a discursive space in which individuals and groups associate to discuss matters of mutual interest and, where possible, to reach a common judgment about them. It is the locus of emergence for rhetorically salient meanings" (1999, 61). While Hauser (1999) does not use the term *genre*, his case studies investigating the rhetorical formation of publics feature constellations of genres that coordinate complex social actions and reflect the emergence of rhetorically salient meanings. For example, in his case study of the controversial Meese Commission Report on pornography, he focuses on how various genres—such as the report issued by the State Department of Justice in 1986 (*Final Report of the Attorney General's Commission on Pornography*), dissenting opinions to the report, evidence (photos, videos), the commission charter, popular-press stories, magazine features, interviews, news conferences, letters from the public, previous court cases, public hearings, and witness tes-timony—all interacted to shape public opinion and action and, in this case, to move the terms of public debate from the issue of censorship to the methodologies of the commission itself, thus limiting public dis-cussion. Overall, while public sphere scholars have not explicitly used a genre lens for exploring public discursive interactions, they share a focus with RGS on "the communicative and epistemic functions mani-fest in the range of discursive exchanges among those who are engaged by a public problem" (Hauser 1999, 109); furthermore, it is this focus on public problems and public exchanges that can inform genre stud-ies by turning scholars' attention to the varied, multiple, and dispersed interactions within public networks of genres.

Public sphere scholars' now well-documented challenges to an ideal-ized, normative, and stable Habermasian public sphere[1] and their explo-ration of the dynamic discursive engagements within multiple publics (see, for example, Felski 1989; Fraser 1996; Hauser 1999; Warner 2002) parallel RGS's challenge to conventional definitions of genres as static systems of classification and move to a more dynamic definition of how genres' formal features "are connected to social purposes and to ways of being and knowing in relationship to these purposes" (Bawarshi and Reiff 2010, 4). Hauser and other public sphere scholars share the belief that "interrogating the process by which rhetorically salient meanings are created and embedded dialogically helps us decipher the persua-sive force of identifications in the process of public opinion formation" (Hauser 1999, 61). RGS scholars, by providing an analytical framework for examining "the persuasive force of identifications" and for exam-ining why and how genres function as "sites of social and ideological action" (Schryer 2002), have contributed to such interrogations. The ideological function of genre has been studied by numerous scholars who are interested in how, as writers reproduce and replicate genres, genres simultaneously work to reproduce and reinforce power relations within and between individuals and social organizations (see, for exam-ple, Artemeva 2006; Bazerman 2001; Benesch 1993, 2001; Casanave 2003; Paré 2002; Schryer 2002; Swarts 2006; Winsor 2000; Yates and Orlikowski 2002).

These culturally embedded meanings and identifications, as pointed out by both RGS and public sphere scholars, can function hegemoni-cally in the service of the status quo, leading to the exclusion of par-ticular perspectives from discursive forums. In recognizing genres as sites of social and ideological intervention, RGS scholars have encouraged a critical consciousness of genres and an awareness of how they both enable and limit access and privilege certain users (Paré 2002; Schryer 2002; Winsor 2000) and have recognized the need for alternative genres, hybrid genres, or "antigenres" (Peters 1997). Similarly, public sphere scholars have studied the emergence of counterpublics, or discursive entities that function as alternatives to wider publics that exclude the interests of potential participants, such as Michael Warner's (2002) work on queer counterpublics, Rita Felski's (1989) work on feminist counterpublic spheres, and Nancy Fraser's (1996) recognition of multiple public arenas, oppositional publics, or "subaltern counterpublics." Just as the constraints and conventions of genres can lead to the creation of alternatives, the norms of dominant groups within the public sphere can lead to alternative norms of public speech (or what Fraser calls "counterdiscourses") and styles of political behavior that enable the formation of oppositional identities and uptakes. To illustrate her point, Fraser focuses on the "feminist subaltern counterpublic," which, through invention and circulation of counterdiscourses (and a constellation of public genres such as books, journal articles, films and video, lectures, meetings, conferences, etc.), is able to invent "new terms for describing social reality" (Fraser 1996, 67). More recently, Fraser has critiqued the correspondence between normative public spheres and existing global realities and has defined a "transnational public sphere" that "overflow[s] the bounds of both nations and states" (Fraser 2014, 8), an idea that has also drawn the interest of media studies scholars, such as danah boyd (2010), who have explored the affordances of global communication across "networked publics." Indeed, a focus on the multiplicity of publics and on marginalized or oppositional publics within public sphere scholarship can inform critical approaches to genre—expanding perspectives on public genres and their uptakes as emergent and enacted through complex ecologies of publics. Conversely, RGS's focus on generic sites of articulation—where genres work to reproduce and reinforce power relations within and between individuals and cultures—can inform public sphere scholarship by focusing attention on the ideological discursive sites where multiple publics are enacted and potentially transformed.

In the chapters that follow, contributors examine the multiplicity of publics, from the transnational publics that coalesce around a digital campaign to end violence against women; to the networked publics of climate-change blogs, web-based public-health campaigns, and Internet discourse on radiation risk; to the overlapping discursive arenas (professional, technical, personal, public) within jury deliberations and within a Canadian public inquiry. Contributors also explore the range of ways dominant genres—such as the English-language dictionary, the public petition, or women's vocational guides—manage public identities and participation and the ways in which marginalized and oppositional groups resist, transform, and deploy alternative genres to perform counterdiscourses—from the interdiscursive, hybrid performances of a news magazine article, to the alternative uptakes within public discourse on Israel-Palestine, to citizens' interventions in urban planning.

UPTAKE AND PUBLIC GENRE PERFORMANCES

Given that both fields recognize the multiplicity of publics and public interactions as well as the ideological function and effects of public discourse, perhaps most relevant to this discussion of the intersection of RGS and public sphere scholarship is the potential for both genre scholars and public sphere scholars to use genre (or what Hauser [1999] calls "discursive indicators") to gain insight into and critically analyze public rhetorical performances—the complex, dynamic, situated, normalized as well as improvisational ecologies of uptakes that mobilize public life. Carolyn Miller has argued that a perspective on genre as situated action has methodological implications: "For the critic, genres can serve both as an index to cultural patterns and as tools for exploring the achievements of particular speakers and writers" (Miller 1984, 165). Miller has advocated what she calls an "ethnomethodological" approach, one that "seeks to explicate the knowledge that practice creates" (155)—knowledge rooted in the materiality of circumstances and conditions of actual use of genres. Similarly, Hauser, in his study of the rhetoric of publicness, explains that what sets apart his rhetorical model of publics is this "empirical framework," which "draws its inferences about publics, public spheres and public opinion from actual social practices of discourse" (Hauser 1999, 275). Through his systematic examination of not only official discourses or genres of institutions, political leaders, or the press but also the everyday or "vernacular" discourses and genres of marginalized publics or counterpublics, Hauser is able to describe the plurality of publics in which participants are engaged in multiple, local, interactive webs of meaning—employing an empirical approach that shares a critical framework with genre analysis, thus illustrating the potentially productive dialogue between RGS and public sphere scholarship that could enrich approaches to studying situated genre uptakes and performances of publics.[2]

An empirical and ethnomethodological attitude toward genre and public performances (one that pays attention to "actual social practices of discourse" and works to "explicate the knowledge that practice creates") calls our attention to uptake, a concept first introduced by J. L. Austin in his theory of speech acts and more recently adapted by Freadman to account for the interconnections, translations, and pathways between genres. In *How to Do Things with Words*, Austin (1962) introduced the idea of uptake as a way to explain how illocutionary force becomes a perlocutionary effect—how, that is, an intentional utterance (saying "it is hot in here") helps to produce an effect (one consequence being that someone opens a window) under certain conditions. Within Austin's theory of speech acts, uptake is offered as a fairly straightforward process secured by the apprehension (and then translation) of an intended illocutionary act. In bringing uptake into dialogue with genre study, Freadman complicates Austin's causal theory of uptake while offering RGS a way of accounting for the interplays and trans-actions between genres. In describing uptake as "the local event of crossing a boundary" (Freadman 2002, 43), Freadman draws attention not only to the relations between genres but also to how individuals move and translate across genres. In this sense, uptake can be understood both as a kind of in-between or trans-actional space as well as the effects or performances that result from this trans-action. This dual nature of uptake is captured in Freadman's formulation of uptake as "the bidirectional relation that holds" between genres (40). By "holding" genres together, uptakes enable meanings that are made possible from that set of relations. The seams between genres that uptakes weave, in other words, make movements and translations between and across genres possible.

Uptake accounts for and enables researchers to study the movements of actions and meanings between and across genres and publics. For example, returning to Hauser's study of the Meese Commission report on pornography, the genres serve as nodes within the public network—such as the report issued by the State Department of Justice, dissenting opinions to the report, evidence (photos, videos), the commission charter, popular-press stories, magazine features, interviews, news conferences, letters from the public, previous court cases, public hearings, and witness testimony. But in order to understand how these genres interacted to shape public opinion and action, we must examine the uptakes between and across these genres in ways that allow us to trace how these genres helped to move the terms of public debate from the issue of censorship to the methodologies of the commission itself. The pathways drawn, managed, and trans-acted between and across these genres facilitated and limited public discussion in ways that enabled certain performances of publics to take place.

Perhaps Freadman's most important contribution to the study of public uptakes is her claim that uptake "selects, defines, or represents its object" (Freadman 2002, 48). Uptake, she writes, "is first the taking of an object; it is not the causation of a response by an intention. This is the hidden dimension of the long, ramified, intertextual memory of uptake: the object is taken from a set of possibilities" (48). By selecting from a set of possibilities, the "holding" that uptakes perform can create a sense of seamlessness between genres that translate meanings and actions in fairly habitual, well-worn paths, especially within systems of genres that exist within institutional settings. At the same time, as Freadman demonstrates, intergeneric uptakes that occur outside of jurisdictional frames can be much more dynamic and unpredictable since it is there "that translation is least automatic and most open to mistake or even to abuse" (44), as Freadman's analysis of the conflict between the executive government and the judiciary in the Ryan death-penalty case reveals. Intergeneric uptakes are much more the norm within public spheres, where the relations that hold between genres are less enforced, where genre translations are more rhizomatic and more subject to mistake, abuse, and recontexualization.

By drawing our attention to what Vijay Bhatia in chapter 1 in this volume calls the "interdiscursive" factors that inform genre performances, uptake challenges us to consider history, materiality, embodiment, improvisations, emotion, and other *agentive* factors that shape genre performances in the spatial and temporal conditions of their use. Anis Bawarshi, in chapter 2, explores the complex material, dispositional, and affective factors that shape routinized uptakes and limit productive public deliberation on contentious topics, while Dylan Dryer, in chapter 3, examines the temporal and dispositional factors that shape various forms of uptakes within urban-planning contexts. Tosh Tachino, in chapter 9, analyzes the constraints and limitations of the "uptake paths" between research and policy genres while Jennifer Nish, in chapter 12, focuses on the distribution of uptakes used to coordinate public action. Uptake compels us to pay ethnomethodological and empirical attention to localized, strategic performances of genres in moments of interaction, an interaction captured in Hauser's claim that the "focus on actual discursive practices of leaders and citizens, borne of real-world experiences, . . . can help us to better understand how publics, public spheres, and public opinion form and function" (Hauser 1999, 281). Both RGS and public rhetoric scholars share an interest in how public performances, particularly those "borne of real-world experiences," are shaped not just by the symbolic landscapes but also by the material land-scapes, an intersection the next section will further explore.

PUBLIC PERFORMANCES, PUBLIC GENRES: NAVIGATING RHETORICAL AND MATERIAL UPTAKES

The intersection between RGS and public rhetoric scholarship contin-ues in recent movements within both areas to focus attention on not just symbolic landscapes but also on material conditions that shape public life and performances. A material approach to the study of pub-lic genres can complicate our understanding of the multifaceted fac-tors that position the performances of public actors with genre systems, produce exclusionary uptakes within these systems, and orchestrate citizens' actions and the multidirectional performances of genre in real space and time. In *Rhetorical Bodies* (Selzer and Crowley 1999), Barbara Dickson defines material rhetoric as "a mode of interpretation that takes as its objects of study the significations of material things and corporal entities—objects that signify not through language but through their spatial organization, mobility, mass, utility, orality, and tactility" (Dickson 1999, 297). Over the past decade, scholars in the field of rhetoric and composition and related fields have proposed a variety of perspectives on the intersections of multiple discourses and material practices, from ecological views of how "writing takes place" (Dobrin 2001), to spatial views that ground writing theory and practice in the material (Reynolds 2004), to perspectives on writing as an embodied practice (Aronson 1999; Brodkey 1996; Brandt 1995; Haas 1996; Marback 1998), to views on the material location of academic discourse (Horner 2000). More recently, scholars have focused on the material conditions influencing public discourse (Asen 2009; Brouwer 2006) and the posthumanistic relations between human and nonhuman (Hawk 2011).

RGS scholar Dylan Dryer has recently drawn attention to how uptakes of public genres (in this case, municipal zoning codes) have their basis in concrete, material conditions, noting that "close atten-tion to the materiality of uptake"—to the "specific material conditions through which readers and writers are 'taken up' into social relations when they 'uptake' a genre"—"helps us better understand the persis-tence of exclusionary systems of genre" (Dryer 2008, 504). Similarly, public scholar Robert Asen's recent work acknowledges the significance of the relationship between discourse and its material conditions, not-ing that scholars should add to their rhetorical study of public and counterpublic discourses and ideologies "a conception of materiality that places discourse in relation to the material conditions from which it arises and that it engages" (Asen 2009, 268). Likewise, Daniel Brouwer foregrounds a critical approach that would examine the links between material disparities and rhetorical practices, arguing that public scholarship should focus on "how various qualities and quantities of various resources delimit the available means of persuasion" (Brouwer 2006, 201). This potential for a materialist perspective to illuminate how public discourse limits participation—or enables participation in a way that forestalls change—is especially useful as a critical framework for studying publics and counterpublics.

In their recent work, *The Public Work of Rhetoric,* John M. Ackerman and David Coogan note that public rhetoricians often enter into public scenes with a "discursive divining rod"; however, "in most of our narratives we discover a pre-existing conspiracy against the common good in public life that cannot be determined through the intellectual prism of the hermeneutic interpretation" (Ackerman and Coogan 2010, 9). They invite rhetoricians to enter into the political and public life of the street and to study the rhetorical geographies and ways in which discursive acts are "conferred by the cultural economies of actual places" (17). Public sphere scholars and RGS scholars can help each other in this endeavor, public sphere scholars perhaps benefitting from a genre approach to studying situated rhetorical formations and RGS, with its privileging of typification, learning more about the varied material factors that affect the contingent, impromptu, multidirectional genre uptakes within publics.

CHAPTER OVERVIEWS

The chapters in part 1, "The Interdiscursivity of Public Genres: Dynamics of Uptakes, Agency, and the Performances of Public Life," advance multiple perspectives on the extratextual and material-historical factors that condition uptakes of public genres and shape public performances. In "Genre as Interdiscursive Performance in Public Space," Vijay Bhatia demonstrates how the concept of "interdiscursivity" (as appropriation of semiotic resources across genres, social practices, and disciplinary and institutional cultures) can enrich the study of public genres. Drawing on a public-media genre—a BBC news article analysis—Bhatia examines the appropriation of resources across disciplinary and public cultures, across media, and across private and public identities. Bhatia's chapter makes a compelling case for the value of interdiscursivity for the study of uptake and public genre performances.

Just as Bhatia draws our attention to the extratextual or interdiscursive factors that inform public genre performances, Anis Bawarshi, in "Between Genres: Uptake, Memory, and US Public Discourse on Israel-Palestine," focuses attention on the historical-material conditions that shape discursive performances, challenging both RGS and public sphere scholars to consider the interdiscursive relations and material, dispositional, and affective factors that may limit productive public deliberation on contentious topics. Bawarshi examines the normalized and routinized uptakes that work to maintain the rhetorical impasse in US public discourse about the Israel-Palestine conflict, in particular the way uptakes, informed by rhetorical memory, can precondition or overdetermine encounters with genres. The chapter suggests how genre and public sphere scholars might more productively intervene in public deliberation about contentious topics.

Further exploring the concept of uptake and an expanded notion of public agency, Dylan Dryer, in "Disambiguating Uptake: Toward a Tactical Research Agenda on Citizens' Writing," argues that a more nuanced understanding of various dimensions of uptake can contribute to more productive public participation and, in turn, that studies of public participation can contribute to and expand RGS's study of agency. Dryer explores various forms of uptake—and the interplay among generic responses—in order to better distinguish among factors that precede and shape encounters with public texts, the responses to public texts and enactments of alternatives, the temporal and dispositional factors that shape these discursive encounters, and the effects of public texts. Drawing on the various forms of uptakes within urban-planning contexts, and with a particular focus on the genre of citizen commentary, Dryer demonstrates a more complex construct of public agency and opens up new, more complex ways of understanding public participation.

Expanding part 1's focus on the extratextual, material, and affective factors that inform public performances, in "Part II: Historicizing Public Genres: Invention, Evolution, and Embodiment of Public Performances," the authors examine the historical-material factors and bodily dispositions that condition uptakes and challenge and complicate understandings of genre invention, genre evolution and change, and embodied genre performances. Examining a genre with wide public use and circulation, the dictionary, Lindsay Russell in "Defining Moments: Genre Beginnings, Genre Invention, and the Case of the English-Language Dictionary" draws our attention to a defining historical moment in which the early dictionary moved outside of highly restricted academic spaces to circulate broadly and serve a variety of publics, thus complicating and challenging RGS scholars' understanding of the "social typification" of genres and focusing instead on the multiple, variegated strategies used to invite public uptake. By focusing on the genre formation and invention of the dictionary as well as on the public debates surrounding the conception of the genre prior to its systematized uses, Russell demonstrates how the study of public genres within their historical and material conditions opens up spaces for reenvisioning genre invention as a form of public participation and generically mediated action.

The historical study of public genres not only enables a reconceptualization of genre invention as a rhetorical, strategic process but can also highlight the interaction between rhetoric and materiality and between rhetorical actions and public actions. Mary Jo Reiff, in "Geographies of Public Genres: Navigating Rhetorical and Material Relations of the Public Petition," examines the process of public engagement through petitioning—and the material location, production, distribution, and circulation of petitions—as a particularly rich site for studying rhetorical interventions in publics. She demonstrates that by grounding historical inquiry in the material, we can better understand the conditions that work to undermine public participation and preclude change and can productively complicate our conventional understanding of genre evolution and change.

Further focusing on the material-historical factors that condition genre performances, in "Bodily Scripts, Unruly Workers, and Public Anxiety: Scripting Professional Embodiment in Interwar Vocational Guides," Risa Applegarth examines how the public genre of the vocational guide—operating in a context of massive economic and cultural shifts after WWI as well as shifting labor and gender relations—manages professional spaces and women's performances in them. In particular, she explores the role vocational guides played in renegotiating public norms and public anxiety as women in the 1920s and 1930s entered professional work spaces, linking embodied performances of the "bodily scripts" provided in vocational guides to professional suitability and competence. Through her examination, we learn more about how genres perform an intermediary function—mediating between domestic and professional spaces and translating public anxiety into discursive practices that get taken up as embodied performances in the public sphere.

The intermediary function genres perform is the subject of "Part III: Intermediary Public Genres: Mobilizing Knowledge across Genre

Boundaries." In "Uncovering Occluded Publics: Untangling Public, Personal, and Technical Spheres in Jury Deliberations," Amy Devitt examines the genre of jury deliberations and their participation in a complex web of personal, technical, and public spheres. Devitt demonstrates that jury deliberations, while publicly consequential acts, are an occluded genre, with exemplars of the genre hidden from public view. While demonstrating how genres can fall short of accounting for the complexities of public participation, the chapter also reveals how genre study can give us access to occluded publics and explores the role of intermediary genres in managing the complex negotiation of shifting relations among personal, technical, and public spheres.

Exploring the interaction between intramediary and intermediary genres, Graham Smart, in "Discourse Coalitions, Science Blogs, and the Public Debate over Global Climate Change," examines how the interplay of uptakes performed via science blogs maintains entrenched positions within discourse coalitions in ways that limit public understanding and engagement. Drawing on concepts from rhetorical genre studies, he examines the discursive relationship between discourse coalitions focused on climate change and analyzes how the use of scientific blogs among these coalitions helps to reproduce and maintain a paradox of exclusive interaction. At the same time, he also demonstrates an alternative set of uptakes that can engage wider audiences and invite more productive public participation.

While Devitt and Smart explore how genres cross boundaries of personal, technical/professional, and public spheres, Tosh Tachino, in "Multiple Intertextual Threads and (Un)likely Uptakes: An Analysis of a Canadian Public Inquiry," explores the knowledge mobilization across boundaries of research genres and public-policy genres as expert knowledge is moved from formal research (in scientific articles) to active use in the process of public-policy decision making; he also examines the constraints and limitations of the "uptake paths" between research and policy genres. Within the intertextual network of public inquiry, this chapter enriches a networked understanding of uptakes and knowledge mobilization within public discourse, providing valuable insights into the ways expert knowledge can be brought into and work to influence public networks of genres.

This focus on the mobilization of knowledge across networks continues in "Part IV: Digital Public Genres: Mediating Public Engagement and Expanding Public Participation" with a focus on digital networks and the performance of genres within networked publics. In "Appropriating Genre, 'Taking Action' Against Obesity: The Rhetorical Work of Digital

Genre Systems in Public Discourse," Monica Brown focuses on a web-based public-health campaign and explores how a promotional site's appropriations of a government health site lend authority to the web campaign while simultaneously undercutting public action. This focus on public discourse within a web-based context contributes to an understanding of how public genres function within and intervene in networked systems of activity and usefully complicates our understanding of web-mediated public engagement.

Further focusing on public discourse within a web-based context, in "Exigencies, Ecologies and Internet Street Science: Genre Emergence in the Context of Fukushima Radiation-Risk Discourse," Jaclyn Rea and Michelle Riedlinger examine the Canadian Internet-based discourses that informed public discussions about the risks of radiation from the Fukushima nuclear incident and the public's active online engagement in creating and distributing risk-assessment information. Through their exploration of how Internet street scientists create/repurpose the multimedia genres they need to intervene in public discourse, their study sheds light on what happens when publics, enabled by new media platforms, legitimately participate in domains that, until recently, have been considered the domains of experts. Furthermore, they demonstrate how changes in technological affordances influence public exigencies and how Internet-based genres become sites of even greater public activity and public participation.

The powerful role new media platforms play in giving agency to particular publics is also the focus of Jennifer Nish's chapter, "Spreadable Genres, Multiple Publics: The Pixel Project's Digital Campaigns to Stop Violence Against Women." Nish explores the rhetorical tactics of an online global organization working to raise awareness of and stop violence against women. Drawing on the concept of spreadable media and taking into consideration the affordances of digital media, she examines the impact of what she calls "spreadable genres" on the formation and coordination of an activist public, with a focus on the genres of tweets and video interviews and their work in distributing messages to multiple publics. Her analysis of spreadable public genres and their multiple uptakes has implications for how we understand genre performance as distributive action and provides insights into the role of genre in the formation of activist publics.

Overall, contributors to this edited volume draw on scholarship in rhetorical genre studies in order to explore how genres shape the formation of publics and counterpublics, including how public genres mediate rhetorical and social interactions; define social exigencies;

inform public opinion, identity formation, and collective action; and serve as sites of resistance and change. At its core, this collection is interested in how genres, as typified rhetorical ways in which individuals recognize and respond to recurrent situations, contribute to the interconnected and dynamic performances of public life.

Notes

1. For comprehensive overviews of critiques of Jürgen Habermas's bourgeois public sphere (as described in his *Structural Transformation of the Public Sphere: An Inquiry into a Category of Bourgeois Society*), see Frank Farmer's (2013) introduction to *After the Public Turn: Composition, Counterpublics, and the Citizen Bricoleur* or Robert Asen and Daniel C. Brouwer's introduction to *Counterpublics and the State* (Asen and Brouwer 2010). Both works identify key challenges to Habermas's conception of the public sphere, from Oskar Negt and Alexander Kluge's conceptualization of a proletarian public sphere (Negt and Kluge 1993), to Nancy Fraser's (2014) and Michael Warner's (2002) widely known and oft-cited critiques.

2. A framework for exploring processes of public engagement—based on the concept of modalities—was recently introduced by public sphere scholars Robert Asen and Daniel Brouwer. Moving beyond the traditional definition of mode as a conduit for a message, they align modality with the rhetorical concept of techne, a productive art and domain of "intervention and invention" that envisions public engagement as "an active purposeful process" (Asen and Brouwer 2010, 19). The modality approach foregrounds purposive action and the "productive arts of crafting publicity," emphasizes *how* publicity is constituted rather than whom or what is publicized, and emphasizes dynamism and fluidity, which is more fitting for an increasingly pluralized public arena.

References

Ackerman, John M., and David Coogan. 2010. *The Public Work of Rhetoric: Citizen-Scholars and Civic Engagement.* Columbia: University of South Carolina Press.

Aronson, Anne. 1999. "Composing in a Material World: Women Writing in Space and Time." *Rhetoric Review* 17 (2): 282–99. http://dx.doi.org/10.1080/0735019990935 9246.

Artemeva, Natasha. 2006. "A Time to Speak, a Time to Act: A Rhetorical Genre Analysis of a Novice Engineer's Calculated Risk Taking." In *Rhetorical Genre Studies and Beyond*, edited by Natasha Artemeva and Aviva Freedman, 188–239. Winnipeg, MB: Inkshed.

Asen, Robert. 2009. "Ideology, Materiality, and Counterpublicity: William E. Simon and the Rise of a Conservative Counterintelligentisia." *Quarterly Journal of Speech* 95 (3): 263–88. http://dx.doi.org/10.1080/00335630903140630.

Asen, Robert, and Daniel C. Brouwer. 2010. *Public Modalities: Rhetoric, Culture, Media, and the Shape of Public Life.* Tuscaloosa: University of Alabama Press.

Austin, J. L. 1962. *How to Do Things with Words.* Oxford: Oxford University Press.

Bawarshi, Anis, and Mary Jo Reiff. 2010. *Genre: An Introduction to History, Theory, Research, and Pedagogy.* West Lafayette, IN: Parlor.

Bazerman, Charles. 1994. "Systems of Genres and the Enactment of Social Intentions." In *Genre and the New Rhetoric*, edited by Aviva Freedman and Peter Medway, 79–101. Bristol: Taylor and Francis.

Bazerman, Charles. 1999. "Letters and the Social Grounding of Differentiated Genres." In *Letter Writing as a Social Practice*, edited by David Barton and Nigel Hall, 15–30. Amsterdam: John Benjamins.

Bazerman, Charles. 2001. "Nuclear Information: One Rhetorical Moment in the Construction of the Information Age." *Written Communication* 18 (3): 259–95. http://dx.doi.org/10.1177/0741088301018003002.

Bazerman, Charles. 2002. "Genre and Identity: Citizenship in the Age of the Internet and the Age of Global Capitalism." In *The Rhetoric and Ideology of Genre: Strategies for Stability and Change*, edited by Richard Coe, Lorelei Lingard, and Tatiana Teslenko, 13–37. Cresskill, NJ: Hampton.

Benesch, Sarah. 1993. "ESL, Ideology, and the Politics of Pragmatism." *TESOL Quarterly* 27 (4): 705–17. http://dx.doi.org/10.2307/3587403.

Benesch, Sarah. 2001. *Critical English for Academic Purposes: Theory, Politics, and Practice.* Mahwah, NJ: Erlbaum.

Bonini, Adair. 2009. "The Distinction Between News and Reportage in the Brazilian Journalistic Context: A Matter of Degree." In *Genre in a Changing World*, edited by Charles Bazerman, Adair Bonini, and Débora Figueiredo, 199–225. Fort Collins, CO: WAC Clearinghouse and Parlor.

boyd, danah. 2010. "Social Network Sites as Networked Publics: Affordances, Dynamics, and Implications." In *A Networked Self: Identity, Community, and Culture on Social Network Sites*, edited by Zizi Papacharissi, 39–58. New York: Routledge.

Brandt, Deborah. 1995. "Accumulating Literacy: Writing and Learning to Write in the Twentieth Century." *College English* 57 (6): 649–68. http://dx.doi.org/10.2307/378570.

Brodkey, Linda. 1996. *Writing Permitted in Designated Areas Only.* Minneapolis: University of Minnesota Press.

Brouwer, Daniel C. 2006. "Communication as Counterpublic." In *Communication as . . .: Perspectives on Theory*, edited by Gregory J. Shepherd, Jeffrey St. John, and Ted Striphas, 195–208. Thousand Oaks, CA: SAGE. http://dx.doi.org/10.4135/9781483329055.n22.

Campbell, Karlyn Kohrs, and Kathleen Hall Jamieson. 1990. *Deeds Done in Words: Presidential Rhetoric and the Genres of Governance.* Chicago, IL: University of Chicago Press.

Caple, Helen. 2009. "Multi-Semiotic Communication in an Australian Broadsheet: A New News Story Genre." In *Genre in a Changing World*, edited by Charles Bazerman, Adair Bonini, and Débora Figueiredo, 247–58. Fort Collins, CO: WAC Clearinghouse and Parlor.

Casanave, Christine. 2003. *Controversies in L2 Writing: Dilemmas and Decisions in Research and Instruction.* Ann Arbor: University of Michigan Press.

Deans, Thomas. 2003. *Writing and Community Action: A Service-Learning Rhetoric and Reader.* New York: Longman.

Dickson, Barbara. 1999. "Reading Maternity Materially: The Case of Demi Moore." In *Rhetorical Bodies*, edited by Jack Selzer and Sharon Crowley, 297–313. Madison: University of Wisconsin Press.

Dobrin, Sidney I. 2001. "Writing Takes Place." In *Ecocomposition: Theoretical and Pedagogical Approaches*, edited by Christian Weisser and Sidney I. Dobrin, 11–25. Albany: SUNY Press.

Dryer, Dylan B. 2008. "Taking Up Space: On Genre Systems as Geographies of the Possible." *JAC* 28 (3–4): 503–34.

Eberly, Rosa. 2000. *Citizen Critics: Literary Public Spheres.* Champaign-Urbana: University of Illinois Press.

Farmer, Frank. 2013. *After the Public Turn: Composition, Counterpublics, and the Citizen Bricoleur.* Logan: Utah State University Press.

Felski, Rita. 1989. *Beyond Feminist Aesthetics: Feminist Literature and Social Change.* Cambridge, MA: Harvard University Press.

Fraser, Nancy. 1996. "Rethinking the Public Sphere: A Contribution to the Critique of Actually Existing Democracy." In *Habermas and the Public Sphere,* edited by Craig Calhoun, 109–42. Cambridge: MIT Press.

Fraser, Nancy. 2014. "Transnationalizing the Public Sphere: On the Legitimacy and Efficacy of Public Opinion in a Post-Westphalian World." In *Transnationalizing the Public Sphere,* edited by Kate Nash, 8–42. Malden, MA: Polity.

Freadman, Anne. 1994. "Anyone for Tennis?" In *Genre and the New Rhetoric,* edited by Aviva Freadman and Peter Medway, 43–66. Bristol: Taylor and Francis.

Freadman, Anne. 2002. "Uptake." In *The Rhetoric and Ideology of Genre: Strategies for Stability and Change,* edited by Richard Coe, Lorelei Lingard, and Tatiana Teslenko, 39–53. Cresskill, NJ: Hampton.

Freadman, Anne. 2012. "The Traps and Trappings of Genre Theory." *Applied Linguistics* 33 (5): 544–63. http://dx.doi.org/10.1093/applin/ams050.

Freadman, Anne. 2014. "Where Is the Subject? Rhetorical Genre Theory and the Question of the Writer." *Journal of Academic Language and Learning* 8 (3): A1–11.

Giltrow, Janet. 2002. "Meta-Genre." In *The Rhetoric and Ideology of Genre: Strategies for Stability and Change,* edited by Richard Coe, Lorelei Lingard, and Tatiana Teslenko, 187–205. Cresskill, NJ: Hampton.

Haas, Christina. 1996. *Writing Technology: Studies on the Materiality of Literacy.* Mahwah, NJ: Erlbaum.

Hauser, Gerard. 1999. *Vernacular Voices: The Rhetoric of Publics and Public Spheres.* Columbia: University of South Carolina Press.

Hawk, Byron. 2011. "Reassembling Postprocess: Toward a Posthuman Theory of Public Rhetoric." In *Beyond Postprocess,* edited by Sidney I. Dobrin, J. A. Rice, and Michael Vestola, 75–93. Logan: Utah State University Press.

Horner, Bruce. 2000. *Terms of Work for Composition: A Materialist Critique.* Albany: State University of New York Press.

Lucas, Stephen E. 1986. "Genre Criticism and Historical Context: The Case of George Washington's First Inaugural Address." *Southern Speech Communication Journal* 51 (4): 354–70. http://dx.doi.org/10.1080/10417948609372672.

Makmillen, Shurli. 2007. "Colonial Texts in Postcolonial Contexts: A Genre in the Contact Zone." *Linguistics and the Human Sciences* 3 (1): 87–103.

Marback, Richard. 1998. "Detroit and the Closed Fist: Toward a Theory of Material Rhetoric." *Rhetoric Review* 17 (1): 79–92. http://dx.doi.org/10.1080/07350199 809359232.

Mathieu, Paula. 2005. *Tactics of Hope: The Public Turn in English Composition.* Portsmouth, NH: Heinemann.

Miller, Carolyn. 1980. "Environmental Impact Statements and Rhetorical Genres." PhD diss., Rensselaer Polytechnic Institute.

Miller, Carolyn. 1984. "Genre as Social Action." *Quarterly Journal of Speech* 70 (2): 151–67. http://dx.doi.org/10.1080/00335638409383686.

Miller, Carolyn, and Dawn Shepherd. 2009. "Questions for Genre Theory from the Blogosphere." In *Genres in the Internet: Issues in the Theory of Genre,* edited by Janet Giltrow and Dieter Stein, 263–90. Amsterdam: John Benjamins. http://dx.doi.org /10.1075/pbns.188.11mil.

Negt, Oskar, and Alexander Kluge. 1993. *Public Sphere and Experience: Toward an Analysis of the Bourgeois and Proletarian Public Sphere.* Translated by Peter Labanyi, Jamie Owen Daniel, and Assenka Oksiloff. Minneapolis: University of Minnesota Press.

Paré, Anthony. 2002. "Genre and Identity: Individuals, Institutions, and Ideology." In *The Rhetoric and Ideology of Genre: Strategies for Stability and Change,* edited by Richard Coe, Lorelei Lingard, and Tatiana Teslenko, 57–71. Cresskill, NJ: Hampton.

Peters, Brad. 1997. "Genre, Antigenre, and Reinventing the Forms of Conceptualization." In *Genre and Writing: Issues, Arguments, Alternatives*, edited by Wendy Bishop and Hans Ostrom, 199–214. Portsmouth, NH: Boynton/Cook.

Ramos, Rui. 2009. "The Organization and Functions of the Press *Dossier*: The Case of Media Discourse on the Environment in Portugal." In *Genre in a Changing World*, edited by Charles Bazerman, Adair Bonini, and Débora Figueiredo, 223–42. Fort Collins, CO: WAC Clearinghouse and Parlor.

Reynolds, Nedra. 2004. *Geographies of Writing: Inhabiting Places and Encountering Differences*. Carbondale: Southern Illinois University Press.

Schryer, Catherine. 2002. "Genre and Power: A Chronotopic Analysis." In *The Rhetoric and Ideology of Genre: Strategies for Stability and Change*, edited by Richard Coe, Lorelei Lingard, and Tatiana Teslenko, 73–102. Cresskill, NJ: Hampton.

Selzer, Jack, and Sharon Crowley, eds. 1999. *Rhetorical Bodies*. Madison: University of Wisconsin Press.

Spinuzzi, Clay. 2008. *Network: Theorizing Knowledge Work in Telecommunications*. Cambridge: Cambridge University Press. http://dx.doi.org/10.1017/CBO9780511509605.

Swales, John. 1998. *Other Floors, Other Voices: A Textography of a Small University Building*. Mahwah, NJ: Erlbaum.

Swarts, Jason. 2006. "Coherent Fragments: The Problem of Mobility and Genred Information." *Written Communication* 23 (2): 173–201. http://dx.doi.org/10.1177/0741088306286393.

Warner, Michael. 2002. *Publics and Counterpublics*. New York: Zone.

Weisser, Christian R. 2002. *Moving Beyond Academic Discourse: Composition Studies and the Public Sphere*. Carbondale: Southern Illinois University Press.

Welch, Nancy. 2008. *Living Room: Reaching Public Writing in a Privatized World*. Portsmouth, NH: Boynton/Cook, Heinemann.

Wells, Susan. 1996. "Rogue Cops and Health Care: What Do We Want From Public Writing?" *College Composition and Communication* 47 (3): 325–41. http://dx.doi.org/10.2307/358292.

Winsor, Dorothy. 2000. "Ordering Work: Blue-Collar Literacy and the Political Nature of Genre." *Written Communication* 17 (2): 155–84. http://dx.doi.org/10.1177/0741088300017002001.

Yates, JoAnne, and Wanda Orlikowski. 2002. "Genre Systems: Chronos and Kairos in Communicative Interaction." In *The Rhetoric and Ideology of Genre: Strategies for Stability and Change*, edited by Richard Coe, Lorelei Lingard, and Tatiana Teslenko, 103–21. Cresskill, NJ: Hampton.

PART I

The Interdiscursivity of Public Genres

Dynamics of Uptakes, Agency, and the Performances of Public Life

1
GENRE AS INTERDISCURSIVE PERFORMANCE IN PUBLIC SPACE

Vijay K. Bhatia

Drawing on Mikhail Bakhtin's (1986) suggestion that texts are invariably dialogic and hence must be looked at and accounted for in the context of other relevant and related texts, it is possible to claim that writers or speakers often interdiscursively appropriate, directly or indirectly, discursive resources, including genre conventions, and often manage as well as manipulate discursive space and participant systems in an attempt to create novel and hybrid genres through rhetorical processes of recontextualization, reformulation, reframing, and resemiotization. Although I have discussed the function of interdiscursive appropriation of discoursal and generic resources in professional contexts elsewhere (see Bhatia 2010), I believe it has an even more significant role to play in public discourses of different kinds in realizing a variety of communicative intentions in various media. Drawing on the analysis of a typical instance of media discourse, this chapter aims to give more substance to this claim by elaborating on the notion of interdiscursivity as appropriation and management of discoursal resources in genre theory and by arguing for a multiperspective framework to analyze interdiscursive performance in public space. In providing a framework that accounts for text-external resources for understanding genre performance, interdiscursivity can contribute to rhetorical genre studies scholars' burgeoning interest in genre uptakes as dynamically localized and interconnected in ways especially useful for the study of public genres this volume undertakes.

Let me first briefly refer to a multiperspective framework I introduced earlier (Bhatia 2004) for the analysis of discourse within which I would like to consider such appropriations of interdiscursivity in public discourse.

DOI: 10.7330/9781607324430.c001

THREE-SPACE MODEL FOR GENRE ANALYSIS

In proposing a three-space multiperspective model for the analysis of written discourse in my earlier work (Bhatia 2004), I underpinned the importance of context in genre theory. The three overlapping concepts of space—which include textual, sociopragmatic (incorporating both genre-based discursive and professional practices), and, more generally, sociocultural—help a discourse analyst to focus more appropriately on one or more of these three dimensions of space to analyze and interpret discourse. In fact, if we look at the three-space model in more detail, we realize that most forms of discourse operate simultaneously within and across four somewhat distinct yet overlapping levels in order to construct and interpret meanings in specific contexts. Drawing on this framework (Bhatia 2004), these levels of realization can be identified as *discourse as text, discourse as genre, discourse as social practice*, and discourse as identity and culture, which can be represented as in Figure 1.1.

The interesting thing about discourse analysis is that although the ultimate product we can see is in the form of a text, it is made possible by a combination of complex and careful selection of resources, which may include lexico-grammatical, rhetorical, and discourse organization, all of which are text internal. In addition to these text-internal resources, other contributors to the construction of discourse are conventions of the genre in question, relevant aspects of the social practice in which the genre is situated, and the culture of the community, discipline, or institution, which constrains the use of textual resources for a particular discursive practice. Thus, any instance of discourse as communication is simultaneously realized, and hence can be analyzed, at four levels: as text, as representation of genre, as realization of social practice, and as indication of social and individual identity as well as culture. Identity includes disciplinary, institutional, and professional identities in addition to individual, ethnic, and, more generally, sociocultural identities.

These distinct levels of discourse realization highlight two kinds of relationship, one between discursive practice and social practice and the other between text-internal and text-external semiotic resources and constraints. Text-internal resources have been researched for quite some time within discourse and genre analytical literature highlighting the notion of intertextuality; however, text-external resources so far have not been treated in as much detail in discourse and genre analytical literature. Text-external resources, as mentioned earlier, include the discourse and genre conventions that constrain not only the construction but also the interpretation, exploitation, and use (including genre uptake) of texts as some of the key aspects of social practices. They also

SOCIO-CULTURAL PERSPECTIVE

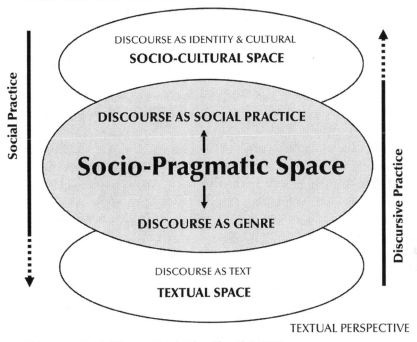

Multi-Perspective Model of Discourse Analysis (Adapted from Bhatia, 2004)

Figure 1.1. Multiperspective model of discourse analysis.

include social identities and various manifestations of culture that motivate these discourses and social practices.

INTERDISCURSIVE PERFORMANCE

The multispace model for genre analysis described above enables us to understand and account for the appropriation of textual as well as other semiotic resources and conventions at various levels of discursive engagement invariably exploited for the construction and interpretation of discursive as well as social, professional, disciplinary, and institutional practices, all of which can reveal interactive patterns of inter-textuality and interdiscursivity. The concept of interdiscursivity, which is sometimes subsumed under intertextuality, is not entirely new and can be traced back to the work of Bakhtin (1986), Candlin and Maley (1997), Fairclough (1995), Foucault (1981), Kristeva (1980), and, more recently, Bhatia (2004; 2010) and several others. However, these two concepts have not been fully explored and sufficiently developed to investigate some of the complexities we find in discursive and social practices within genre studies. To make an initial distinction between these two related concepts, we can begin by assuming that intertextuality refers to the use of prior as well as contemporaneous texts, in particular within the contexts of "genre sets" (Berkenkotter 2008; Devitt 1991), transforming the past into the present. Interdiscursivity, on the other hand, refers to more innovative attempts to create various forms of hybrid and relatively novel genres by appropriating or exploiting established conventions or discoursal resources associated with other genres and social practices. Interdiscursivity thus accounts for a variety of discursive and social practices, often resulting in "mixing," "embedding," and "bending" of generic norms in professional contexts (Bhatia 1995; 1997; 1998; 2004). Interdiscursivity thus can be viewed as appropriation of semiotic resources (which may include textual, semantic, sociopragmatic, and generic) across any two or more different levels of discourse realization, especially those of genre, social practice, and disciplinary and institutional cultures (Bhatia 2010). Appropriations across texts thus give rise to intertextual relations, whereas appropriations across professional genres, practices, and cultures constitute interdiscursive relations. It must be pointed out that in most generic artifacts, intertextuality and interdiscursivity may be present simultaneously.

In order to develop a comprehensive and evidence-based awareness of the motives and intentions of such disciplinary, institutional, professional, and social practices (Swales 1998), we need to look closely at the multiple discourses, actions, and voices that play a significant role in the formation of specific discursive practices within relevant institutional and social frameworks in addition to the conventional systems of genres (Bazerman 1994) often used to fulfill professional objectives of specific disciplinary or discourse communities. This examination is possible only within the notion of interdiscursivity, which is an important function of appropriation of text-external generic resources across genres and social practices.

Before I proceed to discuss specific instances of interdiscursivity in public genres, I would like to give more substance to what I mean by text-external semiotic resources crucial for interpreting interdiscursivity as appropriation of generic resources. These text-external resources primarily include three kinds of factors, which make a particular genre possible (Bhatia 2004): discursive practices, discursive procedures, and social identities and different manifestations of culture.

Discursive practices, on the one hand, are essentially the outcome of specific discursive procedures and, on the other hand, are embedded in specific institutional cultures and realize various forms of identities, institutional as well as individual. Discursive practices include factors such as the choice of a particular genre to achieve a specific objective and the appropriate and effective mode of communication associated with such a genre. Discursive procedures are factors associated with the characteristics of participants authorized to make a valid and appropriate contribution; participatory mechanisms, which determine what kind of contribution a particular participant is allowed to make at what stage of the genre construction process; and the other genres that make a valid and justifiable contribution to the document under construction. Both these factors (discursive practices and discursive procedures) inevitably take place within the context of typical disciplinary, institutional, and professional cultures, which validate a particular genre and establish sociocultural identities.

Within our understanding of genres as interdiscursive practices, we see expert writers constantly operating within and across generic boundaries creating new but essentially related and/or hybrid (both mixed and embedded) forms to give expression to their "private intentions" within socially shared communicative practices and generic norms (Berkenkotter and Huckin 1995; (Bhatia 1994; Fairclough 1995). Interdiscursivity, therefore, spans discursive events and is often based on shared generic or contextual characteristics across two or more discursive constructs. Interdiscursivity thus can be viewed as a function of the *appropriation of generic resources* across three kinds of contextual and other text-external boundaries: genres, social practices, and identities and cultures. However, in the context of public discourse, it is also necessary to identify at least two other forms of management of discursive resources. One of them is the management and manipulation of discursive space and the other is the exploitation of available participant management systems to meet socially shared expectations and objectives—often mixing private and public discourses, on the one hand, and meeting and invariably exploiting the expectations of multiple audiences on the other. The exploitation of interdiscursive space is quite evident in the coconstruction of discursive practices leading to a creative manipulation of semiotic resources within the corporate world, especially in the context of annual corporate reports, which typically incorporate various disciplinary discourses, such as those of accounting, finance, public relations, and law within the same interdiscursive space in order to achieve the reports' professional objectives (Bhatia 2014). Participant management, on the other hand, is seen as a typical discursive resource to balance the expectations of various audiences, especially keeping in mind

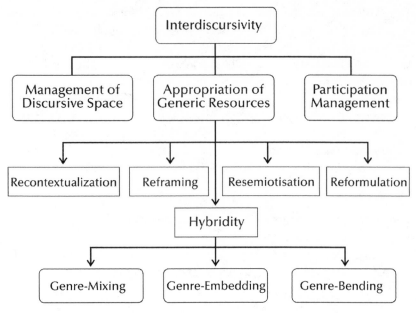

Figure 1.2. Range of genre appropriations.

the interpretation and uptake of discursive intentions, as is often the case in the construction of legislative discourse. It may also be pointed out that often these appropriations, whether text internal or text external, discursively operate simultaneously to realize the intended meaning. The full range of appropriations can be represented as in Figure 1.2 above, which has been adapted from the one in Bhatia (2012, 25).

In a similar fashion, WU (2011) refers to interdiscursivity as "the mixing of diverse genres, discourses, or styles associated with institutional and social meanings in a single text" (96). He mentions the case of medical interviews in China, in which the interdiscursive relations between the "standard medical interview genre and counseling, between the discourse types of the traditional Chinese medicine and the Western medicine" (96) are commonly displayed.

It is interesting to note that some of the important aspects of interdiscursivity, particularly the relationship between genres and actions, have been extensively explored in rhetorical genre studies within the notion of uptake on genres. Anne Freadman (1994) was perhaps the first one to introduce uptake to genre study by using the analogy of tennis to describe how genres get their meanings in relation to one another. For her, genres are like "games" that constitute their own rules for play within what she calls "ceremonials" for the exchange of texts that she regards as "shots." In a series of articles since then, Freadman's main objective has been to explore how individuals use genres to interact within particular contexts (what she refers to as "discursive events" [Freadman 2012]) to create meaning, just as "shots" are picked and returned in tennis within specific spatial and temporal convergences. Anis Bawarshi and Mary Jo Reiff use the notion of uptake to analyze complex transactions that mediate meanings and actions between genres (Bawarshi and Reiff 2010). Charles Bazerman (1997) takes a similar position when he talks about the nature of the interrelationship between different genres as "discursively structured activities." He claims everyday genres, such as sales receipts, have specific relationships with tax laws, corporate records, financial reports, and even economic indicators.

In what follows, I would like to take specific instances of interdiscursive performance from a variety of public contexts not only to illustrate that it operates at all levels—generic, social practice, and social identity and culture—but also to claim that it allows a more rigorous and comprehensive analysis of genres in social practice. At the same time, analysis of interdiscursive performance also encourages evidenced-based studies of public discourse and institutional practices and cultures through the genres they often use. I would like to take up instances of interdiscursivity from a number of media genres from different contexts, which result from an appropriation of generic resources across genres, practices, and/or cultures in and across public and private spheres.

INTERDISCURSIVE PERFORMANCE IN PUBLIC DISCOURSE

One of the most important and pervasive aspects of public discourse is the use of a private voice in the public domain. Media discourse, with its human interest in everyday affairs and in specialized content, often turns specialized disciplinary discourses into popularized versions to make them accessible to general readers. Another characteristic of media discourse is the use of personal opinions, often unverified, appropriated and interdiscursively transformed into public opinions in various contexts, as in letters to the editor, reviews of current developments, commentaries on current affairs, and even editorials. Other contexts of such hybrid discourses in the public domain are Internet public forums, talk shows on television, and, more recently, tweets, weblogs, and so forth. For our discussion here, issues such as how public opinions are interdiscursively represented in the media—through a variety of techniques (such as opinion polling and people-on-the-street interviews) and modes of construction, interpretation, and exploitation—are key instances of hybrids of private and public voices. It is also interesting to study and understand how such private discourses generated by these techniques are interdiscursively turned into public discourses, who contributes what to these opinions, and what makes these discursive events possible. How politicians and government officials invoke and contest the notion of public opinion in political debates is also interesting. Let us briefly look at some of the studies that highlight such interdiscursive events.

Ib Bondebjerg (1996), referring to television media, makes a relevant point, claiming that "soft, human interest journalism has arrived on television and private life stories have been lifted into public discourses, changing the established forms of journalism. At the same time new forms of television documentary—building on the documentary film tradition—have emerged, where hybridization of factual and fictional elements are found" (28). He further points out,

> Even though we need the difference between fact and fiction, and it is very fundamental in our social and communicative behaviour, it is also true that the difference is not basic on all levels. At a textual level, within segments of a text, it may be hard to draw a clear line, and even though the context, the communicative situation and the act of reference are different in most cases, it is also important to note that we use our life categories and our basic experiences and schemas when we relate both to fictional and factual forms. Our use of, and response to, programmes of a hybrid nature may both influence our public knowledge of social matters and our emotional, interpersonal understanding of life. Programmes like these raise the question of how public discourse and private fascination are combined on the textual and experiential level of interaction between programme and viewer. (Bondebjerg 1996, 28)

Reasserting Jürgen Habermas's (1987; 1989) assertion, he continues: "The hybridization of private and public discourse is often seen as a sign of simple decline, where the commercial powers of the system suppress the forces of the lifeworld" (Bondebjerg 1996, 28) in order to entertain rather than to give information, thus blurring the boundaries between factual forms and fiction, between private and public.

Candlin and Maley (1997) discuss the interdiscursive relations between bargaining, counseling, therapeutic, and legal genres in their study of mediation practices in Australia, claiming that the interdiscursive use of different social practices represents an attempt to incorporate strategies from related professional spheres (see also chapter 9's discussion of how professional scientific research is mobilized and actively used in the process of public-policy decision making). In addition to the role of a specialist, collaborator, and mediator, the doctor must also facilitate mutual understanding across different levels of specialist knowledge and understanding, convince patients about their diagnoses, motivate and promote different treatment options, and reassure patients about continued treatment.

Srikant Sarangi (2000), in a similar manner, points out that as health and social-care professionals are undergoing changing practices, the discourses are also changing within the social institution of health and family welfare. He rightly claims that caring professions like social work are adopting the role of service providers in conjunction with a market economy model, and this has implications for community care and consumer ethics. He further points out that genetic counseling constitutes "information giving," "advice seeking," and "decision making," each of which, he points out, is realized through different discourses motivated by strategic choices inspired by increasingly changing institutional contexts and sociopolitical developments.

Similarly, in professional legal contexts, members of the legal profession are adopting the role of service providers within a market economy model, and their practices, standards of services, attitudes toward their professional expertise, and professional identities have also undergone changes (for more on the intersection of public, personal, and technical within the legal sphere, see chapter 7 in this volume). In a similar fashion, Maurizio Gotti (2014), focusing on popularization for the purposes of making specialized knowledge accessible to nonspecialist readers for information purposes through recontextualization, makes an interesting point when he claims that an interdiscursively constructed popular version is characterized by its "lack of discussion . . . of new scientific knowledge added to the discipline's conceptual base" (16). He attributes this to the lack of shared disciplinary knowledge on the part of lay readers and to the essentially informative purpose of such texts. In his view, "Popularization often involves not only a reformulation of specialized discourse, but also a 'recontextualization' (Calsamiglia and Van Dijk 2004, 370) of scientific knowledge originally produced in specific contexts to which the lay public has limited access. This recontextualization implies a process of adaptation of popularization discourse to the appropriateness conditions of the new communicative events and to the constraints of the media employed, which have become quite varied in their nature and are often used in an integrated way" (Gotti 2014, 22–23). We often find other instances of such popularization in brochures and leaflets issued by governments in order to provide information regarding health policies (see chapter 10 in this volume for an analysis of a promotional website's appropriations of a government health site) and guidelines on new legislation, among many other such efforts. Popularizations, thus, are by far the most prolific category in which we find large-scale appropriations of disciplinary discourses for information or entertainment purposes in public space. Additional examples include business and scientific reports in newspapers and magazines for lay readers; sports reports in newspapers, which combine information for entertainment purposes; science fiction, both in print forms as well as on television; travel-related television programs; television programs and movies on law; medical-issue-related programs, such as hospital dramas; detective and crime-investigation-based dramas; documentaries and dramas based on real-life events and issues created for informative and entertainment purposes, to name only a few.

Another case of generic hybrids in public discourse is the appropriation of private discourse for public consumption, which includes letters to editors, representing personal opinions in public space. Even editorials, comments in newspapers, news analyses, and reviews of movies, restaurants, and other consumer products can be regarded as legitimate appropriations. Other cases of such extensive appropriations in new media include Facebook, Twitter and weblogs, which are becoming increasingly popular and have become the most powerful instruments of appropriation of private discourse in public space (see the discussions of science blogs in chapter 8, the emergence of Internet street science in chapter 11, and the formation of public digital campaigns in chapter 12).

Bawarshi and Reiff (2010, 261) report on a study by Débora de Carvalho Figueiredo (2009) in which she investigated personal accounts of three women about their cosmetic plastic surgery that appeared in the public media in Brazilian women's magazines, and she found that the personal accounts in the media performed "the social action of creating idealized identities that interpolate and imbricate individuals by and into gendered narratives" (quoted in Bawarshi and Reiff 2010, 158). Similarly, interdiscursivity can also manifest itself through recontextualization and resemiotization of information resulting in generic transfer, or what Kimberly Emmons (2009) calls "inter-generic translation" when she points out that "a consultation interprets patient *talk* as a series of *symptoms*; a diagnosis responds to *symptoms* with a *prescription*; a pharmacist transforms a *prescription* into a *medication*; and a patient ingests the *medication* in accordance with the *directives* on the bottle, thereby incorporating into the body a material response to an initial, purely rhetorical locution" (136). "In each of these translations," she adds, "a process legitimizes the connections between genres; both context (the office, laboratory, and pharmacy) and convention (the textual forms of professional legitimacy and the social rituals of prescribing), for example, must sanction the doctor's ability to write a prescription, and the pharmacist's to fill it" (136).

Another category of interdiscursive appropriation is in the form of hybrid genres, which includes genre mixing, genre embedding, or genre bending (Bhatia 2004) in conventional as well as in new media. In my discussion of professional discourse (Bhatia 1995), I give examples from several settings where genre mixing and embedding have become increasingly common. I also mention several instances in which one may find an increasing use of promotional strategies in genres traditionally considered nonpromotional in their communicative purposes. The examples include job advertisements and academic introductions, in which I found rather explicit indications of promotional elements, which traditionally have been regarded as purely informative, or at best persuasive, but certainly not promotional in the marketing sense. A closer look at these instances indicates that informative functions are more likely to be colonized by promotional functions rather than are any other functions. As I point out (Bhatia 1993), the most popular promotional strategy in advertising has been *to describe and evaluate a product or service in a positive manner*, which may be seen as the information-giving function of language. These two functions of language, informational and promotional, are therefore unlikely to create tension, even if they may not be entirely complementary to each other. A number of such instances of mixed genres are getting established, and these genres are being given innovative names, such as *infomercial, infotainment,* or *advertorial.* Although it may appear that this kind of genre mixing is more common in genres that are less likely to create functional tension, it would be wrong to assume that will always be the case. It is possible to view this subtle colonization of genres in terms of appropriation and ultimate mixing of genres, depending upon the degree of invasion one may find in individual members of a colony.

Advertorials are prime examples of such mixed genres. Others include job advertisements, which sometimes function as both a promotion for the company and a job description. Recent academic job advertisements from universities are typical of such efforts. In new media, websites, which are typical of mixed genres, serve a number of different purposes, including informative, promotional, and marketing. Examples of embedded genres we typically find in advertisements that exploit embedded generic forms include scientific reports, celebrity endorsements or testimonials, sometimes poetic forms, letter forms, and so forth. Sujata S. Kathpalia (1992) calls these "pretend genres" as they are not exactly what they appear to be; the real purpose is promotion and marketing.

INTERDISCURSIVE SPACE AND PARTICIPATION MANAGEMENT: AN ILLUSTRATION

Bawarshi and Reiff (2010), referring to the recent interest in studies of genre and new media, rightly point out how "participation in genres and genre systems is not only shaped by activity systems, social groups, and organizations—whether academic, work-place, or public—but by medium, with researchers using genre as a tool to explore how communicative practices across contexts are influenced by new media" (160). They rightly point out that these studies "seek to explore how established print genres are imported into a new medium or how genre variants or even new genres develop and emerge in electronic environments" (160), which they refer to as the "principle of genre re-mediation," that is, how familiar genres are imported into new mediums. In addition to the management of private discourse in public space, it is also possible to exploit the system of participant management, particularly in the context of new media.

To give more substance to some of these interdiscursive aspects of genres in public space, I would now like to take an example from the BBC News online magazine, which seems to be very rich in multimodality, generic hybridity, and the mixing of several different private and public genres and styles. It is essentially a hybrid genre that combines aspects of news report, editorial, letters to the editor, and other kinds of comment on or analysis of issues. At the same time, it mixes different forms of new media, electronic as well as visual. Using Erving Goffman's famous metaphor of "on-stage" and "off-stage" performance, one can see these performances interdiscursively exploited in this genre of news magazine in which an off-stage performance, that is, private discourse, becomes an on-stage act in public space. This dynamic mode of communication allows the pushing of boundaries imposed by conventional communication modes toward incorporating multiparty issues, agendas, and so forth to encourage multiparty dialogue in a virtual space where self-representation takes on new value.

The article, entitled "No Country for Single Women," begins with a headline followed by a not-so-typical summary or lead, which introduces the key idea, issue, or problem that is the focus of the hybrid of a feature article and a news report, embedding private discourse in a public space. It may appear to be like a summary we so typically find in the everyday news report to indicate the nature of the report. In this case, though, it is something more than just a report; it also makes use of personal narrative. Let us look at the lead: "For many young people, India is a land of opportunity. Male or female, if you're well educated and resourceful there's the chance of a well-paid career. Just one problem, says Suruchi Sharma—if you're a woman, you must marry by your mid-20s" (BBC 2014). The feature opens with a dialogue, thus bringing in another genre.

> "Single? Why, what's your age?"
> "28."
> "Okay, that's too bad. How are you managing it? Couldn't find anyone?"

Thus far, we have already seen a mixture of three genres—news report, feature article, and dialogue—which is one of the key aspects of appropriation across genres within my conceptualization of interdiscursivity. It also is an excellent illustration of what I have referred to above as management of interdiscursive space. The article then proceeds to recontextualize the dialogue, creating a personal narrative account that is a mix of informal and casual style, often deviating into a dialogue format. It then moves forward in the form of a private discourse, including a few personal pictures of the narrator and the family for public consumption.

> Welcome to the conversation that a single woman in India, in her late 20s, faces almost all the time. Yes, it's a big deal if you're 28 and unmarried. You're looked upon as a big failure. I am serious.
> I live in Mumbai, the biggest metro city in India. I belong to a typical urban middle-class family. My life is the same as that of many young women who move away from home and pursue their dream of an independent life.
> How does it feel to be living in the city on my own? It's awesome! I'm independent with a lifestyle I used to dream of. (BBC 2014)

After this brief opening, the news-cum-feature article begins to shape into an editorial style of argumentative discourse almost completely based on the private experiences of a twenty-eight-year-old protagonist. It is different from a typical editorial, as it does not represent the voice of the newspaper but that of a common person. One may be tempted to identify some similarities with what is commonly known as the *letter to the editor*, and yet it is not a letter to the editor, although it does highlight an issue. Unlike letters to the editor, its style is more like a mixture of several different styles, in particular a hybrid of narration and argumentation: "But there is one pressure that just refuses to leave us alone, a question that follows us everywhere: 'What are your marriage plans?' In India, a girl's identity revolves around her marriage. As children, we are all raised to understand that we must end up with the right partner, and must go to a nice family as a daughter-in-law" (BBC 2014).

Another interesting aspect of this article is that it has embedded at various places asides relevant to the theme and intended to involve readers in the ongoing narrative discussion of the issue in question. These asides are separated from the ongoing discussion, are not meant to be digressions in a conventional sense, and are clearly textually mapped, as they are thematically related and mark a significant attempt to take readers to other interdiscursive resources. These asides are some of the key resources used to make the feature article not only interdiscursive but interactional as well. The interactive asides are typically marked by indications such as "Find out more" and "Listen-BBC World service":

- The BBC's Rupa Jha talks to four single women living in India
- India's Invisible Women will be on BBC World News on Friday 7 March at 20:30 GMT, Saturday 8 March at 11:30 GMT and Sunday 9 March at 17:30 and 22:30 GMT
- Listen on BBC World Service throughout Friday 7 March

Yet another interesting aspect of this interdiscursively complex artifact is that it often refers to different media sources as well, namely the "matrimonial website": "If you look at any matrimonial website (a common trend in India these days) you will find the terms 'family-oriented,' 'homely,' 'not too much into career'—these are the qualities in a bride people most often look for" (BBC 2014). There is also an attempt to identify yet another social problem, that of the difficulty single women have when trying to rent apartments, which is presented as a discriminatory social practice: "People don't like to rent apartments to single, professional women—they are afraid that someone like me will behave immorally" (BBC 2014).

At this stage there is another attempt to involve readers in yet another interdiscursive context, this time encouraging a more interactive initiative on their part: "Whether it's freedom from surveillance or freedom to be single, the BBC is investigating what freedom means in the modern world. We want to know what freedom looks like to you. Please send us your own images, videos, animations or artwork. Find out how to get involved here." The article then continues the personal narration about the family support Suruchi, who is the narrator, gets at all times: "I am lucky that my family is extremely supportive. My parents stand by me when it comes to waiting for the right guy to come along, but they too face extreme pressure from relatives and everyone in their circle. 'When is Suruchi getting married?' They get asked this question every day, and it makes them anxious. They begin to wonder if they are doing the wrong thing by letting their daughter make her own choices" (BBC 2014).

The article ends with an invitation to readers from other countries, who are directed to a forum to share their own private stories or experiences using other forms of new media, such as Twitter and Facebook, which demonstrates how media writers use "management participation mechanisms" to involve extended interaction with much wider participation: "Follow @BBCNewsMagazine on Twitter and on Facebook. Is it hard being single—male or female—in your country? Tell us why, using the form below." This feature article based on the private experiences of an individual has been turned into an interdiscursively and interactively rich piece of public discourse to involve readers in an ongoing interaction with BBC in a public space.

CONCLUDING REMARKS

In this chapter, I have made an attempt to propose a framework to study one of the most dominant aspects of discourse and genre in public space, in particular focusing on media discourse for a number of reasons. It is probably the most predominant and versatile form of public discourse, apart from advertising. Its versatility is evident not simply from the copresence of a number of media genres in a more or less well-defined public space but also from the hybrid nature of some of the genres. In more recent times, we have also seen the prominence of the interdiscursively versatile multimodal and creative involvement of other forms of media channels, such as online discourses—communication through twitter, blogs, Facebook, and many other media resources—which have opened up possibilities of what I (Bhatia 2004, 2010) have identified as the mixing, embedding, and bending of genres. I attempted to see this kind of versatility in the form of using various media as well as discourses addressing multiple audiences, often involving them interactively, and at the same time, innovatively proposing novel responses in the form of various kinds of hybridity in genre construction. I chose to focus on the online BBC news magazine, which seems to illustrate all these diverse tendencies in a single instance of a hybrid public genre.

As the discussion above indicates, the BBC news magazine article "No Country for Single Women" illustrates a number of new developments, which seem to have been well established in a relatively short period of time, and is a key example of a genre as interdiscursive performance in public space. It is rich in its use of interdiscursive resources, especially in using private discourse in a public context. Although it is predominantly based on an individual and private experience, it is creatively mixed with certain aspects of public concern, in particular the way the private discourse is interdiscursively mediated by frequent recontextualization, reframing, reformulation, and resemiotization of important generalizations, which make this private discourse relevant to public contexts and encourage audience participation using a variety of new media resources. This creative bringing together of private voice and public response is yet another form of interdiscursivity quite typical of media genres.

To sum up, the chapter focuses on genre as interdiscursive performance bringing together instances from professional, institutional, disciplinary, and public domains to make the claim that interdiscursivity, as appropriation of text-external generic resources, includes discursive practices and procedures, professional and social practices, and even various conceptualizations of culture in the construction, interpretation, use, and exploitation of genres in order to respond to typical and not-so-typical situational configurations, thereby creating novel responses. Many of these novel and creative responses are hybrids of various kinds, which include the mixing, embedding, and even bending of genres. Interdiscursivity is thus seen as a key resource used in various forms in business, law, newspapers, advertising, and even in academic settings. It is especially noticeable in annual corporate reports, new forms of legislative documents, medical consultations, mediation and arbitration practices, and several other creative hybrids such as advertorials, infomercials, sponsored features, and many more.

This chapter also highlights yet another aspect of interdiscursivity in genre theory, which extends the scope of interdiscursive appropriations in at least two additional directions: towards the management of interdiscursive space, on the one hand, and toward the management of multiple voices, on the other, thus extending the boundaries of interdiscursive performance in public space. Although this process of interdiscursive performance has attracted attention from discourse and genre theorists relatively recently, it is a lot more visible and creatively used in public discourse than it ever was in professional and disciplinary contexts. This visibility and creativity is certainly the influence of the introduction of new media in public and professional discourse, which makes it possible for expert writers to manipulate and manage discursive space creatively and at the same time involve and address multiple audiences more effectively than ever before.

References

Bakhtin, M. M. 1986. *Speech Genres and Other Late Essays*. Austin: University of Texas Press.

Bawarshi, Anis, and Mary Jo Reiff. 2010. *Genre: An Introduction to History, Theory, Research, and Pedagogy*. West Lafayette, IN: Parlor.

Bazerman, Charles. 1994. "Systems of Genres and the Enhancement of Social Intentions." In *Genre and the New Rhetoric*, edited by Aviva Freedman and Peter Medway, 79–101. London: Taylor and Francis.

Bazerman, Charles. 1997. "Discursively Structured Activities." *Mind, Culture, and Activity* 4 (4): 296–308. http://dx.doi.org/10.1207/s15327884mca0404_6.

BBC. 2014. "No Country for Single Women." http://www.bbc.com/news/magazine-2 6341350.

Berkenkotter, Carol. 2008. *Patient Tales: Case Histories and the Uses of Narrative in Psychiatry*. Columbia: South Carolina: South Carolina University Press.

Berkenkotter, Carol, and Thomas N. Huckin. 1995. *Genre Knowledge in Disciplinary Communication: Cognition/Culture/Power*. Mahwah, NJ: Erlbaum.

Bhatia, Vijay K. 1993. *Analysing Genre—Language Use in Professional Settings*. London: Longman.

Bhatia, Vijay K. 1994. "Dynamics of Genre Manipulation." *Central Institute of English and Foreign Languages Bulletin* 6 (1): 25–42.

Bhatia, Vijay K. 1995. "Genre-Mixing in Professional Communication: The Case of 'Private Intentions' v. 'Socially Recognised Purposes.'" In *Explorations in English for Professional Communication*, edited by Bertha Du Babcock, Paul Bruthiaux, and Tim Boswood, 1–19. Hong Kong: City University of Hong Kong.

Bhatia, Vijay K. 1997. "Genre-Mixing in Academic Introductions." *English for Specific Purposes* 16 (3): 181–95. http://dx.doi.org/10.1016/S0889-4906(96)00039-7.

Bhatia, Vijay K. 1998. "Discourse of Philanthropic Fundraising." *New Directions in Philanthropic Fundraising* 22:95–110.

Bhatia, Vijay K. 2004. *Worlds of Written Discourse: A Genre-Based View*. London: Continuum International.

Bhatia, Vijay. 2010. "Interdiscursivity in Professional Communication." *Discourse and Communication* 4 (1): 32–50.

Bhatia, Vijay K. 2012. "Critical Reflections on Genre Analysis." *Iberica* 24:17–28.

Bhatia, Vijay K. 2014. "Managing Interdiscursive Space in Professional Communication." In *Evolution in Genres: Emergence, Variation, Multimodality*, edited by Paola Evangilisti Allori, John Bateman, and Vijay K. Bhatia, 95–114. Bern: Peter Lang.

Bondebjerg, Ib. 1996. "Public Discourse/Private Fascination: Hybridization in 'True-Life-Story' Genres." *Media Culture & Society* 18 (1): 27–45. http://dx.doi.org/10.1177/016344396018001003.

Calsamiglia, Helena, and Teun A. Van Dijk. 2004. "Popularization Discourse and Knowledge about the Genome." *Discourse & Society* 15 (4): 369–89. http://dx.doi.org/10.1177/0957926504043705.

Candlin, Christopher N., and Yon Maley. 1997. "Intertextuality and Interdiscursivity in the Discourse of Alternative Dispute Resolution." In *The Construction of Professional Discourse*, edited by B. L. Gunnarsson, Per Linell, and Bengt Nordberg, 201–22. London: Longman.

Devitt, Amy J. 1991. "Intertextuality in Tax Accounting: Generic, Referential, and Functional." In *Textual Dynamics of the Professions: Historical and Contemporary Studies of Writing in Professional Communities*, edited by Charles Bazerman and James Paradis, 336–57. Madison: University of Wisconsin Press.

Emmons, Kimberly. 2009. "Uptake and the Biomedical Subject." In *Genre in a Changing World*, edited by Charles Bazerman, Adair Bonini, and Débora Figueiredo, 134–57. Fort Collins, CO: WAC Clearinghouse and Parlor.

Fairclough, Norman. 1995. *Critical Discourse Analysis: The Critical Study of Language.* London: Longman.

Figueiredo, Débora de Carvalho. 2009. "Narrative and Identity Formation: An Analysis of Media Personal Accounts from Patients of Cosmetic Plastic Surgery." In *Genre in a Changing World*, edited by Charles Bazerman, Adair Bonini, and Débora Figueiredo, 255–76. Fort Collins, CO: WAC Clearinghouse and Parlor.

Foucault, Michel. 1981. *The Archaeology of Knowledge.* New York: Pantheon Books.

Freadman, Anne. 1994. "Anyone for Tennis?" In *Genre and the New Rhetoric*, edited by Aviva Freedman and Peter Medway, 43–66. London: Taylor & Francis.

Freadman, Anne. 2012. "The Traps and Trappings of Genre Theory." *Applied Linguistics* 33 (5): 544–63. http://dx.doi.org/10.1093/applin/ams050.

Gotti, Maurizio. 2014. "Reformulation and Recontextualization in Popularization Discourse." *Ibérica* 27:15–34.

Habermas, Jürgen. 1987. *The Theory of Communicative Action.* Boston: Beacon.

Habermas, Jürgen. 1989. *The Structural Transformation of the Public Sphere: An Inquiry into a Category of Bourgeois Society.* Cambridge: MIT Press.

Kathpalia, Sujata S. 1992. "A Genre Analysis of Promotional Texts." PhD diss., National University of Singapore.

Kristeva, Julia. 1980. "Word, Dialogue and Novel." In *Desire in Language*, edited by Leon S. Roudiez. Translated by Thomas Gora, Alice Jardine, and Leon S. Roudiez, 64–91. Oxford: Blackwell.

Sarangi, Srikant. 2000. "Activity Types, Discourse Types and Interactional Hybridity: The Case of Genetic Counseling." In *Discourse and Social Life*, edited by Srikant Sarangi and Malcolm Coulthard, 1–27. London: Pearson Education Limited.

Swales, John M. 1998. *Other Floors Other Voices: A Textography of a Small University Building.* London: Erlbaum.

WU, Jianguo. 2011. "Understanding Interdiscursivity: A Pragmatic Model." *Journal of Cambridge Studies* 6 (2–3): 95–116.

2
BETWEEN GENRES
Uptake, Memory, and US Public Discourse on Israel-Palestine

Anis Bawarshi

In *After the Last Sky*, and speaking as a Palestinian, Edward Said writes, "There has been no misfortune worse for us than that we are ineluctably viewed as the enemies of the Jews. No moral and political fate worse, none at all, I think: no worse, there is none" (Said 1986, 134). As I see it, this is as much a rhetorical fate as a moral and political fate, a rhetorical fate that, primarily in the West and especially in the United States, has pitted attempts to represent Palestinian suffering and victimization against competing representations of Jewish suffering and victimization. Within this rhetoric of incommensurability—this rhetorical dilemma of representing oneself as a victim of a victim and the competing memories and power imbalances at work there—attempts to represent or critique Israel's treatment of Palestinians are often silenced or ignored, more often taken up as a threat to Israel's right to exist and labeled as anti-Semitic, either because they rely on references to Jewish power or because they purportedly single out Israel for criticism. This rhetorical impasse, managed by a powerful set of uptakes, informs US public discourse about Israel-Palestine.

For a while now, I have been interested in this rhetorical impasse and the ways it plagues public discourse on the Israel-Palestine conflict in the United States, especially when this discourse has such consequential implications for Palestinians and Israelis and their prospects for peace.[1] For me, this interest is both an academic and a personal one. As a Palestinian-Lebanese American married to a Jewish woman, with two children who are both Jewish and Palestinian, I have grappled with this impasse in my home life, as my partner and I have often struggled with, and have become increasingly better at, engaging in deliberation about this conflict. As a rhetorician and genre researcher, I have confronted this impasse repeatedly, as public discourse about this conflict, across various contexts and genres, often degenerates into heated

DOI: 10.7330/9781607324430.c002

accusations, personal attacks, and name calling, even on academic list-servs devoted, no less, to the teaching of academic writing and civic discourse, such as WPA-L (writing program administrators' discussion list) and Rhetoricians for Peace. The degree to which these exchanges reflect a seemingly habitual, totalizing pattern of uptakes (whether in response to a teaching-award announcement in memory of Rachel Corrie, a twenty-three-year-old student from Washington State who was killed in 2003 by an Israeli bulldozer; or to Jimmy Carter's book, *Palestine: Peace Not Apartheid*; or to former DePaul University profes-sor and historian Norman Finkelstein's tenure controversy; or to Bob Simon's January 2009 *60 Minutes* report on the West Bank occupation; or to the 2013 American Studies Association resolution to endorse a boycott of Israeli academic institutions; or to US Secretary of State John Kerry's recent use of the word *apartheid* in reference to the risks of failed peace; or to numerous other events) compels us to think about how the patterns function and how we might work to delay or disrupt them in productive, more discerning ways—at the very least in ways that distinguish more carefully between, for instance, a racist screed by white supremacist David Duke and a critique of Israel by historian and son of Holocaust survivors Norman Finkelstein. In this chapter, I will analyze some of the rhetorical patterns and normalized uptakes that have become entrenched within US public discourse about the Israel-Palestine conflict, and then I will examine the challenges faced by genre and public sphere scholars who wish to intervene in these uptakes in ways that encourage more productive inquiry and public deliberation about this and other contentious topics.

UPTAKE AND GENRE

At the epicenter of this chapter is the question of genre's relationship to uptake. As Anne Freadman (1994; 2002; 2012) has noted in her ground-breaking work on genre and uptake, genres condition uptakes, espe-cially within activity systems such as schools, academic disciplines, and workplaces in which related genres coordinate uptakes in fairly predict-able ways for the achievement of shared object-motives, as when class-room assignment prompts get taken up as student papers, which then get taken up as teacher feedback, which then is potentially taken up as revised papers, which then gets taken up as grades in a grade book, and so on. Apprentices learn these uptakes as part of their genre acquisition and participation in systems of activity. As Janet Giltrow has observed, activity systems often include what she terms "meta-genres," genres such as manuals and handbooks that provide shared background knowledge and guidance in how to produce and negotiate genres and genre uptakes within genre sets and systems. Metagenres can take the form of explicit guidelines or tacitly shared discourse about genres. As Giltrow defines them, metagenres are "atmospheres surrounding genres" that function on the boundaries between activity systems to smooth over potential tensions individuals experience within and between activity systems (Giltrow 2002, 195). Freadman's scholarship has helped genre scholars better understand how genres are defined not only by their typified features but also, and more consequentially, by the uptakes they condition and secure.

Within speech act theory, uptake traditionally refers to how an illocutionary act (saying, for example, "it is hot in here" with the intention of getting someone to cool the room) gets taken up as a perlocutionary effect (someone's subsequently opening a window) under certain conditions. The important thing to note in this commonly used example is how a perlocutionary effect involves the embodiment of an illocutionary act—there is a body in motion and time that takes up an utterance, and that uptake is subject to a complex set of conditions that inform its movement. Such embodiment and emplacement are crucial to uptake. In applying uptake to genre theory, Freadman draws on the force of this understanding to argue that genre performances are more complex and dynamic than genre research has generally accounted for and to draw our attention to the *interplays* between genres.

As Freadman is careful to note, uptake does not depend on causation (as in a call for papers leads to a proposal) but rather on *selection.* Uptake, she explains, "selects, defines, or represents its object. . . . Uptake is first the taking of an object; it is not the causation of a response by an intention. This is the hidden dimension of the long, ramified, intertextual memory of uptake: the object is taken from a set of possibilities" (Freadman 2002, 48). By shifting our attention from causation to selection, Freadman offers uptake as a complex scene of agency, one informed by learned inclinations and embodied dispositions; memories; attachments; access to certain tools; one's sense of self, authority, and cultural capital; one's perceived sense of timing, stakes, motivation, task relevance; and other affective, temporal, historical, and material factors that make uptakes complex sites of selection and genre performance. Following Freadman, genre scholars have described uptake as the taking up or contextualized, strategic performance of genres in moments of interaction: both the result of genre action and the cognitive, social, psychological, and material *trans-action* that enables genre action (see, for example, Bastian 2015; Bawarshi 2008, forthcoming; Berkenkotter and Hanganu-Bresch 2011; Dryer 2008; Emmons 2009; Kill 2006; Rounsaville 2012; Seidel 2007). Uptake, then, as a *relational* sense or force ("the bidirectional relation that holds" between genres, as Freadman [2002, 40] describes it), is a vital part of genre knowledge, but because it takes place within a complex scene of agency, it also exceeds genre knowledge and is informed by one's sense of self, one's memory of prior uptakes, the timing and stakes of a discursive event and its participants (Freadman 2012), and other affective and material factors that make uptakes, while to some extent habitual and conditioned by genre, also momentary, unpredictable, and, as we will see in the analysis this chapter offers, subject to transformations and relations of power.

The complex relationship between genres and uptakes becomes even more important to consider when we move outside the boundaries of institutional activity systems, whether professional or academic, and into public domains where uptakes are less "disciplined" and brokered by agreed-upon metagenres and where processes of apprenticeship (what Lave and Wenger [1991] have described as "legitimate peripheral participation") are less structured or even nonexistent. As an examination of US public discourse on the Israel-Palestine conflict reveals (exemplified by my analysis of a report and editorial responses to it as well as a political science/personal memoir book and responses to it), uptakes within public spheres are less conditioned by genres, and indeed, dominant uptakes often trump or elide important genre distinctions in ways that can limit public deliberation. Genres that could serve usefully in mediating public discourse become subordinate to dominant uptakes. Such a study can teach us about the limits of genre but also about genre's possibilities in delaying, intervening in, and offering alternative uptakes in ways that can offer more productive public deliberation around contentious, emotionally fraught topics.

While research in genre studies has taught us a great deal about what genres are and how genres relate to one another in complex ways, we do not know as much about the complex uptake performances that take place between and around genres. By drawing our attention to what Vijay Bhatia in his chapter in this volume calls the "interdiscursive" factors that inform public genre performances and by accounting for the interconnections, translations, and pathways between genres, uptake enables researchers to study the movements of actions and meanings across genres. As Anne Freadman recently put it, "No genre can do more than predict the kind of uptake that would make it happy, and no speaker or writer can completely secure an uptake. This is partly because no discursive event is a pure example of any genre, and partly because of the unpredictable historical complexity of its moment and its ongoing action. We cannot . . . reflect productively on uptake outside of discussions of genre, nor is it productive to theorize the action of genres without uptake. Genre is destabilized by uptake even as it asserts its power" (Freadman 2012, 560). An examination of the uptakes that work to maintain the rhetorical impasse in US public discourse about the Israel-Palestine conflict—in particular the way uptakes can be used to precondition or overdetermine our encounters with genres—can thus expand our understanding of genre and agency within public deliberation.

UPTAKES, RHETORICAL MEMORY AND THE ISRAEL-PALESTINE CONFLICT

Freadman (2002, 48) argues that uptakes have memories—"long, ramified, intertextual" memories—and these memories are powerfully at work in rhetorics of Israel-Palestine. In *I Saw Ramallah*, for example, Palestinian poet Mourid Barghouti (2000, 91) explains that the experience of exile turns place into time: "I do not live in a place," he writes, "I live in a time." Amira Hass provides an example of what Barghouti means. She recounts a conversation in which one Palestinian asks another, "Where are you from?" and each answers the other by identifying the name of his family village. Hass writes, "Both the men were born in the Gaza Strip and knew of the village only from their parents and grandparents. But in mentioning the names, the two took their place in an essential human chain that challenges history and defies the passage of time with an individual and collective inner truth that refuses to die" (Hass 1996, 161). Living "in a time" conflates place and memory in complicated and often competing ways, as when Palestinian narratives clash with narratives about Israel's War of Independence in 1948, which imagine Palestinians left their homes willingly or on the advice of Arab leaders (for revisionist historical accounts of Israel's War of Independence, see the work of Israeli new historians Benny Morris [1989]; Ilan Pappe [2006]; and Tom Segev [2000]), or, in then-Israeli Prime Minister Golda Meir's claim, in a June 15, 1969, *Sunday Times* interview, that Palestinians did not exist: "There was no such thing as Palestinians. When was there an independent Palestinian people with a Palestinian state? It was either southern Syria before the First World War, and then it was a Palestine including Jordan. It was not as though there was a Palestinian people in Palestine considering itself as a Palestinian people and we came and threw them out and took their country away from them. They did not

exist." Meir's claim compels us to ask, what happens to Palestinian rhetorical memories when these confront another, more powerful set of
rhetorical memories? This question is not only about competing memories or about who is more right and who is more wrong. Certainly,
the impasse that plagues public discourse about Israel-Palestine in the
United States suffers plenty from a lack of historical and factual knowledge and from competing truth claims. But more than that, the question has to do with how rhetorical memories work to shape our encounters with what we read, hear, and see and how we take these up in our
responses and actions. A powerful affective dimension is at work here
that, in some cases, is manipulated by those who want to silence dialogue
about Israel-Palestine in the United States but just as often works in
more habitual, less conscious ways as deeply held attachments to ensure
dominant uptakes that maintain a rhetoric of incommensurability and
stifle debate. Understanding how these uptakes are steeped in "long,
ramified, intertextual" memories that often trump or elide important
genre distinctions can shed light on the processes of uptake selection
and the relations of power that inform them.

THE ISRAEL-PALESTINE CONFLICT IN US PUBLIC GENRES

The mainstream US public discourse surrounding the Israel-Palestine
conflict and the set of uptakes that manage it is exemplified by the
controversial case of John Mearsheimer and Stephen Walt's report,
"The Israeli Lobby." The report was first published in article form in
the *London Review of Books* in March 2006 and then posted online, in
an extended format, on the Harvard Kennedy School of Government
website, where Walt is endowed professor of international affairs
(Mearsheimer is endowed professor of political science at the University
of Chicago; in 2008, Mearsheimer and Walt published a book-length
version of their report, titled *The Israel Lobby and U.S. Foreign Policy*). In
general, the report argued that US support of Israel has been unwaver-
ing, has jeopardized US security, and has been driven by the unmatched
power of the Israel "lobby," which Mearsheimer and Walt define as the
"loose coalition of individuals and organizations who actively work to
steer U.S. foreign policy in a pro-Israel direction" (Mearsheimer and
Walt 2006a, n.p.). Threaded through this argument is a critique of
Israel's policies toward Palestinians.

Space does not permit a fuller contextualization, but uptakes of the
report in various public genres were heated and ranged across contexts
and modalities, from mainstream media to Op-Ed pieces to response

letters and e-mails. Although met with some reputable support, the report was largely condemned in the United States. One of the most prominent charges against Mearsheimer and Walt is that they perceive the lobby as a well-organized Jewish conspiracy. A response letter published in the *London Review of Books* noted, "Accusations of powerful Jews behind the scene are part of the most dangerous traditions of modern anti-Semitism" (Pipes 2006). Likewise, the Anti-Defamation League called the article "a classical conspiratorial anti-Semitic analysis involving the canards of Jewish power and Jewish control" (Anti-Defamation League 2006), a charge echoed by Eliot Cohen (professor at Johns Hopkins School of Advanced International Studies), Harvard law professor Alan Dershowitz, Representative Eliot Engel of New York, and many others.

Dershowitz also accused Mearsheimer and Walt of recycling accusations that "would be seized upon by bigots to promote their anti-Semitic agendas" (Dershowitz 2006, 4) and compares the article to *The Protocols of the Elders of Zion*, a classical anti-Semitic text that scapegoated Jews as an untrustworthy class of international conspirators plotting against the gentile nations for world domination by controlling banks, stock exchanges, and so forth (*The Protocols* was, after the Bible, the world's most widely circulated book between 1918 and 1939). In a *Washington Post* editorial, Eliot Cohen summed it up as follows: "If by anti-Semitism one means obsessive and irrationally hostile beliefs about Jews; if one accuses them of disloyalty, subversion, or treachery, of having occult powers and of participating in secret combinations that manipulate institutions and governments; if one systematically selects everything unfair, ugly, or wrong about Jews as individuals or as a group and equally systematically suppresses any exculpatory information—why yes, this paper is anti-Semitic" (April 5, 2006).

Yet these uptakes seem incommensurate with what is included in Mearsheimer and Walt's report, which explicitly states that the Israel lobby's "activities are *not* a conspiracy of the sort depicted in tracts like the 'Protocols of the Elders of Zion'" (Mearsheimer and Walt 2006a, n.p.) and which rejects the notion that the lobby is some sort of secret cabal. The report also notes that "there is a strong moral case for supporting Israel's existence." Yet to understand the reactions to the report, we must remember Freadman's (2002) observation that uptakes have memories. We do not simply respond to the immediate demands of a rhetorical situation, an utterance, a text, a genre. Uptakes have memories in the sense that they are learned recognitions and inclinations that, over time and through affective attachments and formations of power, become habitual and take on a life of their own (what Dylan Dryer in his chapter in this volume calls "uptake residues" or sedimentations) outside the genres that would work to condition or secure them. As much as genres shape our uptakes, our uptake memories and their residues shape our genre encounters, helping us select from, define, and make sense of those encounters in ways that genre research has yet to fully acknowledge.

In this case, we can see how Mearsheimer and Walt's report triggers uptake memory. For instance, early in the report, Mearsheimer and Walt argue that Israel does not behave like a loyal ally. They write, "Israeli officials frequently ignore U.S. requests and renege on promises (including pledges to stop building settlements. . . .). Israel has provided sensitive military technology to potential rivals like China. . . . According to the General Accounting Office, Israel also 'conducts the most aggressive espionage operations against the U.S. of any ally'. . . . Israel is hardly the only country that spies on the US, but its willingness to spy on its principal patron casts further doubt on its strategic value" (2006a, n.p.). The argument and evidence notwithstanding, this excerpt, coming early in the text, includes what Mikhail Bakhtin (1986, 91) terms "echoes and reverberations" of Jewish stereotypes—that Jews are disloyal, shifty, manipulative—that contain and trigger rhetorical memory of modern anti-Semitism. These residues or sedimentations inform and animate the uptakes.

A similar example can be seen when Mearsheimer and Walt (2006a, n.p.) later write, "Thanks in part to the influence Jewish voters have on presidential elections, the Lobby also has significant leverage over the executive branch. Although they make up fewer than 3 percent of the population, they make large campaign donations to candidates of both parties." Again, the word *influence* collocated with *Jewish* here triggers rhetorical memory that shapes how readers encounter and take up the text. So by the time readers get to the part in the article where Mearsheimer and Walt claim that "the Lobby's perspective prevails in the mainstream media" (2006a, n.p.), this claim can easily get taken up instead as "Jews control the media"—not because the report ever states this but because it has previously triggered a set of uptakes rooted in historical-material conditions that can secure this response.

These residues, appearing in a report on the role of the Israel lobby that also critiques Israel's policies toward Palestinians, enable a set of uptakes that link support for Palestinian rights and self-determination with perceived anti-Semitism. In this set of uptakes, critique of Israeli policy taps into threatening stereotypes. Since Palestinian representation is linked to critique of Israeli policy, what Dryer in this volume calls "uptake capture" (the consequences of uptake that result in "lingering effects" on what individuals "see—or indeed are *able* to see—as the realm of the possible") leads to the conclusion that Palestinian representation is anti-Semitic. Any salient arguments Mearsheimer and Walt make are thus lost in this rhetorical interplay. And when former KKK leader David Duke writes of the Mearsheimer and Walt report, "I have read about the report and read one summary already, and I am surprised how excellent it is. . . . It is quite satisfying to see a body in the premier American University essentially come out and validate every major point I have been making since even before the war even started" (Foxman 2007, 81), his words drive the threat even deeper. Mearsheimer and Walt rejected Duke's efforts to use their report to promote his racist agenda, writing, "We have no control over who likes or dislikes our article, but we regret that Duke used it to promote his racist agenda, which we utterly reject" (Mearsheimer and Walt 2006b). But uptakes can be rhizomatic and difficult to control, especially in the public sphere where the mechanisms for their regulation and distribution are more diffuse—managed less by metagenres, genres, and forms of apprenticeship and more by political, ideological, and religious attachments, subjectivity, access to media, forms of intimidation, and the power of individuals to shape discursive events.

The uptakes I have described at work in the Mearsheimer and Walt controversy are triggered by rhetorical memories of very real, horrific, and continuing anti-Semitism. At the same time, these uptakes invariably create a rhetoric of incommensurability that too often silences attempts to represent Palestinian injustice and advocate for Palestinian rights. What makes these uptakes so powerful is that they circulate across and trump context and genre distinctions in ways that often block attempts to use genres to effect public deliberation. The anti-Semitic uptake of Mearsheimer and Walt's report invalidates its genre status as an article by reputable historians through a kind of metonymy that makes *anti-Semitism* stand for and erase the whole. Rather than take up the article as an article, the responses take up the article as an anti-Semitic illocutionary act. In so doing, such an uptake elides significant differences between the article and a racist screed, rendering both as deserving of the same response. The uptake in this case permits the genre not to matter.

DISRUPTING UPTAKES/RECONTEXTUALIZING UPTAKE MEMORY

Genres and uptakes are closely connected, and genres often help condition uptakes (indeed, through habitual uptakes, genres reliably invoke one another). But uptakes, as we see in the case of the Mearsheimer and Walt controversy, can likewise trump or outlast or overpower genre distinctions when they are used to select, define, or represent objects in ways that take up certain utterances and block others across various contexts and genres. As Freadman notes in her discussion of uptake, this is the strategy of power.

Such strategies of power alert us to the ways uptakes are complex sites of agency that challenge a view of causation as mainly rooted in genre. For instance, in Freadman's definition of uptake as "the bidirectional relation that *holds* between" genres (Freadman 2002, 40; emphasis added), the pivotal term *holds* suggests a relational force or interplay that operates between genres. What makes uptakes especially interesting is that they compel us to pay attention to the historical-material conditions and dynamics of agency and power that function between, hold together, and shape genre performances. Uptake, then, is a vital part of but also exceeds genre knowledge. Such a historical-materialist view of uptake invites us to examine causation in more complex ways—including how forms of cognition become "sedimented at a corporeal level where they are repeated as habits . . . lodged in bodily memory" (Coole and Frost 2010, 34)—and to recognize the interlocking systems and forces at play in performances of genre, especially within publics.

As "the local event of crossing a boundary" (Freadman 2002, 43), uptake draws our attention not only to the relations between genres but also to how individuals move and translate across genres—to the pathways drawn, managed, and trans-acted across genres that enable and limit public discussion. It is especially when they occur across intergeneric boundaries, Freadman notes, that uptake translations are "least automatic and most open to mistake or even to abuse" (44) since they are most subject to relations of power. As a result, we need to pay attention to how uptakes are brokered. Certain routinized uptakes, especially within bounded and regulated institutional contexts, follow well-worn, expected directions and are thus habitually received. But as Rebecca Nowacek (2011) has demonstrated in terms of genre and knowledge transfer, other uptakes need to be explicitly "sold" and validated, and here too power comes into play in terms of which uptakes are sanctioned, who is granted authority to sell and see uptakes, the institutional affordances that enable or prevent the seeing and selling, and so on. However, as we will see in the following example, while the brokering of uptakes can be used as a strategy of power to maintain dominant uptakes, it can also be used to disrupt dominant uptakes through a process of uptake recontextualization.

Just as uptakes can trump or outlast or overpower genre distinctions when they are used to select, define, or represent objects in ways that take up certain memories and block others across various contexts and genres, so too can uptakes become strategies for counteracting power, as when uptakes from one context are brought to bear on another (see Jennifer Nish's chapter in this volume for an examination of distributive uptakes and genre spread). In her study of how discourses about depression are taken on and then taken up by women, Kimberly Emmons (2009) makes a useful distinction between generic and discursive uptakes. Generic uptakes refer to the movement of genres (such as the symptoms list) into new situations, as when a symptoms list is recontextualized from professional to public contexts. Discursive uptakes, however, refer to the taking up of key phrases from one genre into another, as when the women in Emmons's (2009) study use the phrase *chemical imbalance* to describe their symptoms. In a similar way to how *anti-Semitism* can become a kind of discursive uptake used to discourage debate across genres and contexts, other discursive uptakes can be used to provoke debate across contexts and genres.

We see such a recontextualization of uptake memory at work in Jimmy Carter's 2006 book, *Palestine: Peace Not Apartheid*. While Carter's book is more of a personal reflection and accounting of his involvement in the region than it is a rigorously cited historical study, it gains its power by presenting two disrupting and challenging uptakes, both of which are invoked in the book's title: *Palestine* and a*partheid*. The mere mention at the time of the name *Palestine* by a former US president constitutes a significant uptake since it acknowledges the existence of a Palestinian homeland. Even more powerfully, Carter's use of the word *apartheid* also triggers uptake memory by transferring and applying a term for South African legally enforced racial segregation and using it to represent the conditions under which Palestinians are increasingly forced to live under occupation, especially in the West Bank. Indeed, the image of Israel's "security fence" surrounding the West Bank depicted on the book's cover, juxtaposed with the book's title, suggests fairly directly that the walled barrier (which Carter refers to as "imprisonment wall" [2006, 174] and "segregation wall" [193]) is both a symbol of apartheid and an impediment to peace.

Interestingly, the word *apartheid* appears minimally throughout the book: the index lists three references—by my informal count, it was four. Yet the presence of the word in the book's title permitted into US mainstream public discourse questions, comparisons, and debates about segregation and inequality that were previously less visible. (It is hard to imagine, for example, that Bob Simon's January 2009 *60 Minutes* report on the West Bank occupation and his depiction of settlements and set-tler-only roads would have aired if not for the apartheid uptake Carter's book permitted.)

By bringing uptake memory from one context (South African apart-heid) to another (occupied Palestinian territories), Carter's book per-forms what Jennifer Nish in this volume describes as a distributive uptake and in so doing creates the possibility for a different debate to take place. Along the way, Carter disrupts a number of other dominant uptakes. For instance, he brings the language of colonialism (to coun-terbalance the language of defense and security) to bear on the Israeli occupation of Palestinian territory; he challenges the perception that Yasir Arafat was responsible for the failure of the so-called peace pro-cess, having rejected Ehud Barak's "generous offer" (Carter 2006, 152); he reconfigures the narrative of historical events to highlight Israel's resistance to peace efforts (see, for example, his depiction of events that followed the Arab League resolution in 2002 [156–58]); and he allows Palestinian perspectives to emerge for a mainstream audience not used to hearing them (e.g., Carter frequently uses indirect speech to report what Palestinian representatives have told him: "Abbas informed me," "he reminded me," "he responded," "He also asked"). While none of these counteruptakes were especially revelatory or new to those who are aware of debates about the conflict, they were made especially powerful because they were performed by a former US president and addressed to a mainstream US public.

While Carter cites provocative acts by Arab militants, acknowledges corruption among Palestinian leaders, condemns terrorism as a seri-ous threat to Israel and an obstacle to peace, and insists that "the secu-rity of Israel must be guaranteed" (Carter 2006, 207), and while Carter cites his commitment to Israel's security through his negotiation of the Israeli-Egyptian peace treaty and is careful to explain that "the driving purpose for the forced separation of the two peoples [Israelis and Palestinians] is unlike that in South Africa—not racism, but the acquisition of land" (189–90)—critics accused Carter of being one sided, distorting facts, and contriving an accusation of ethnic cleans-ing against Israel in its dealing with the Palestinians. Alan Dershowitz's description of Carter in his *The Case Against Israel's Enemies: Exposing Jimmy Carter and Others Who Stand in the Way of Peace* is an example of how this uptake worked with the term *apartheid.* To depict Carter as an obstacle to peace when he helped negotiate a peace deal between Israel and Egypt would seem incommensurate, yet it also reveals the power of uptake to function as both a site of instantiation and regulation of power and a site of intervention.

Dershowitz rejects *apartheid* as an "explosive and incorrect term" (Dershowitz 2008, 23), arguing that it "fuels anti-Semitism in the Arab world" (47) and contributes to the irrational hatred of Israel. Instead of engaging in an argument about how the presence of settler-only roads in the West Bank, for example, serves as a kind of apartheid, Dershowitz responds instead to the uptake memory triggered by the word *apartheid*. Arguing that "racism is the sin qua non of apartheid" (26), Dershowitz proceeds to dispute the presence of racism in Israel: "But Israel, unlike its neighboring Arab nations, does not use religious coercion; neither is there segregation or discrimination against minorities who are not Jewish" (25). By focusing on the legal definition of apartheid and its specific systematic practice in South Africa, Dershowitz and others can then reject the analogy wholesale, claiming that the apartheid system in South Africa "does not remotely resemble Israel" (26). While Carter explains that "the driving purpose for the forced separation of the two peoples [Israelis and Palestinians] is unlike that in South Africa—not racism, but the acquisition of land" (Carter 2006, 189–90)—and it seems clear that Carter is applying the term *apartheid* only to the occupied Palestinian territories, not to Israel as a whole, the uptake memory triggered by the word *apartheid* presents Dershowitz with an opportunity not only to reject the analogy but also to turn it around against itself, from being a critique of Israeli occupation and segregation in the West Bank to being an existential threat to Israel. As Dershowitz argues, "To accuse Israel of apartheid is therefore to strike at the foundations of the state itself. It implies . . . that Israel is illegitimate, racist, and deserving of destruction. Just as the apartheid system in South Africa had to be dismantled entirely, the analogy posits, 'apartheid Israel' must be utterly destroyed" (2008, 23). An analogy Carter purportedly uses to provoke debate about the conflict, with the purported goal of outlining a path to peace and security, is taken up as a threat to Israel's existence. In invoking different parts of the public memory of apartheid, Carter and Dershowitz dramatize how uptake functions as a site of selection and power as well as of brokering, but even with Dershowitz's refusal to take up Carter's intended analogy, the act of transference itself and the fact that Dershowitz had to contend with it even in his rejection allowed Carter to move the debate. We can note the residue of that uptake today in US Secretary of State John Kerry's recent use of the word *apartheid* in reference to the risks of failed peace as well as in frequent references to apartheid in arguments for and against the campaign for boycott, divestment, and sanctions against Israel in the United States.

GENRES AND THE POSSIBILITY OF DELAYING UPTAKES

Attempts to study public deliberation about the Israel-Palestine conflict in the United States must contend with the uptakes that operate
or "hold" between genres. Such study reveals the dynamic, less predictable, rhizomatic nature of uptakes as they operate within the public
sphere, where the mechanisms for their coordination are more diffuse—managed less by metagenres and genre knowledge and more by
"long, ramified, intertextual" memories (Freadman 2002), differential
access to media (how often, when, and where positions are represented;
who gets to speak; how the issues are framed), public coercion (threats
to political and professional aspirations for those who speak out), and
the power of individuals to shape the discourse (individuals whose subject positions and affiliations grant them permission to broker uptakes
more freely than others). In addition, they compel us to pay attention
to the historical-material conditions and complex dynamics of agency
and power that function between, hold together, and shape public
genre performances. It is interesting, for example, to examine the role
powerful figures play, much more so than genres, in the distribution of
uptakes that shape US public discourse around this conflict. Individuals
such as Alan Dershowitz and Jimmy Carter perform the function of
what might be called *uptake sponsors* who work to maintain and broker
dominant (or resistant) uptakes). Drawing on Jennifer Nish's notion of
spreadable genres and distributive uptakes, uptake sponsors are individuals or institutions that work to condition, secure, and distribute certain
uptakes in ways that can traverse and exceed genre and context.

In light of these complex uptakes, what can genre and public sphere
scholars do to intervene in these uptakes in ways that encourage more
productive inquiry and public deliberation about this and other contentious topics? As I see it, the answer has to do in part with identifying and confronting the uptakes that secure and maintain habitual
responses. This means we need to acknowledge when these uptakes are
appropriate (as in the case of David Duke) and when they are used to
silence dialogue (as in the case of responses to Mearsheimer and Walt,
or Jimmy Carter, or Bob Simon's *60 Minutes* episode, or the American
Studies Association academic boycott resolution). Freadman (2002, 48)
explains that uptake represents its object. In this case, the power of
sponsored uptakes elides differences between David Duke and Jimmy
Carter, representing them both as posing the same or a similar threat.
The difference between Duke and Carter should *matter*, especially if we
want to have more nuanced and productive discussion about Israel in
the United States. But identifying uptakes is not enough. We also need

to intervene in these normalized uptakes—that is, delay, alter, or avoid triggering the habitual responses while also being accountable to evidence-based arguments. Part of that approach involves being careful in our rhetorical choices so as to avoid loaded, memory-triggering words, but part of it is also about imagining alternative uptakes as well as allowing genre and context distinctions to *matter*—to help us distinguish between uptakes in more nuanced, genre- and context-specific ways so as to allow for a greater selection of responses (something art and humor, for example, afford).

Art, in particular, allows us to linger longer in our encounters with genres, to experience provocative, even challenging and potentially threatening, ideas and situations in ways less quick to trigger habitual uptakes. Habitual uptakes are akin to what Daniel Kahneman (2011) has called "fast thinking," a form of routinized thinking that enables us to negotiate daily life without cognitive overload. But Kahneman also describes the power of "slow thinking" to allow us to take stock, reflect on what we know and do not know, and select from a broader set of uptake choices as we puzzle through experiences that disorient us. Ari Folman and David Polonsky's graphic novel and film *Waltz with Bashir* provides a powerful psychological account, from an Israeli soldier's perspective, of Israel's invasion of Lebanon, including Ariel Sharon's complicity in the Sabra and Shatila Palestinian refugee camp massacre (Folman and Polonsky 2009). Likewise, Joe Sacco's (2006) graphic novel *Palestine* offers an unflinching depiction of Palestinian life under occupation, while the popular and award-winning Israeli primetime sitcom *Arab Labor* depicts the life of an Israeli Arab journalist as he negotiates his Arab identity and the cultural divide between Israelis and Palestinians in Israel. In allowing their audience to delay the habitual uptakes, these artistic representations make possible the opportunity for alternative uptakes to take hold, alternative uptakes that have the potential to become recontextualized to other genres and contexts.

In this chapter I have tried to describe uptake as a dynamic site of agency that invites us to recognize the interlocking systems and forces at play in performances of genre in ways that exceed genre knowledge alone and get us closer to what Bhatia (2010) has termed "interdiscursive" performances informed by embodied memories, material and historical conditions, affective attachments, and other extratextual factors. As sites of agency, uptakes involve both the instantiation and regulation of power and the potential for intervention—a rhizomatic view of uptakes that accounts for and allows us to identify the relations and meanings secured by dominant uptakes. Such "thick" attention to and critical engagement with uptakes is particularly difficult because uptakes, as habits of remembering that mediate our encounters, are less textually, materially "visible" and predictable and more deeply held as attachments. The key is to delay the uptakes long enough for us to critically examine their sources and motivations as well as to consider what is permitted and what is excluded by these uptakes, how they operate in relation to genres (or not), and how they are shaped by power relations in the in-between spaces where public genre performances play out.

Note

1.   An earlier, differently focused version of this chapter appears in *Toward a Critical Rhetoric on the Israel-Palestine Conflict*, edited by Matthew Abraham (Parlor, 2015).

References

Anti-Defamation League. 2006. "A Review of Mearsheimer and Walt's 'The Israel Lobby and U.S. Foreign Policy': An Anti-Jewish Screed in Scholarly Guise." http://www.adl.org/israel-international/anti-israel-activity/c/mearsheimer-and-walts.html.

Bakhtin, M. M. 1986. "The Problem of Speech Genres." In *Speech Genres and Other Late Essays*, edited by Caryl Emerson and Michael Holquist, 60–102. Austin: University of Texas Press.

Barghouti, Mourid. 2000. *I Saw Ramallah.* New York: Anchor Books.

Bastian, Heather. 2015. "Capturing Individual Uptake." *Composition Forum* 31.

Bawarshi, Anis. 2008. "Genres as Forms of In[ter]vention." In *Originality, Imitation, Plagiarism: Teaching Writing in the Digital Age*, edited by Caroline Eisner and Martha Vicinus, 79–89. Ann Arbor: University of Michigan Press.

Bawarshi, Anis. forthcoming. "Accounting for Genre Performances: Why Uptake Matters." In *Trends and Traditions in Genre Studies*, edited by Natasha Artemeva and Aviva Freedman. Edmonton: Inkshed.

Berkenkotter, Carol, and Cristina Hanganu-Bresch. 2011. "Occult Genres and the Certification of Madness in a 19th-Century Lunatic Asylum." *Written Communication* 28 (2): 220–50. http://dx.doi.org/0.1177/0741088311401557.

Bhatia, Vijay. 2010. "Interdiscursivity in Professional Communication." *Discourse & Communication* 4 (1): 32–50. http://dx.doi.org/10.1177/1750481309351208.

Carter, Jimmy. 2006. *Palestine: Peace Not Apartheid.* New York: Simon and Schuster.

Coole, Diana, and Samantha Frost. 2010. *New Materialism: Ontology, Agency, and Politics.* Durham, NC: Duke University Press. http://dx.doi.org/10.1215/9780822392996.

Dershowitz, Alan. 2006. "Debunking the Newest – and Oldest – Jewish Conspiracy: A Reply to the Mearsheimer-Walt 'Working Paper.'" 1–46. http://www.comw.org/war report/fulltext/0604dershowitz.pdf.

Dershowitz, Alan. 2008. *The Case Against Israel's Enemies: Exposing Jimmy Carter and Others Who Stand in the Way of Peace.* Hoboken, NJ: Wiley and Sons.

Dryer, Dylan. 2008. "Taking Up Space: Genre Systems as Geographies of the Possible." *JAC: Rhetoric, Writing, Culture, Politics* 28 (3/4): 503–34.

Emmons, Kimberly K. 2009. "Uptake and the Biomedical Subject." In *Genre in a Changing World*, edited by Charles Bazerman, Adair Bonini, and Débora Figueiredo, 134–57. Fort Collins, CO: WAC Clearinghouse and Parlor.

Folman, Ari, and David Polonsky. 2009. *Waltz with Bashir: A Lebanon War Story.* New York: Metropolitan Books.

Foxman, Abraham H. 2007. *The Deadliest Lies: The Israel Lobby and the Myth of Jewish Control.* New York: Palgrave.

Freadman, Anne. 1994. "Anyone for Tennis?" In *Genre and the New Rhetoric,* edited by Aviva Freadman and Peter Medway, 43–66. Bristol: Taylor and Francis.

Freadman, Anne. 2002. "Uptake." In *The Rhetoric and Ideology of Genre: Strategies for Stability and Change,* edited by Richard Coe, Lorelei Lingard, and Tatiana Teslenko, 39–53. Cresskill, NJ: Hampton.

Freadman, Anne. 2012. "The Traps and Trappings of Genre Theory." *Applied Linguistics* 33 (5): 544–63. http://dx.doi.org/10.1093/applin/ams050.

Giltrow, Janet. 2002. "Meta-Genre." In *The Rhetoric and Ideology of Genre: Strategies for Stability and Change,* edited by Richard Coe, Lorelei Lingard, and Tatiana Teslenko, 187–205. Cresskill, NJ: Hampton.

Hass, Amira. 1996. *Drinking the Sea at Gaza: Days and Nights in a Land Under Siege.* New York: Henry Holt.

Kahneman, Daniel. 2011. *Thinking, Fast and Slow.* New York: Farrar, Straus and Giroux.

Kill, Melanie. 2006. "Acknowledging the Rough Edges of Resistance: Negotiation of Identities in First-Year Composition." *College Composition and Communication* 58 (2): 213–35.

Lave, Jean, and Etienne Wenger. 1991. *Situated Learning: Legitimate Peripheral Participation.* Cambridge: Cambridge University Press. http://dx.doi.org/10.1017/CBO97805118 15355.

Mearsheimer, John, and Stephen Walt. 2006a. "The Israel Lobby." *London Review of Books* 28 (6). http://www.lrb.co.uk/v28/n06/john-mearsheimer/the-israel-lobby.

Mearsheimer, John, and Stephen Walt. 2006b. "Letters." *London Review of Books* 28 (9). http://www.lrb.co.uk/v28/n06/john-mearsheimer/the-israel-lobby.

Morris, Benny. 1989. *The Birth of the Palestinian Refugee Problem 1947–1949.* Cambridge: Cambridge University Press.

Nowacek, Rebecca. 2011. *Agents of Integration: Understanding Transfer as a Rhetorical Act.* Carbondale: Southern Illinois University Press.

Pappe, Ilan. 2006. *The Ethnic Cleansing of Palestine.* Oxford: Oneworld.

Pipes, Daniel. 2006. "Letters." *London Review of Books* 28 (7). http://www.lrb.co.uk/v28 /n06/john-mearsheimer/the-israel-lobby.

Rounsaville, Angela. 2012. "Selecting Genres for Transfer: The Role of Uptake in Students' Antecedent Genre Knowledge." *Composition Forum* 26. http://composition forum.com/issue/26/selecting-genres-uptake.php.

Sacco, Joe. 2006. *Palestine.* Seattle: Fantagraphics Books.

Said, Edward W. 1986. *After the Last Sky: Palestinian Lives.* New York: Pantheon Books.

Segev, Tom. 2000. *One Palestine, Complete: Jews and Arabs Under the British Mandate.* Translated by Haim Watzman. New York: Henry Holt.

Seidel, Chalet K. 2007. "Professionalizing the Student Body: Uptake in a Nineteenth Century Journalism Textbook." *Linguistics and the Human Sciences* 3 (1): 67–85.

3
DISAMBIGUATING UPTAKE
Toward a Tactical Research Agenda on Citizens' Writing

Dylan B. Dryer

"Culture" is the history of the fact that more often than not we do not share contexts and of our means of dealing with that fact.
—Anne Freadman 2002

INTRODUCTION: CONSIDERING UPTAKE

In the thirty years since Carolyn R. Miller's "Genre as Social Action" effectively launched rhetorical genre studies (RGS), studies of *how* genres mediate "private intentions and social exigence" and connect "the private with the public, the singular with the recurrent" (Miller 1984, 163) have reshaped our understanding of what writing even means. Writing is now routinely described as *situated, embedded, enmeshed,* and *imbricated* in social and material contexts. From the undergraduate who arranges her furniture to pen herself in so she cannot leave her writing desk (Prior and Shipka 2003), to the English major repurposing her array of fan-fiction skills across her educational career and into her own classroom (Roozen 2009), to skilled professionals improvising and automating responses to a rapidly changing work environment (Spinuzzi 2010), writing studies has oriented to a "broad framework that links textual forms, literate and semiotic practices, identities, and social formations in dynamic and historical trajectories" (Prior and Bilbro 2012, 31; see also MacMillan 2012). This framework has enabled productive lines of inquiry into these forms, practices, identities, and social trajectories and accounts for the increasing importance of the concept of uptake to RGS since—as we will see—the term is used to invoke, if somewhat imprecisely, just such complex linkages.

Anne Freadman (1994) first alerted RGS to the implications of Austin's observation that speech acts don't exist apart from their *effects.* "The performance of an illocutionary act," says Austin, *"involves* the securing of an uptake" (Austin 1962, 116; emphasis added)—"involves,"

DOI: 10.7330/9781607324430.c003

that is, as in *is necessary to*: where there is no uptake, no speech act can be said to have occurred. Freadman—like Miller a decade earlier—was challenging the usefulness of the dominant formalist construct of genre. As interest in genre conventions *qua* conventions waned in favor of the social relations those conventions reflect and produce, Freadman argued that "genre" is a concept better applied to "the interaction of, minimally, a pair of texts" than it is to any single text's "standardized morphology" (Freadman 2002, 40). Freadman called this interaction "uptake," offering us a construct of genre as *movement*—interrelationships drawing together configurations of conventions into (perceived) recurrence in particular places and times. In one of Freadman's frequently cited examples, the proposal is the uptake of a call for papers; again, the point is that the *interplay* accords generic status. A genre stops being a genre if, as she says, its value ceases to be negotiated (since negotiations, even adversarial or parodic ones, assume a value in need of settling).

By this logic, only in their uptakes do genre sets, systems, colonies, and ecologies have (what we are pleased to call) their lives, their "ramifications" (Freadman 2002), their modifications and hybridizations, their dissolution, and their otherwise inexplicable persistence. Uptakes are exceptionally difficult to pin down; as Anis Bawarshi explains, they "configure, normalize, and activate relations and meanings within and between systems of genres" and elude scrutiny because "they are learned recognitions of significance that over time and in particular contexts become habitual" (Bawarshi 2006, 653). Uptake could be likened to a speculative element at the bottom of the periodic table (ununoctium, say, which exists only for milliseconds under highly controlled conditions). Or like subatomic particles, genre uptakes reveal themselves in fleeting moments of alignment with, or disruption of, writers' "complex and sometimes conflicting templates of languages, Englishes, discourses, senses of self, visions of life, and notions of . . . relations with others and the world" (Lu 2004, 28; for an attempt to induce generic profiles this way, see Reiff and Bawarshi 2011).

In attempting to operationalize such insights, the broad framework now dominant in writing studies has overtaxed RGS's conceptual vocabulary for delineating specific interactions among forms, practices, identities, and social formations—any and all of which we seem, confusedly, to mean by the word *uptake*. In disambiguating such uses below (some of which extend beyond Freadman's [1994; 2002; 2012; 2014] ongoing work with the concept), my aim is not to isolate a correct definition of the term but to illustrate that variation in its use points to different elements of the phenomenon. If our aim is to better understand these complex interactions, we require a more precise vocabulary: one that will enable us to ask more specific questions and to deploy more focused research methods than we have so far.

CITIZEN-WRITERS

Citizens' written participation in public deliberation and governmental decision-making illuminate these different elements of uptake in productive ways. As the editors' introduction to this collection points out, RGS has mostly confined itself to immediately or proximally available academic or workplace contexts and writers. In that spirit, public-sector genres fit neither the curriculum nor the "extracurriculum" (Gere 1994); that is, they are self-sponsored in the sense of being voluntary but are also strongly framed by legal requirements and public institutions, and thus the usual constructs of agency don't easily apply.[1]

Like the well-studied genre systems of healthcare, those of land-use administration touch all lives. Urban planners work among complex systems of documents to shape the built environments of cities and thus the lives that can be lived there (for a startling glimpse of this complexity, see Turner 2006, 145). Among that welter of largely occluded forms, boilerplates, and document chains (consultant/facilitator requests for proposals, solicitation e-mails, surveys, agendas, draft ordinances, meeting minutes, talking points, report-outs, zoning codes, comprehensive plans, maps of planned developments and overlay districts, etc.), we find those that solicit and sift citizens' input on pending land-use decisions.[2] For in the United States, European Union, and Commonwealth—as increasingly elsewhere—it is matter of regulatory compliance at the highest levels that citizens be consulted in municipal decision making about the built environment (building, demolishing, authorizing, rezoning, writing or revising an ordinance, etc.). *Consulted* is broadly construed and ranges from a brightly colored flyer posted on a nearby public right of way, to surveys, to opportunities to make oral or written comments to public officials and/or private stakeholders, to consultations, citizen juries, and/or steering or advisory committees, all of which mobilize diffuse reading and writing practices.

In the United States, such laws have been in place since the HUD reforms of the mid-1960s, which makes this salvo by two prominent scholars in public policy and urban planning worth considering at length.

It is time to face facts we know, but prefer to ignore. Legally required methods of public participation in government decision making in the

US—public hearings, review and comment procedures in particular—do not work. They do not achieve genuine participation in planning or other decisions; they do not satisfy members of the public that they are being heard; they seldom can be said to improve the decisions that agencies and public officials make; and they do not incorporate a broad spectrum of the public. Worse yet, these methods often antagonize the members of the public who do try to work with them. The methods often pit citizens against each other, as they feel compelled to speak of the issues in polarizing terms to get their points across. This pattern makes it even more difficult for decision makers to sort through what they hear, much less to make a choice using public input. Most often these methods discourage busy and thoughtful individuals from wasting their time going through what appear to be nothing more than rituals designed to satisfy legal requirements. They also increase the ambivalence of planners and other public officials about hearing from the public at all. Nonetheless, these methods have an almost sacred quality to them, and they stay in place despite all that everyone knows is wrong with them. (Innes and Booher 2004, 419)

RGS would predict productive uptakes here; in fact, everything seems to be in place: material support, recognizable scenes, established precedents, clearly defined roles, and investment in (putatively) shared motives. Yet at the same time Judith E. Innes and David E. Booher invoke typified utterances, "public hearings, review and comment procedures," they invoke equally typified metageneric commentary: such utterances are "rituals" that "everyone knows" don't work. There are plenty of questions for both Innes and Booher (2004) and RGS: what constitutes "genuine participation" in the context of legal compliance? If "polarization" is a pattern, might citizens be responding to tacit polarization embedded in the framing of the "issues" or to the inadvertent telegraphing of planners' "ambivalence" about involving citizens in the first place? Can "rituals" be satisfying in more than one way? And what accounts for these methods' persistence, anyway, since "everyone knows" what's wrong with them?

Such questions point to a construct of social relations and language use (or text and context, or participation forum and citizen) that is dynamic and mutually constitutive. Research that has advanced this construct typically assumes recurrent contexts from which genres, as it is now usually said, "arise" (Reiff and Bawarshi 2011; Smith 2011; Tardy 2003; Wardle 2009) or "emerge" (Bazerman 2009; Devitt 2009; Fuzer and Barros 2009; Schryer 2002). Yet Freadman's epigraph above warns us not to be too sanguine about how "mutual" these interactions actually are. Instead, she advises us to see genres as one of the means by which the emergent is continuously reorganized in the terms of the dominant and the residual, and culture itself as the range of relations all of us take in relation to that ongoing reorganization. While "emerge" and "arise" avoid both Scylla (assigning simplistic agency to the human actor) and Charybdis (assigning deterministic control to the genre), they do so at the cost of black-boxing the writer's brain—passing it over with phrases like *writers coming to understand conventions* or *writers coming to be acclimated*. Such descriptions are accurate without satisfying the question of *how* this happens. *That* question is extraordinarily complex, necessarily involving textual forms (and talk about those forms) and the various literacies and technologies involved in composing and distributing those forms, all of which are located in specific material sites mobilizing the cognitive architecture and the multiple motivations of anyone engaging in such composing and talking. Neither RGS nor our colleagues in urban planning have been equipped to see the social scene of "public participation in government decision making" (Innes and Booher 2004, 419) for what it truly is: ongoing assumptions embedded in the genre systems of public participation continuously laboring to refashion the present in spite of contributions from those who don't necessarily share those assumptions.

Imprecision about the elements of this concatenation among uses (or avoidances), encounters, responses, and effects (short- and long-term) of texts leads us to confuse various parts with the whole. To make that argument, I'll briefly map current uses of *uptake* so as to illuminate the problems a different construct of agency can help solve. I'll then apply that frame to genres of citizen commentary in order to show a convergence in thinking among different scholars of the public's writings and conclude by considering some implications of this convergence for studies of uptake in the public sphere. These studies are of more than theoretical interest: an enormous amount of public and public-sector writing on these topics will take place in the next decades as sea-level rise forces us to triage our coastal cities' built resources. RGS must help shape the texts that invite citizens to contribute meaningful writing and ensure that citizens' writing is taken up in the most productive ways.

DISAMBIGUATING UPTAKE

Uptake has a long tradition of use in the social sciences, K–12 education, and in second-language acquisition,[3] where it tends to mean measurable *use* or *adoption* of something that's been offered: an updated policy, a social good, a research finding, an innovation. Here we find studies of how tenth-grade teachers "assign writing tasks that result in uptake of academic vocabulary" (Wolsey 2010, 194) or suggestions that "effective policy makers . . . anticipate local uptakes and collateral effects" (Luke 2011, 376). Because these researchers are primarily concerned with facilitating particular uses or deterring particular activities, they focus on opportunities and constraints in the conventions that precede and shape the encounter, lines of inquiry we might restrict to the term *uptake affordances* (cf. Prior 2009, 25, 28). Papers that directly cite Freadman, on the other hand, usually use *uptake* to refer to another genre—that is, a text produced in response to other texts (Berkenkotter and Hanganu-Bresch 2011, 222) or an "intermediary" genre that facilitates the uptake of one genre by another (Tachino 2012). Here we are likely to find a sentence like "an underlying assumption in the genre of the writing assignment across the curriculum is for students to construct discourse for a wider audience and to develop an appropriate uptake text that fulfills the generic expectations of that audience" (Clark 2005). In such uses, I suggest that what is being described is more precisely an *uptake artifact.*

Two additional senses of the word are apparent when we shift attention from text-objects to composers. First, it appears that sometimes we mean by *uptake* something like *deliberate repurposing of.* Natasha Artemeva's case study of a novice engineer "illustrates a successful—though risky— uptake . . . undertaken by a novice who has developed sufficient understanding of professional genres and the hierarchy of the engineering workplace to be able to subvert local practices" (Artemeva 2006, 162). The *act* of producing an utterance or text in response to uptake affordances we should call *uptake enactments.* A second set of uses describes cognitive or affective *consequences* of uptake: in other words, what do successive uptakes do *to* readers and writers? Kimberly Emmons argues, for example, that "the intimate, embodied power" of uptake means defining it "not as the relation between two (or more) genres, but as the disposition of subjects that results from that relation" (Emmons 2009, 137). "It is by examining the processes of uptake that inform our most habitual responses," writes Melanie Kill, "that we have the best chance of making conscious choices to change and challenge limiting and self-defeating patterns of interaction" (Kill 2006, 233). These researchers are, I suggest, really describing *uptake capture,* a term that emphasizes uptake's temporal dimensions. Repeated encounters with genres have lingering effects on what writers see—or indeed are *able* to see—as the realm of the possible in academic (Berkenkotter, Huckin, and Ackerman 1988; Casanave 1992; Dryer 2012; Leki 2003), workplace (Dias and Paré 2000; Paré 2002; Schryer 2002), and personal (Regaignon 2015) lifeworlds.

One connotation remains: what Freadman calls "memory." Freadman understands memory to operate across very long timescales. Consistent with her 2002 demonstration of uptake as "long, ramified, intergeneric memories," she has recently argued that context should be "defined not only as a single 'occasion' but as a sequence of events in time and across a variety of temporal sequences" (Freadman 2012, 558). A judicial sentence becomes an execution, she finds, because of "*the genres that constitute collective memory* and the uptakes they condition" (2002, 51; emphasis added). Freadman's suggestion is unsettling; we are all implicated in these memories, yet these memories (or "histories" [cf. 2012, 547]) belong to no one of us. Observed from this altitude, any instance of any of these dimensions of uptake is an incremental contribution to social formations: uptake affordances, artifacts, enactments, and captures all help maintain, modify, and destabilize cultural institutions—phenomena we might describe as *uptake residues*. Unfortunately for the necessary basic research still to be done on these recognitions, the more normalized the *uptake affordance*, the more instantaneous and "natural" the moment of *uptake capture*, the more powerful the *uptake artifact*, the more habitual the *uptake enactment*, and the more deeply sedimented the *uptake residues*.

Writing studies' interest in civic writing focuses mostly on *uptake capture*. For example, Derek Wallace finds it "hard to escape the conclusion" that a task force's handling of public response to a utility-privatization proposal was only a "system designed to extrude and then re-ingest [citizens' comments] to satisfy an institutionalized requirement to consult and be consulted" (Wallace 2003, 169). Wallace's reading of citizens' writing was until recently the dominant one in research and scholarship on urban studies, but in the next section we will see evidence of a gradual shift toward a perspective more like that of Spoel and Barriault (2011). These scholars, who in reminding us that citizens are always "motivated by complex clusters of values, interests, and emotions," help signal both the complexities and the promise of more nuanced understanding of individual and institutional language practices (106). To accelerate this shift, we must attend to the multifaceted ways uptake unfolds so we can investigate each dimension empirically and study public participation in ways that do justice to its complexity.

REFRAMING PARTICIPATION "RITUALS"

Beginning with the still widely cited article by Sherry R. Arnstein (1969), disciplines like urban studies and planning, environmental sciences, and resource economics share a substantial body of work measuring the ideal of citizen participation against the actual experiences of citizens

and practices of municipalities. Some examine ways in which nondomi-
nant rhetorical strategies work against citizens' ability to be heard (Tauxe
1995, 472–79); others highlight inequitable distributions of "organizational and financial resources" that allow the well-enfranchised to arro-
gate the terms of the discussion (Fainstein 2003, 187) or the ways in
which special interests specifically (e.g., a chamber of commerce) or
generally (the upper-middle class) deploy experts to turn the discussion
to the outcome they desire (Rydin and Pennington 2000, 156).

   Nonetheless, the editors of a more recent special issue of *Planning
Practice & Research* speculate that the era of exposés of "the 'dark-side'
in neo-liberal planning practice" is drawing to a close (Brownill and
Parker 2010, 276). It appears that contemporary researchers in these
fields are less interested in documenting public participation's failure
to meet its ideal and more interested in diagnosing specific sites of failure.[4] Much of this research is technocratic—concerned with tinkering
with uptake affordances to optimize information "handoff" (e.g., Loh
2012), the design of participatory mechanisms (Chaskin et al. 2012,
897), or planners' understanding of appropriate resource allocation
(McGovern 2013, 319). But others are beginning the hard work of
challenging the very construct of "participation" itself. For example,
Jarkko Bamberg (2013) challenges urban planners' assumptions that
public participation is only for "delivering information and producing
knowledge for planning" (48) while other scholars work toward a better
understanding of the ways the "more visible social and economic closure mechanisms" reproduce "cognitive closure mechanisms" (Hanssen
and Saglie 2010, 516). Instead of creating additional routes for participation, suggest Beebeejaun and Vanderhoven (2010, 295), "we might
start to think about . . . exploring what is said in more complex and
productive ways."

   Such scholars seem more likely now to talk about frames or filters
than hegemony. Jeremiads about neoliberal city-states' diversion of
social critique by foisting responsibilities on untrained volunteers have
given way to more measured questions about the construct of participation embedded in the public-outreach toolkits available to planners.
Meanwhile, a few empirical investigations of occluded genres like meeting agendas are problematizing long-standing assumptions about correlations between median income and political priorities (Jun and Musso
2013) and the "rational choice" models that guide decision-making
procedures (Parker and Murray 2012, 24). Brownill and Parker (2010)
charge public officials with clarifying the means and ends of particular designs of specific applications of participatory opportunities and

venture an interesting definition of participation: "being *involved and being aware* of how planning and related policy will shape one's own environment" (281; emphasis added).

That this list of articles sounds increasingly as if it could belong at a recent symposium on rhetorical genre studies signals a convergence: a mutual reorientation toward the complexities of language practices. It also signals an opportunity in which breakthroughs in RGS's understanding of uptake can contribute to public participation and in which studies of public participation can contribute to RGS's struggle with agency (see Freadman 2014). Urban planners and rhetorical genre theorists alike are teaching themselves to see language practices as reflecting and producing complex "surrounds" of uptake affordances, artifacts, enactments, captures, and residues.

Freadman reminds us that "uptake is first the taking of an object; it is *not* the causation of a response by an intention" (Freadman 2002, 48). As RGS and urban studies alike try to do better justice to the complexity of what it means for a writer to write or a citizen to participate, the reciprocal relations they are uncovering resonate, I suggest, with contemporary cognitive science. Reading that neuroscientists now accept that "the bounds of cognition . . . include the body in an environment" (Berninger and Winn 2006, 108), we gain another insight into the exceptional complexity of what it means to "decide" to take up a genre.[5] Marilyn Cooper (2011) finds that brain researchers generally agree that we act not so much *on* the world but *into* what she calls a "surround"— a social and physical space present in our minds before we are aware of it that is already cuing us to actions that seem proper, fitting, useful, expedient, unavoidable, compulsory—and which, in a matter of milliseconds, we will believe we decided to do.[6]

Understanding "cognitive processes and brain dynamics as embodied nonlinear self-organizing systems interacting with the surround" (Cooper 2011, 421) offers a way to understand how "stabilized for now" (Schryer 1993, 208) reading and writing practices "emerge" and "arise." We can instead think of undergraduate education, or workplace acclimatization, or even those unworkable "rituals" Innes and Booher (2004) declaim as a surround of countless uptakes of generic affordances: texts taken up to read and write, artifacts produced and taken up in response, the accompanying washes of "neuromodulators such as histamine, dopamine, endorphins, vasopressin and norepinephrine" by and through which brains make sense of the surround of textual practices by forming and reinforcing neural pathways (Cooper 2011, 431). To take academic writing as a case in point, if freshmen wonder how they can possibly write within academic genres, the *uptake residue* four years later can be found in seniors who believe they cannot *not* write within those genres.

It seems both possible and productive to draw together these various threads of RGS and public-sector research under this concept of the surround—such as, textual, social, and built environments cueing citizens and public officials toward certain language practices that may be rebuilt (or negotiated, or rewritten) to cue us toward others. To this end, the next section returns to the five uptake distinctions mapped above, suggesting in each case how specific insights and certain (increasingly shared) methods might coordinate cooperation between RGS and the public sphere. While Kaifeng Yang (2005) argues that public administrators' trust of citizens "may be one of the biggest obstacles to authentic citizen involvement" (273), a better angle of approach (since genres constitute the realm of the intersubjective) is the very texts municipalities use to invite, orchestrate, and report on citizens' involvement. The disambiguated categories of uptake mapped above can be mobilized with insights from RGS and planning alike to model different ways of thinking about citizens' writing in this dimension of the public sphere.

TOWARD A RESEARCH AGENDA ON PUBLIC-SPHERE UPTAKE

Anyone with experience of public planning will find this description familiar:

> The public mostly wants clear answers to its questions, not speculation; it wants to hear as much about fundamental decisions as details, and it wants to know that the planners, elected officials and policy-makers know what they are doing, even though it will often accuse them otherwise. For the most contentious of issues, these publics also want to vent their emotions either because something important about their world is threatened or because they are simply frustrated with government. They are there to express their concerns, not to deliberate. They are there for acknowledgment and validation, not for (just for) information. They are there to discuss the kinds of places in which they want to live, with whom they want to live, and the changes they are willing to tolerate, not technical arguments. (Beauregard 2013, 13)

But RGS, sensitive to the ways the reconstitution of genres perpetuates the path-dependence of entire systems of belief (like the "polarizing" discourse of citizens or the "sacred" qualities of participation "rituals") should detect in Beauregard's world-weary description neurological routines fostered by commonplace ways of making sense of what citizens want and what they say. The danger here is taking what the public "wants" as natural and inevitable when it is socially produced—and as such, subject to contestation and change. So reframed, what the public "wants" or what they are "there for" is available for empirical inquiry (see Hanssen and Saglie 2010; McComas 2003).

Considering *uptake affordances* (the opportunities and constraints in the conventions that precede and shape the uptake encounter), Pierre Bourdieu's critique of polling practices applies: "[a]sking everyone the same question," he writes, implies "agreement about which questions are worth asking," and to such questions, respondents "take the positions which we are predisposed to take in function of our position in a certain domain" (Bourdieu 1979, 124–28). (Orchestrating a series of "perspectives" on an issue, he argues, will yield a series of such "positions" useful only for inducing the "real" question being responded to.) Open-ended, often anodyne questions about impressions of neighborhoods or relative enthusiasm for conceptual renderings remain routine ways to prompt citizen input. But just as Heather Bastian (2010; 2015) has found that *unusual* writing situations have potential to deroutinize *uptake enactments*, Cooper and others have suggested that disruptions to the "skillful coping" of everyday cognition (mostly handled by nonconscious processes of "AM patterns, basins of attraction, neuron assemblies, and neuromodulators") can bring such processes "to awareness" (Cooper 2011, 429). What's needed here are not more efficient ways to harvest community beliefs and perceptions but "probing questions that elude framing" (Kaufman and Smith 1999, 178) and that unsettle rituals of participation that trigger the predisposed position.

In helping to design scaffolding for public participation (surveys, think pieces, discussion questions, charrettes, design juries) RGS might contribute *disruptakes*—uptake affordances that deliberately create inefficiencies, misfires, and occasions for second-guessing that could thwart automaticity-based *uptake enactments*. As I have argued elsewhere, even small adjustments to the wording of such prompts would deroutinize their *uptake enactment at the moment of their presentation.*[7] Delays—even of minutes—could offer citizens and planners alike the chance to perceive a fuller range of discursive and cultural resources as germane to the discussion but which their long habituation with the conventional has made, neurologically speaking, hard to perceive as relevant or appropriate. Calling on our colleagues in technical communication and applied linguistics, we are now in the realm of testable hypotheses. For example, usability testing with stratified sampling could test whether particular *uptake affordances* (e.g., invitations for reflective writing, member-validated word choices, or comparisons of "cognitive mapping" exercises [Reynolds 2004, 82–85]) might be usefully adapted to different kinds of urban-planning initiatives (neighborhood branding, rezoning, community planning, quality of life studies, etc.).

Recalling that *uptake artifacts* (the genre[s] that result from uptake) are both medium and outcome of the social processes discussed here, Freadman herself has suggested the uses of a corpus of *uptake artifacts* ("a corpus of [physicians'] referral letters," she wagered, would reveal "all sorts of ways of indicating to one another not only their medical judgments, but their assessments as to the patient's supposed character, his/her way of handling suffering," and so on [1994, 50]). Machine parsing the syntactic and discursive patterns in a collection of citizens' responses could offer planners a productively disinterested perspective on citizens' input. As Ken Hyland (2012) points out, corpus analysis can go beyond interviews or observations of specific *occasions* of writing to locate what is independently variant and therefore what individuals and collectivities actually, consistently *do*. Freeware like Antconc (Anthony 2014) can immediately show not only which words (or strings of words) are most likely to appear in a given collection but also the contexts in which they appear and the relative frequency of neighboring terms (word frequency, concordancing, and collocation, respectively). Examining citizens' responses this way could interrupt cognitive routines that impose ritualistic qualities on citizens' comments. Until their contexts of use are mapped carefully, for example, it may not become apparent that words like *development, safety, affordable,* or *jobs* are aligned with sharply different priorities. With time, these corpora could be compiled into a reference corpus with fields and tables cross-indexed by region, project, type of question, stakeholder, and so on against which it would be possible to see the recurring terms and collocations that distinguish citizens' word choices about specific initiatives or neighborhoods from discursive formulations that seem more conventional to these contexts.

Richard Buttny (2010), who actually uses the word *uptake* in the sense of *enactment* (the *act* of producing an utterance or text in response to uptake affordances), finds evidence in his case study of a rezoning hearing that citizens' use of metadiscourse had functional roles in developing solidarity and (because their rhetorical tactics sometimes provoked unscripted rationales and rationalizations from officially impassive board members) a better understanding of where those board members actually stood on the issue (654). This striking example of the unpredictability of language practice and of language users' multiple motives and resources should interest RGS ethnographers in a better understanding of how the writers of uptake artifacts reconstruct their *uptake enactment* strategies, an exploration for which stimulated-elicitation interviews (Reiff and Bawarshi 2011) are well suited. Attention to citizens' everyday strategic repurposing is a useful antidote to the tendency to prematurely assign stability to, in this case, citizens' "identities, desires, beliefs, and values" (Lu and Horner 2013, 597). Although few citizens might themselves put it quite this way, three decades of RGS-informed studies of students and workers suggest widespread awareness that reading and writing practices bleed across permeable lifeworlds of work, home, school, and recreation. Ambivalence and resistance are legitimate responses to that knowledge; moreover, ambivalence and resistance can be knowledge-making practices in their own right. Seemingly off-topic or inappropriate responses can be read as indicators of the boundaries of the frame envisioned by planners, boundaries that may therefore warrant another look.

As noted above, there is as substantial a literature in urban studies on the susceptibility of public-participation processes to seizure by dominant interests as there is in writing studies on seizure of knowledge-making capacities by dominant language practices. Against the cognitive and affective consequences of *uptake capture* (the way repeated encounters with genres have lingering effects on what writers see or are even *able* to see), opportunities exist to join those interested in creating the conditions for building social capital. After all, "citizen participation may be fostered as much by the creation of opportunity structures that build confidence in the efficacy of participation as by the intrinsic levels of civic culture" (Docherty et al. 2001, 2246). Citizens invited on short notice often encounter a new way of talking about their city for the first time in an unfamiliar and sometimes formal context, can feel overwhelmed by technical detail and patronized by "experts," and can leave unsure of what has been decided. Clearly the factors that "influence citizens' attitudes toward public meetings as decision making processes, including citizens' enthusiasm or willingness to take part in future meetings, bear further investigation" (McComas 2003, 181).

Those taking up McComas's challenge, like Carolyn G. Loh (2012) and Stephen J. McGovern (2013), have pinpointed some of the places at which citizen involvement is most likely to break down, especially at the transitions between initial *uptake enactments* and the more technocratic realms of planning design. But from the perspective of *uptake capture*, the well-documented difficulties public officials face in getting anyone other than "avid proponents and opponents of a measure affecting them personally . . . representatives of organized interest groups, and . . . a handful of diehard board watchers" (Innes and Booher 2004, 424) to show up for public hearings is an understandable consequence of citizens' lived experience of encounters with official genres. Given urban studies' vested interest in discovering why these meetings go awry— seemingly invariably, as innumerable case studies testify—focus groups (see Emmons 2009) using coding from nodes could excavate the affective and cognitive experiences of *uptake capture*. It would be possible, after all, to examine an array of citizen/city-hall interactions so as to trace the social and discursive experiences that build and—through perceived repetition—*literally* reinforce citizens' "neurodynamic structures." Such information would help us to better understand those moments in which citizens become convinced that the meeting is going wrong—a conviction, recall, that solidifies *before* citizens are consciously aware of it.

The essential point is that *uptake captures* and the dispositions that result are *mitigable*—reversible, even. For example, Vivien Lowndes et al.'s synthesis of research in public participation finds multiple points of contact where the relationship between citizen and institution is more malleable than conventional wisdom would predict. Municipalities, in one scenario, could offer multiple *kinds* of invitations and/or venues in which to participate (since not all citizens will perceive an invitation in the same way, or even perceive it as an invitation at all [Lowndes et al. 2006, 288]). Lowndes et al. also validate Iain Docherty et al.'s findings, cited above: the kind, quality, and amount of citizens' commentary is elastic and thus less a known quantity to be collected and more an *effect* of the social relationships in the community invited to participate (and, moreover, that those relationships can be *built*) (Lowndes et al. 2006, 286–88).

For even RGS has chronically underestimated the inertia of what Dorothy Smith and Catherine F. Schryer call "documentary society"— the ways "texts penetrate and organize the very texture of daily life as well as the always-developing foundations of the social relations and organization of science, industry, commerce, and the public sphere" (Smith and Schryer 2008, 116). Participant-ethnographers could apply insights from the categories and methods described above to document the formation, maintenance, and strategic disruption of *uptake residue* (the accretion and sedimentation of memory that conditions uptakes) on a citywide scale (Grabill [2007] and Flower [2008] provide glimpses of what this might look like). If, as systemic-functional linguistics has it, "culture is a system of genres" (Martin 2009), the way to understand what Freadman meant by "culture" in this chapter's epigraph is as civic institutions' capacity, through all the dimensions of uptake I have mapped here, to habituate new readers and writers into contexts they did not initially share.

History teaches us that there were moments in which what came to pass could have been otherwise. As the seas rise, the contextualizing urban surrounds that cities provide will change rapidly. While the moments of decision-making are approaching, they still contain multiple possibilities. Since we all must live in the *uptake residues*, this edited collection orients RGS to a pragmatic understanding of the reconstitution of public genres and equips us to disrupt routinized *uptake affordances, artifacts,* and *captures* that will favor the elite and to facilitate *uptake enactments* that keep other possibilities alive for us all. And there is hope, after all: perhaps these rituals of participation have a sacred quality because we do believe there is a point in talking with each other. Perhaps what we see here is not just a matter of blind adherence but signs of optimism, trust, and faith. Perhaps the public has more faith in planners and more to contribute to the process than they are imagined to have—or that the documents currently written for them encourage them to demonstrate.

Notes

1.   RGS's difficulty with agency (see, again, Freadman 2014) has hindered its ability to keep the full complexities of the phenomenon of textual recurrence firmly in view, which will become obvious once we relocate the situation of writing from the academic (or occasionally) workplace sites that have traditionally been its purview.

2.   There are well-developed literatures in rhetoric and writing studies and in public communication and administration on the problematics of risk communication and environmental impacts—probably because the stakes are highest, most immediate, and because the scenes of contact among experts, elected officials, and the public are so fraught (see esp. Katz and Miller; 1996, Rice 2012). My concern here is the more routine moments of city planning and administration, where participation is more likely to be seen as a "technicality" because the future impacts of the change are unknowable.

3.   Uptake has a technical application in biochemistry, where it refers to the absorption of molecules into cells (for example, thanks to aggressive marketing of antidepressives, most people have heard of serotonin reuptake inhibitors). That particular sense dominates its overall use in academic research but is not of interest here.

4.   For example, planners have been attentive to the ways in which GIS mapping and map-annotation technologies have changed what participation can mean (though they have also ruefully noted the persistence of prior constructs of participation in spite of these new technologies). This enthusiasm is recoalescing around VGL (voluntary geographic labeling, e.g., review features in Google Earth), though tempered from the perspective of GIS veterans who have sounded cautionary notes about "the epistemologies, vocabularies, and categories of data structures [that] do not or cannot encompass the experiences, knowledge claims, and identities of some social groups or places" (Elwood 2008, 178).

5. Such research has largely borne out the work of early philosophers of the mind, whose names readers in writing studies may find more familiar than the names of their modern successors.
6. For example, goal setting (a cognitive task of considerable interest to early process researchers) is now understood to occur *before* the emotions and the intentions we experience as caused by external stimuli (Cooper 2011, 429).
7. For example, instead of "In your opinion, what is the most critical issue for the Plan Area?" citizens could be asked, "What issue(s) could you imagine working on together with your neighbors and the City to address in your neighborhood? What could the City provide that would make that work easier to organize and complete?" (Dryer 2010, 50).

References

Anthony, Laurence. 2014. AntConc (Version 3.2.4) [Computer Software]. Tokyo: Waseda University. http://www.laurenceanthony.net/.

Arnstein, Sherry R. 1969. "A Ladder of Citizen Participation." *AIP Journal:* 216–24.

Artemeva, Natasha. 2006. "A Time to Speak, a Time to Act: A Rhetorical Genre Analysis of a Novice Engineer's Calculated Risk Taking." In *Rhetorical Genre Studies and Beyond*, edited by Natasha Artemeva and Aviva Freedman, 189–240. Winnipeg, MB: Inkshed.

Austin, J. L. 1962. *How to Do Things with Words.* Cambridge, MA: Harvard University Press.

Bamberg, Jarkko. 2013. "Engaging the Public with Online Discussion and Spatial Annotations: The Generation and Transformation of Public Knowledge." *Planning Theory & Practice* 14 (1): 39–56. http://dx.doi.org/10.1080/14649357.2012.738306.

Bastian, Heather. 2010. "The Genre Effect: Exploring the Unfamiliar." *Composition Studies* 38 (1): 27–49.

Bawarshi, Anis. 2006. "Taking Up Language Differences in Composition." *College English* 68 (6): 652–56. http://dx.doi.org/10.2307/25472181.

Bawarshi, Anis. 2015. "Capturing Individual Uptake: Toward a Disruptive Research Methodology." *Composition Forum* 31 (Spring). http://www.compositionforum.com/issue/31/individual-uptake.php.

Bazerman, Charles. 2009. "Genre and Cognitive Development: Beyond Writing to Learn." In *Genre in a Changing World*, edited by Charles Bazerman, Adair Bonini, and Débora Figueiredo, 279–94. West Lafayette, IN: Parlor and WAC Clearinghouse. http://dx.doi.org/10.4000/pratiques.1419.

Beauregard, Robert. 2013. "The Neglected Places of Practice." *Planning Theory & Practice* 14 (1): 8–19. http://dx.doi.org/10.1080/14649357.2012.744460.

Beebeejaun, Yasminah, and David Vanderhoven. 2010. "Informalizing Participation: Insights from Chicago and Johannesburg." *Planning Practice and Research* 25 (3): 283–96. http://dx.doi.org/10.1080/02697459.2010.503415.

Berkenkotter, Carol, and Cristina Hanganu-Bresch. 2011. "Occult Genres and the Certification of Madness in a 19th-Century Lunatic Asylum." *Written Communication* 28 (2): 220–50. http://dx.doi.org/10.1177/0741088311401557.

Berkenkotter, Carol, Thomas Huckin, and John Ackerman. 1988. "Conventions, Conversations, and the Writer: Case Study of a Student in a Rhetoric PhD Program." *Research in the Teaching of English* 22 (1): 9–44.

Berninger, Virginia W., and William D. Winn. 2006. "Implications of Advancements in Brain Research and Technology for Writing Development, Writing Instruction, and Educational Evolution." In *Handbook of Writing Research*, edited by Charles A. MacArthur, Steve Graham, and Jill Fitzgerald, 96–111. New York: Guilford.

Bourdieu, Pierre. 1979. "Public Opinion Does Not Exist." In *Communication and Class Struggle. Vol 1: Capitalism, Imperialism,* edited by Armand Mattelart and Seth Siegelaub, 124–29. New York: International General.

Brownill, Sue, and Gavin Parker. 2010. "Why Bother with Good Works? The Relevance of Public Participation(s) in Planning in a Post-Collaborative Era." *Planning Practice and Research* 25 (3): 275–82. http://dx.doi.org/10.1080/02697459.2010.503407.

Buttny, Richard. 2010. "Citizen Participation, Metadiscourse, and Accountability: A Public Hearing on a Zoning Change for Wal-Mart." *Journal of Communication* 60 (4): 636–59. http://dx.doi.org/10.1111/j.1460-2466.2010.01507.x.

Casanave, Christine Pearson. 1992. "Cultural Diversity and Socialization: A Case Study of a Hispanic Woman in a Doctoral Program in Sociology." In *Diversity as Resource: Redefining Cultural Literacy,* edited by Denise E. Murray, 148–82. Alexandria, VA: TESOL.

Chaskin, Robert, Amy Khare, and Mark Joseph. 2012. "Participation, Deliberation, and Decision Making: The Dynamics of Inclusion and Exclusion in Mixed-Income Developments." *Urban Affairs Review* 48 (6): 863–906. http://dx.doi.org/10.1177/1078087412450151.

Clark, Irene. 2005. "A Genre Approach to Writing Assignments." *Composition Forum* 14 (2). http://compositionforum.com/issue/14.2/clark-genre-writing.php.

Cooper, Marilyn M. 2011. "Rhetorical Agency as Emergent and Enacted." *College Composition and Communication* 62 (3): 420–49.

Devitt, Amy J. 2009. "Re-fusing Form in Genre Study." In *Genres in the Internet: Issues in the Theory of Genre,* edited by Janet Giltrow and Dieter Stein, 27–48. Amsterdam: John Benjamins. http://dx.doi.org/10.1075/pbns.188.02dev.

Dias, Patrick, and Anthony Paré. 2000. *Transitions: Writing in Academic and Workplace Settings.* Cresskill, NJ: Hampton.

Docherty, Iain, Robina Goodlad, and Ronan Paddison. 2001. "Civic Culture, Community and Citizen Participation in Contrasting Neighborhoods." *Urban Studies* 38 (12): 2225–50. http://dx.doi.org/10.1080/00420980120087144.

Dryer, Dylan B. 2010. "Composing Citizens: Epistemic Work in the Interstices of Comprehensive-Planning Genre Systems." *Community Literacy Journal* 5 (1): 25–56.

Dryer, Dylan B. 2012. "At a Mirror, Darkly: The Imagined Undergraduate Writers of Ten Novice Composition Instructors." *College Composition and Communication* 63 (3): 420–52.

Elwood, Sarah. 2008. "Volunteered Geographic Information: Future Research Directions Motivated by Critical, Participatory, and Feminist GIS." *GeoJournal* 72 (3/4): 173–83. http://dx.doi.org/10.1007/s10708-008-9186-0.

Emmons, Kimberly K. 2009. "Uptake and the Biomedical Subject." In *Genre in a Changing World,* edited by Charles Bazerman, Adair Bonini, and Débora Figueiredo, 134–57. West Lafayette, IN: Parlor and WAC Clearinghouse.

Fainstein, Susan S. 2003. "New Directions in Planning Theory." In *Readings in Planning Theory.* 2nd ed. Edited by Scott Campbell and Susan S. Fainstein, 173–95. Oxford: Blackwell.

Flower, Linda. 2008. *Community Literacy and the Rhetoric of Public Engagement.* Carbondale: Southern Illinois University Press.

Freadman, Anne. 1994. "Anyone for Tennis?" In *Genre and the New Rhetoric,* edited by Aviva Freedman and Peter Medway, 43–66. London: Taylor & Francis.

Freadman, Anne. 2002. "Uptake." In *The Rhetoric and Ideology of Genre,* edited by Richard Coe, Lorelei Lindgard, and Tatiana Teslenko, 39–53. Cresskill, NJ: Hampton.

Freadman, Anne. 2012. "The Traps and Trappings of Genre Theory." *Applied Linguistics* 33 (5): 544–63. http://dx.doi.org/10.1093/applin/ams050.

Freadman, Anne. 2014. "Where Is the Subject? Rhetorical Genre Theory and the Question of the Writer." *Journal of Academic Language & Learning* 8 (3): A1–11.

Fuzer, Cristiane, and Nina Célia Barros. 2009. "Accusation and Defense: The Ideational Metafunction of Language in the Genre Closing Argument." In *Genre in a Changing World*, edited by Charles Bazerman, Adair Bonini, and Débora Figueiredo, 78–96. West Lafayette, IN: Parlor and WAC Clearinghouse.

Gere, Anne. 1994. "Kitchen Tables and Rented Rooms: The Extracurriculum of Composition." *College Composition and Communication* 45 (1): 75–92. http://dx.doi.org /10.2307/358588.

Grabill, Jeffrey T. 2007. *Writing Community Change: Designing Technologies for Citizen Action.* Cresskill, NJ: Hampton Press.

Hanssen, Gro Sandkjaer, and Inger-Lise Saglie. 2010. "Cognitive Closure in Urban Planning." *Planning Theory & Practice* 11 (4): 499–521. http://dx.doi.org/10.1080/14 649357.2010.525373.

Hyland, Ken. 2012. "Corpora and Academic Discourse." In *Corpus Applications in Applied Linguistics*, edited by Ken Hyland, Chau Meng Huat, and Michael Handford, 30–46. London: Continuum International Publishing.

Innes, Judith E., and David E. Booher. 2004. "Reframing Public Participation: Strategies for the 21st Century." *Planning Theory & Practice* 5 (4): 419–36. http://dx.doi.org /10.1080/1464935042000293170.

Jun, Kyu-Nahm, and Juliet Musso. 2013. "Participatory Governance and the Spatial Representation of Neighborhood Issues." *Urban Affairs Review* 49 (1): 71–110. http:// dx.doi.org/10.1177/1078087412453704.

Katz, Steven B., and Carolyn Miller. 1996. "The Low-Level Radioactive Waste Siting Controversy in North Carolina: Toward a Rhetorical Model of Risk Communication." In *Green Culture: Environmental Rhetoric in Contemporary America*, edited by Carl Herndl and Stuart Brown, 111–40. Madison: University of Wisconsin Press.

Kaufman, Sandra, and Janet Smith. 1999. "Framing and Reframing in Land Use Change Conflicts." *Journal of Architectural and Planning Research* 16 (2): 164–80.

Kill, Melanie. 2006. "Acknowledging the Rough Edges of Resistance: Negotiation of Identities for First-Year Composition." *College Composition and Communication* 58 (2): 213–35.

Leki, Ilona. 2003. "Living through College Literacy: Nursing in a Second Language." *Written Communication* 20 (1): 81–98. http://dx.doi.org/10.1177/0741088303253571.

Loh, Carolyn G. 2012. "Four Potential Disconnects in the Community Planning Process." *Journal of Planning Education and Research* 32 (1): 33–47. http://dx.doi.org/10.1177 /0739456X11424161.

Lowndes, Vivien, Lawrence Pratchett, and Gerry Stoker. 2006. "Diagnosing and Remedying the Failings of Official Participation Schemes: The CLEAR Framework." *Social Policy and Society* 5 (2): 281–91. http://dx.doi.org/10.1017/S147474640500 2988.

Lu, Min-Zhan. 2004. "An Essay on the Work of Composition: Composing English against the Order of Fast Capitalism." *College Composition and Communication* 56 (1): 16–50. http://dx.doi.org/10.2307/4140679.

Lu, Min-Zhan, and Bruce Horner. 2013. "Translingual Literacy, Language Difference, and Matters of Agency." *College English* 75 (6): 586–611.

Luke, Allan. 2011. "Generalizing across Borders: Policy and the Limits of Educational Science." *Educational Researcher* 40 (8): 367–77. http://dx.doi.org/10.3102/001318 9X11424314.

MacMillan, Stuart 2012. "The Promise of Ecological Inquiry in Writing Research." *Technical Communication Quarterly* 21 (4): 346–61. http://dx.doi.org/10.1080/105722 52.2012.674873.

Martin, J. R. 2009. "Genre and Language Learning: A Social Semiotic Perspective." *Linguistics and Education* 20: 10–21.

McComas, Katherine A. 2003. "Citizen Satisfaction with Public Meetings Used for Risk Communication." *Journal of Applied Communication Research* 31 (2): 164–84. http://dx.doi.org/10.1080/0090988032000064605.

McGovern, Stephen J. 2013. "Ambivalence over Participatory Planning within a Progressive Regime: Waterfront Planning in Philadelphia." *Journal of Planning Education and Research* 33 (3): 310–24. http://dx.doi.org/10.1177/0739456X13481246.

Miller, Carolyn R. 1984. "Genre as Social Action." *Quarterly Journal of Speech* 70 (2): 151–67. http://dx.doi.org/10.1080/00335638409383686.

Paré, Anthony. 2002. "Genre and Identity: Individuals, Institutions, and Ideology." In *The Rhetoric and Ideology of Genre*, edited by Richard Coe, Lorelei Lindgard, and Tatiana Teslenko, 57–71. Cresskill, NJ: Hampton.

Parker, Gavin, and Claudia Murray. 2012. "Beyond Tokenism? Community-Led Planning and Rational Choices: Findings from Participants in Local Agenda-Setting at the Neighbourhood Scale in England." *TPR* 83 (1): 1–28.

Prior, Paul. 2009. "From Speech Genres to Mediated Multimodal Genre Systems: Bakhtin, Voloshinov, and the Question of Writing." In *Genre in a Changing World*, edited by Charles Bazerman, Adair Bonini, and Débora Figueiredo, 17–34. West Lafayette, IN: Parlor and WAC Clearinghouse.

Prior, Paul, and Rebecca Bilbro. 2012. "Academic Enculturation: Developing Literate Practices and Disciplinary Identities." In *University Writing: Selves and Texts in Academic Societies*, edited by Montserrat Castello and Christiane Donahue, 19–31. Bingley, UK: Emerald Group.

Prior, Paul, and Jody Shipka. 2003. "Chronotopic Lamination: Tracing the Contours of Literate Activity." In *Writing Selves/Writing Societies: Research from Activity Perspectives*, edited by Charles Bazerman and David R. Russell, 180–238. Fort Collins, CO: WAC Clearinghouse.

Regaignon, Dara Rossman. 2015. "Anxious Uptakes: Nineteenth-Century Advice Literature as a Rhetorical Genre." *College English* 78 (2): 139–161.

Reiff, Mary Jo, and Anis Bawarshi. 2011. "Tracing Discursive Resources: How Students Use Prior Genre Knowledge to Negotiate New Writing Contexts in First-Year Composition." *Written Communication* 28 (3): 312–37. http://dx.doi.org/10.1177/0741088311410183.

Reynolds, Nedra. 2004. *Geographies of Writing: Inhabiting Places and Encountering Difference*. Carbondale: Southern Illinois University Press.

Rice, Jeff. 2012. *Digital Detroit: Rhetoric and Space in the Age of the Network*. Carbondale: Southern Illinois University Press.

Roozen, Kevin. 2009. "Fan fic-ing English Studies: A Case Study Exploring the Interplay of Vernacular Literacies and Disciplinary Engagement." *Research in the Teaching of English* 44 (2): 136–69.

Rydin, Yvonne, and Mark Pennington. 2000. "Public Participation and Local Environmental Planning: The Collective Action Problem and the Potential of Social Capital." *Local Environment: The International Journal of Justice and Sustainability* 5 (2): 153–69. http://dx.doi.org/10.1080/13549830050009328.

Schryer, Catherine F. 1993. "Records as Genre." *Written Communication* 10 (2): 200–234. http://dx.doi.org/10.1177/0741088393010002003.

Schryer, Catherine F. 2002. "Genre and Power: A Chronotopic Analysis." In *The Rhetoric and Ideology of Genre*, edited by Richard Coe, Lorelei Lindgard, and Tatiana Teslenko, 73–102. Cresskill, NJ: Hampton.

Smith, Dorothy, and Catherine F. Schryer. 2008. "On Documentary Society." In *Handbook of Research on Writing: History, Society, School, Individual, Text*, edited by Charles Bazerman, 113–28. New York: Erlbaum.

Smith, Tania. 2011. "Building Academic Community through a Town Hall Forum: Rhetorical Theories in Action." In *Writing in Knowledge Societies*, edited by Doreen

Starke-Meyerring, Anthony Paré, Natasha Artemeva, Miriam Horne, and Larissa Yousoubova, 389–414. Fort Collins, CO: WAC Clearinghouse.

Spinuzzi, Clay. 2010. "Secret Sauce and Snake Oil: Writing Monthly Reports in a Highly Contingent Environment." *Written Communication* 27 (4): 363–409. http://dx.doi.org/10.1177/0741088310380518.

Spoel, Philippa, and Chantal Barriault. 2011. "Risk Knowledge and Risk Communication: The Rhetorical Challenge of Public Dialogue." In *Writing in Knowledge Societies*, edited by Doreen Starke-Meyerring, Anthony Paré, Natasha Artemeva, Miriam Horne, and Larissa Yousoubova, 87–112. Fort Collins, CO: WAC Clearinghouse.

Tachino, Tosh. 2012. "Theorizing Uptake and Knowledge Mobilization: A Case for Intermediary Genre." *Written Communication* 29 (4): 455–76. http://dx.doi.org/10.1177/0741088312457908.

Tardy, Christine M. 2003. "A Genre System View of the Funding of Academic Research." *Written Communication* 20 (1): 7–36. http://dx.doi.org/10.1177/0741088303253569.

Tauxe, Caroline S. 1995. "Marginalizing Public Participation in Local Planning: An Ethnographic Account." *Journal of the American Planning Association* 61 (4): 471–81. http://dx.doi.org/10.1080/01944369508975658.

Turner, Susan M. 2006. "Mapping Institutions as Work and Texts." In *Institutional Ethnography as Practice*, edited by Dorothy E. Smith, 139–62. New York: Rowman & Littlefield.

Wallace, Derek. 2003. "Writing and the Management of Power: Producing Public Policy in New Zealand." In *Writing Selves/Writing Societies: Research from Activity Perspectives*, edited by Charles Bazerman and David R. Russell, 159–78. Fort Collins, CO: WAC Clearinghouse.

Wardle, Elizabeth. 2009. "'Mutt Genres' and the Goal of FYC: Can We Help Students Write the Genres of the University?" *College Composition and Communication* 60 (4): 765–89.

Wolsey, Thomas. 2010. "Complexity in Student Writing: The Relationship Between the Task and Vocabulary Uptake." *Literacy Research and Instruction* 49 (2): 194–208. http://dx.doi.org/10.1080/19388070902947360.

Yang, Kaifeng. 2005. "Public Administrators' Trust in Citizens: A Missing Link in Citizen Involvement Efforts." *Public Administration Review* 65 (3): 273–85. http://dx.doi.org/10.1111/j.1540-6210.2005.00453.x.

PART II

Historicizing Public Genres

*Invention, Evolution, and Embodiment
of Public Performances*

4
DEFINING MOMENTS
Genre Beginnings, Genre Invention, and the Case of the English-Language Dictionary

Lindsay Rose Russell

BEGINNINGS

For genre theorists of all kinds, thinking about beginnings has been tricky. This is, in part, because the beginnings of most genres distantly predate our participation in them and rarely appear to influence our day-to-day genre use. The dictionary genre, for example, is possibly as old as writing itself—dictionary-like lists survive on Sumerian clay tablets from the second millennium BCE; encyclopedic dictionaries were circulating in China by the second century BCE; the word *dictionary* (*dictionarius, dictionarium, dictionarie*) dates to the thirteenth century; and the first monolingual English-language dictionary (Cawdrey 1604) appeared early in the seventeenth century.[1] And yet, when I look up the meaning of a word in a dictionary, I need not know anything at all about when or why the first instantiations of the dictionary appeared in order to accomplish the task at hand. *Wiktionary* will confirm for me that *myopic* means "nearsighted; unable to see distant objects unaided," even though I and quite probably the thirty-or-so editors[2] who have contributed to this particular definition of *myopic* might be remarkably nearsighted concerning any or all historical facts about the dictionary genre. In other words, collective ignorance of this public genre's history appears to in no way affect the aims the genre allows us to accomplish.

Partly attributable to this popular indifference to genre history, genre scholars' difficulty in theorizing genre beginnings is likely also a product of the field's dominant methods and priorities. Scholars understand a genre as a system for getting things done; it is "a socially recognized, repeated strategy for achieving similar goals in situations socially perceived as being similar" (Bazerman 1988, 62). Hence, related desires play out as recurrent actions: I want to know more about a word; I look it up in the dictionary. You want to know more about a word; you look

DOI: 10.7330/9781607324430.c004

it up in the dictionary. I want you to know that I know more about a word than you do; I tell you to look it up in the dictionary. This well-oiled system doesn't just structure repetition, it structures expectation. According to Carolyn Miller, "[W]hat we learn when we learn a genre is not just a pattern of forms or even a method of achieving our own ends. We learn, more importantly, what ends we may have" (Miller 1984, 165). The clay-tablet dictionary, the collegiate dictionary, the dictionary sitting open on a library pedestal, the online dictionary—these are all socially recognized forms similar insofar as they strategically signal a genre that not only allows us to look up words but also gives us the idea and the warrant to do so in the first place. As a shared system, a genre thus enables a host of actions, relations, and expectations, but it also "laminates" those layers (Prior 1998, 24), compressing the slew of complex, dispersed, and fluid activities enacted by, in, and across people, places, times, and artifacts into a single smooth plank. We can, for example, handily dismiss a word as not in the dictionary even when we have no lexicon or lexicographer at the ready to support such a deployment of the genre's authority. In rhetorical terms, a genre's manufactured "lamination of experience" extracts us from "the mangle of practice" (Bazerman 1998, viii)[3] and facilitates our "trajectories of literate activity" (Prior and Shipka 2003, 187). In colloquial terms, genres help us get over it (complexity) and get on with it (daily activity).

For participants and theorists alike, then, genres primarily structure our *present* activities and project our *future* possibilities; they are not chiefly about the *past*. But, of course, their authority to influence what we do and will do is, at least in part, predicated on the idea that genres have already done this work for others. We presume a genre has a past (one that legitimates our genre performances in the present and future), but the particulars of that past are largely irrelevant. For genre participants, genre histories are important, but the sketchiest notion of them will suffice. In genre studies, however, theorizing beginnings and invention is indeed important, not because generic origins reveal generic truths but because the many and messy beginnings of a genre lead us toward a finer appreciation of the diversity of generic action and the ongoing rhetorical interventions we make in the system of genres available to us.[4] Attending to the social rather than the individual, to systems of action rather than sets of texts, to recurrence rather than occurrence, to the normative rather than the novel has meant that genre studies tends to minimize scenes of genres beginning, having already marginalized the individuals, texts, and novel occurrences that animate those scenes. Bracketing beginnings also eliminates from consideration the rhetorical processes of invention, including the active negotiation of generic features and intentional, individual attempts to produce social typification. In other words, when we focus on genres as (temporarily) stabilized social structures that "help do our rhetorical thinking for us" (Miller 1994, 72), we tend to ignore the rhetorical thinking that goes into genre invention itself. Precisely because rhetorical studies understands a genre to be a laminating system, a totalizing illusion, we need to look at the system before its parts are compressed and concealed, the illusion while illusionists are staging the trick.

I develop my argument in two parts, the first a review of extant scholarship addressing "genre emergence." I argue that while we have cultivated an important set of analytical terms—*antecedent genre, recurrent need, shared exigence, social typification, technological affordance, kairotic confluence*—these terms do not yet fully explain the rhetorical work involved in the making of a genre because they too often cast genres as inevitable artifacts of surrounding contexts or agentless processes. Public genres such as the dictionary seem particularly vulnerable to deterministic interpretation within this framework. Because their development is often unbounded by institutional structures and their use (by anyone and everyone) is expansive to infinite, the emergence of public genres is often read as the product of forces beyond individual rhetorical action. While their appearance is indeed a social feat, it is not simply the "natural" or "lucky" outcome of some fortuitous contextual shifts but crucially also the result of rhetorical choices made by genre inventors. I argue that genre invention is a regular mode of genre participation, that it is not circumscribed by the rules of biological reproduction but rather animated by variegated strategies to invite public uptake, and that attending to scenes of manufacture allows us to see the individual rhetorical staging of social action as well as public debates concerning the diverse potentials of a nascent genre—before the systematizing memory of genre erases that sense of diversity and debate.

I turn from this critique of keywords in part I to consider in part II an important beginning of the dictionary genre that demonstrates the potentials of analyzing defining moments. Heeding calls from the highly restricted academic spaces of early modern England for a monolingual English dictionary, early lexicographers ultimately projected a far more general audience, exigence, and environment for dictionary use. Instead of facilitating the studies of men and boys of the highest social order, the genre was proposed as public, meant to circulate broadly and serve a variety of ends among an array of speakers. The process of bringing the genre into being was, in other words, not simply responsive but inventive. Early enactors strategically styled the dictionary as inclusive of a range of users, and that inclusivity has, to a surprising extent, continued to animate the genre: dictionaries are regularly consulted in classrooms and at copydesks; they are cited in courtrooms and at pulpits; the most skeptical of scholars offer dictionary epigraphs as chapter openings; the most inventive of muck-spouts use dictionaries to settle barroom battles over obscene language; creative writers browse dictionaries; and everyday readers reproduce dictionary definitions in the margins of paperback fiction. In most of these situations, dictionary content goes unquestioned, as do the particulars of any given dictionary (its authorship, date of compilation, method of composition, philosophy of description/prescription, etc.) as well as the motivations and repercussions of the genre writ large (the reasons to catalog a language, the limits to cataloguing a language, the unexpected side effects of cataloguing a language, etc.). But any genre purporting to document public knowledge for general use deserves a critical eye: its smooth authority is wrought in multiple, muddled beginnings, each saturated by different interests and biases. When we forget such genres are invented, we are liable to forget they are also open to critique and, possibly, to conscientious revision.

INEVITABILITY, ANTECEDENCE, RECURRENCE, ECOLOGY, EMERGENCE

How Have We Already Accounted for the Ways in Which Genres Begin, and What Are the Limitations of These Accounts?

Anthony Paré describes genres as totalizing "illusions of normalcy": "The automatic, ritual unfolding of genres makes them appear normal, even inevitable; they are simply the way things are done" (Paré 2002, 59, 61). Part cognitive impulse to classify and part social imperative for (inter)action, genres so regularly and recognizably facilitate our personal and social lives that living seems impossible without them. Hence, the time before genres appears inaccessible, illegible, or unimaginable to us. While genres in general might be an inevitable feature of human existence, particular genres are not. English speakers got along without dictionaries for centuries; many still get along without dictionaries. And yet, in attempts to account for the development of particular genres, scholars often return to the idea that genres are bound to appear, the fated outcome of some prior event or some particular climate.

Genre theory understands discourses new and old to be always already genred. "From where do genres come?" asks Tzvetan Todorov.

"Why, quite simply, from other genres" (Todorov 1976, 161). Here, Todorov asserts what many others—before and since (e.g., Bakhtin 1986; Devitt 2004; Fowler 1982; Jamieson 1975)—have claimed: that any new genre will be tethered to, if not predicated on, an old genre. Faced with new ideologies, situations, settings, technologies, or needs, rhetors look to and draw on the rhetorical resources of prior genred experiences. Hence new genres are really existing genres—"antecedent genres" (Jamieson 1975), "existing, flourishing genres" (Popken 1999, 105)—that have, more or less dramatically, shifted shape. By this thinking, the earliest English-language dictionaries could be understood as descendants of foreign-language guides, of annotations about word meanings penned in the margins of manuscripts and printed texts, of vocabulary lists appended to early textbooks, and so on. The new genre is but a random variation in the system, one that has since proven itself well suited to survival.

Shape shifting from one genre to another is usually understood as the result of an emergent common exigence or a swelling recurrent need. According to Amy Devitt, old genres and new problems work hand in hand; the "combination of a preexisting context of genres and newly developed, unfulfilled needs enables the construction of newly identified genres" (Devitt 2004, 92–93). Much like the "*fitting* response" Lloyd Bitzer imagines as a necessary reaction to an "imperfection marked by urgency" (Bitzer 1968, 6, 10), genres arise when a new desire takes hold of the popular imagination and not only requires but to some extent determines the response. The new problem the dictionary ostensibly solved for English speakers was their imperfect knowledge of a progressively unwieldy language. In the fourteenth century, English had been "a vernacular widely held to be insufficient" (Blank 2012, 274), but by the Renaissance, self-conscious efforts to enrich the lexical resources of the language—by converting words from one class to another (e.g., making verbs of nouns), borrowing words from other languages (e.g., Latin, French, Italian), and inventing new words for developing fields (e.g., medicine, fashion, architecture)—were successfully enlarging the language. As many as twenty-five thousand new words had entered the lexicon in the space of a century, and more than one hundred dictionaries were published to help speakers keep pace (Blank 2012, 274; Nevalainen 2006, 49). Here, the new genre is but the required response to an extant situation.

The emphasis on concrete genre antecedents and recurrent social needs has been contextualized by genre theorists, such that prior genres and emergent exigencies take their place within ever more complex "constellations," "ecologies," and "networks" wherein some "kairotic confluence" results in "genre emergence." In the words of Carolyn Miller and Dawn Shepherd, genres are "provoked by differing complexes of social, psychological, economic, and technological change"; they "[arise] from the combination of exigence and affordances, along with the modeling of forms and topoi offered by antecedent genres" (Miller and Shepherd 2009, 265, 283). In the case of the English-language dictionary, unprecedented lexical growth met with a number of other ideological and material changes in early modern England. Easier travel and altered economic structures resulted in social mobility, dialect leveling, and an increasing intolerance for linguistic variation; ideological investments in "proper English" joined with nationalist sentiments about making English worthy of a growing empire. Dictionaries that drew on older pedagogical and scholarly genres promised to accomplish, simultaneously, sociolinguistic uplift of the English masses and erudite declaration of the inherent perfection of the English language to the world. And, of course, the printing press and booming book trade made all of this possible in progressively bigger volumes, available in progressively greater quantities, and affordable for a progressively larger number of people. It was only within such a milieu that the genre of the dictionary could publicly emerge. A new genre is, then, a necessary outcome of related circumstances.

These critical concepts of genre emergence have been useful within genre studies, drawing our attention to genres as nodes in the circulation of power, as imbricated in the work of other (especially older) genres, as collective ideas that pattern behavior, and as points of cultural confluence. These notions also accord with how genre participants themselves relate histories of their social practice. Lexicographers, for example, often narrate the history of the dictionary in terms of ancestral genres, newly felt needs, and complex contextual motivations.[5] When James Murray, primary editor of the *Oxford English Dictionary*, was called upon to deliver a prestigious public lecture at Oxford in 1900, he spoke about "The Evolution of English Lexicography." In the lecture, Murray argues that marginalia, schoolbooks, glossaries, vocabularies, and language guides are "the fountain-heads of English lexicography" (in rhetorical terms, they are antecedent genres to the dictionary) (7–9). He carefully catalogs the "new conditions" under which "lexicographical activity at once bursts forth with vigour," noting, for example, the ascendance of English at the end of the fourteenth century by which time it was a language deployed in literature, spoken in courts of law, taught in classrooms, and therefore worthy of a dictionary (in rhetorical terms, these constellations of social change provoked the dictionary) (15–16). Murray also indicates the recurrent exigence felt by English speakers at the end of the sixteenth century (using terminology that will appear familiar enough to rhetorical scholars): "the Renascence of ancient learning had itself brought into English use thousands of learned words, from Latin, Greek, Hebrew, Arabic, and other languages, 'ink-horn terms,' as they were called by Bale and by Puttenham, unknown to, and not to be imbibed from, mother or grandmother. A work exhibiting the spelling, and explaining the meaning, of these new-fangle 'hard words' was the felt want of the day; and the first attempt to supply it marks, on the whole, the most important point in the evolution of the modern English Dictionary" (27). Murray here narrows in on the moment of generic exigence when a pervasive problem is met by an obvious solution: inadequate knowledge and inadequate teachers are to be remedied by this genre, pedagogical and capacious.

But here, and throughout the lecture, Murray also narrows in on the importance of (borrowing his phrasing) singular attempts to supply the genre. Even as he narrates a smooth history of the English dictionary that conveniently culminates in the publication of the *OED*, Murray is careful to attend to moments of difference, disruption, departure, and new direction. He seeks again and again to understand how individual authors produced individual texts that fundamentally changed how we thought of the English dictionary and the work it might do in the world. According to Murray, before Robert Cawdrey's (1604) *Table Alphabeticall*, "no one appears . . . to have felt that Englishmen could want a dictionary to help them to the knowledge and correct use of their own language" (Murray 1900, 26). Before Samuel Johnson's (1755) *Dictionary*, "The notion that an English Dictionary ought to contain *all* English words had apparently as yet occurred to no one; at least no one had proposed to carry the idea into practice" (Murray 1900, 34). And before Murray's own *OED* (Murray et al. 1889–1928), "No one could find out from all the dictionaries extant how long any particular word had been in the language, which of the many senses . . . was the original, or how or when these many senses had been developed" (Murray 1900, 45). In Murray's theory of genre formation, the large-scale social forces at play and the felt wants of the day are crucial components, but *as* (if not more) crucial are these singular inventive performances by which the illusion of genre, rendered reality in text, is carefully constructed by individual people so as to project and perform social norms that do not yet exist. This pair of critical moves—the focus on points of beginning and the interpretation of acts of invention—seems to me too infrequent in genre scholarship.

To focus on genres beginning, genre scholars may need to pull their attention away from genre circulation. The idea that rhetors are always already operating within "the social and rhetorical conditions that we call genres" (Bawarshi 2003, 7) has encouraged scholarship that explores genres in action to the exclusion of genres beginning. We have been, to quote Anis Bawarshi, "less interested in the 'time before genre'—that time no longer exists—and more interested in what happens once genres are in circulation" (10). Interest in the automatic, ritual unfolding of genres thus pulls our focus to circulation, initiation, and participation and defers consideration of genre invention in favor of understanding new genres as products of the extant system. Circulating genres and circulating ideas about genre will determine when and how an old genre reanimates. By this thinking, there is little new about "new genres"; their emergence is marked by similarity, not difference, so their beginnings become almost indiscernible within ongoing antecedent circumstances.

When genre beginnings vanish into systems of genre circulation, a key scene of genre invention also disappears. We don't simply lose the mystical moment of invention—when "the mind of an atomistic individual" articulates its desire—we also lose sight of the social processes of invention: when rhetors create, find, or remember the substance of discourse; when they project social relationships with real or imaginary, individual or collective, others; when they negotiate "socio-culture in a unique way to generate something"; when they invite, and indeed depend upon, audiences to complete a social act that is yet only initiated (LeFevre 1987, 1, 46–47). These complex rhetorical negotiations are obscured by our current emphases on antecedent genres, recurrent exigencies, and kairotic confluences. Within these paradigms, rhetorical agents tend to play rather minimal roles. They are subsumed by the cultural moments that call forth new genres; presumed rather passive as they perceive, recognize, or construe emergent shared desires; or permitted choices that have little consequence, as their "discourses [will] bear the chromosomal imprint of ancestral genres" regardless of whether rhetors have made an "appropriate" antecedent genre choice (Jamieson 1975, 406, 414). This minimal role for the rhetor is, of course, paired with a minimal role for rhetoric. How rhetors actively propose or secure the emergence of a new genre is eclipsed by a sense of genres as inevitable artifacts of environment or improbable artifacts of chance. Likening genres to organic material—understanding them as life forms (they are born, survive, die) or as species (they emerge, dominate, evolve)—can set in motion a host of inappropriate expectations: about genre beginnings as irregular points of interest in a generic *bildungsroman* that presumes the eventual consolidation of a coherent, stable (generic) identity and about genre invention as a quasi-biological process, bound by reproductive isolation, single ancestors, and suites of essential attributes.[6] Likewise, likening genres to matters of fortune—understanding them as emergent only at some "right moment" or when a "lucky combination of contexts and individuals" renders their performance possible (Devitt 2004, 101)—narrows the way we might understand genre formation to be a rhetorical process rather than an environmental byproduct. By this set of ideas, the intentions and consequences of rhetorical work are buffeted by the winds of circumstance. Invention is supplanted by determinism. But, of course, the dictionary is not inevitable nor is it eternal. It is *rhetorical*: a "partisan, meaningful, consequential text" (Blair 1999, 18). And moments of invention make legible the genre's partiality, polysemy, potentials, and pitfalls. Analysis of genre invention seems, then, particularly important in the case of general-reference genres such as the dictionary, precisely because they wield public authority partly by concealing their partiality, polysemy, and pitfalls.

In so summarizing the ways our current terminology encourages the containment of genre invention, I do not mean to suggest that antecedent genres, genre ideologies, intersubjective construals of type, and complex cultural contexts are anything less than powerful forces at play on rhetors who would propose new genres. I do, however, mean to open a space in which we might think about how individuals, perceiving their work to be outside of accepted genres, project and attempt to stage the circumstances for new kinds of generically mediated action. We know invention happens within genres (e.g., people invent themselves as writers or they invent the things they describe in generic discourse), but the invention *of* genres is another and no less important mode of genre participation. In the lived experience of genre, people often understand themselves to be proposing new modes of social interaction, and, in attending to those moments of genre invention, I believe we gain a finer appreciation for how rhetors shape shared expectations. The rhetorical processes of genre invention are rarely constrained by biological patterns of (re)production or linear narratives of progression; they are animated by promiscuous strategies of creation, and they initiate traditions of manifold genre performance.

DEFINITION

What Do the Beginnings of the Dictionary Genre Tell Us about Genre Invention?
As this discussion has already illustrated, the genre of the dictionary
does not have a precise point of origin. It does, however, have several
notable scenes of beginning. For the English-language dictionary, these
include the earliest *glossae collectae* or collections of glosses (eighth century), the earliest Latin school dictionaries (fifteenth century), the earliest monolingual dictionaries (seventeenth century), the first dictionary
to call itself a *dictionary* (Elyot 1538), the first dictionary to offer a "complete" inventory of English (Kersey 1702), and so on. Hence within a
smooth history of circulation, there are notable moments of roughness
when dictionary makers and users see themselves as doing something
without generic precedent but with generic potential. It is to one of
these moments I would like to turn in order to demonstrate the kinds
of rhetorical strategies that become visible within such periods of self-
conscious genre invention.

In the English-speaking world, the idea of an English dictionary
existed long before anyone had produced one. Latin and Latin–English
dictionaries had been in use in England since the mid-fifteenth century almost exclusively among scholars and students (male, moneyed,
etc.). Not surprisingly, the earliest English speakers to imagine, wish for,
and intend to compile English dictionaries were, then, schoolmasters:
William Bullokar, in 1580, supposed that a dictionary would "cause that
English speech shall be the perfectest" (Bullokar 1580, C1v); Richard
Mulcaster suggested in 1582 that it would be "a thing very praiseworthy
in my opinion, and no less profitable than praiseworthy, if some one well
learned and as laborious a man, would gather all the words which we use
in our English tongue . . . into one dictionary" (166); Bullokar himself
planned to "set hand to perfecting a Dictionary (1586, A4v)," but no
evidence remains that he did so (Starnes and Noyes 1946, 10).[7] In the
end, the one well-learned and laborious man to gather words would be
Robert Cawdrey, and, though he was a schoolmaster, he ultimately envisioned the dictionary to have an audience and exigence well beyond the
schoolhouse.

His 1604 dictionary bears the full title: *A Table Alphabeticall, containing
and teaching the true writing and understanding of hard usuall English words,
borrowed from the Hebrew, Greek, Latin, or French, &c. With the interpretation thereof by plain English words, gathered for the benefit & help of Ladies,
Gentlewomen, or any other unskillful persons. Whereby they may the more easily
and better understand many hard English words, which they shall hear or read
in Scriptures, Sermons, or elsewhere, and also be made able to use the same aptly*

themselves. Cawdrey here specifies a public audience and an exigence that had not been invited by the earlier generation of schoolmasters— ladies in church being quite a different matter than boys in school or scholars in studies. The prominence of women as a primary audience for the dictionary is confirmed by Cawdrey's dedication, where he addresses the *Table Alphabeticall* to five "right honourable, Worshipful, virtuous, & godly Ladies," the daughters of Cawdrey's friend, Lucy Harington, and sisters of Cawdrey's former pupil, James Harington (A2r–A2v). But the dedication and address to the reader, both of which preface the alphabetized content, also suggest complexly compounding audiences and exigencies for the genre. In addition to women who seek better comprehension of religious language, Cawdrey suggests that "strangers that blame our tongue of difficulty and uncertainty may hereby plainly see & better understand those things which they have thought hard"; that all English speakers might benefit from a description of "true Orthography"; that "children hereby may be prepared for the understanding of a great number of Latin words"; that "others" will be brought general "delight & judgment . . . by the use of this little work"; and that those who "have occasion to speak publicly before ignorant people" ("especially Preachers") might be better able to "never affect any strange inkhorn terms, but labour to speak so as is commonly received" (Cawdrey 1604, A2r, A3r).

If Cawdrey's dictionary seems a cauldron of possibilities, this is partly because it is a collage of extant works. The contents of the *Table Alphabeticall*—including its prefatory material—have been shown (e.g., Starnes and Noyes 1946, 13–19) to rely heavily on four other publications: a manual of Ciceronian rhetoric (Wilson 1553), a treatise on the English language (Mulcaster 1582), a Latin–English dictionary (Thomas 1587), and a textbook that includes a grammar, catechisms, prayers, and a vocabulary list (Coote 1596). Cawdrey most definitely borrows form and content from these sources; he also welcomes some of their audiences (preachers, scholars, and children) and claims some of their purposes (to aid in comprehension and composition of English and Latin); however, there is much about the *Table Alphabeticall* that is not characteristic of these earlier works. The primary audience of ladies and gentlewomen, for example, was not common to rhetorics, language treatises, Latin dictionaries, nor schoolbooks. A handful of bilingual language guides had been addressed to women (Russell 2014, 103–4); John Florio's Italian–English dictionary, for example, is dedicated to Lucy Harington Russell (1598, a3r, b3v), the niece of Cawdrey's patrons. Cawdrey himself had also addressed other publications to women; for instance, his treatise on catechisms features a dedication to Elizabeth Golding (Cawdrey 1580, ☞3r). Cawdrey thus certainly reproduced parts of prior work, but his heady combination of reproductions also repurposed what had been borrowed for new audiences.

What is important to notice here is that Cawdrey's proposal of a dictionary genre is not manacled to antecedent modes. The generic material for the dictionary, unlike genetic material, is not handed down from a reproductive pair within a related species but rather composed of the particular rhetorical features Cawdrey draws from across a wide range of texts and kinds. As Jonathan Hope has said, "it is very easy to mate linguistic sparrows with rats to get bats"; a linguistic genre, "unlike a biological species, does not have to have a single immediate evolutionary ancestor" (Hope 2000, 50–51). I believe it to be not at all incidental that the English dictionary, in its earliest articulations, would so spectacularly break from the singular ancestry of the schoolbook (from whence dictionary pleas had been so frequent) by demonstrating characteristics from within and across pedagogical, scholarly, evangelical, domestic, linguistic, literary, and leisurely genres. Cawdrey was plainly heeding the schoolbook call to perform the genre, but he was also gesturing to a host of potentials appropriate to a distinctively different kind of work, a general reference suitable to a variety of publics and purposes.

Cawdrey and other early English-language-dictionary makers might have felt some anxiety about a genre with such narrow content and expansive audience (comprised of just words and their definitions but valuable to women, children, foreigners, speakers, preachers, bad spellers, entertainment seekers, tastemakers, scholars, students, maybe even some sparrows). Mixed genre was a prevailing mode of thought in the Renaissance (Colie 1973, 19–21), but dictionaries were strangely unmixed. The earliest Italian–English dictionary maker had certainly worried that the dictionary was an idea "yet . . . unapproved"; Florio's preface to *A Worlde of Wordes* characterizes his text as an orphan, a "bouncing boy" who "hath tongue to answer, words at will, and wants not some wit, though he speak plain what each thing is" (Florio 1598, a3r, a4v). But Florio's boy, "born, bred, and brought forth" to serve the general public in daily language use, is without family, and Florio can only hope for his eventual adoption (a5r). The orphan is sent off to readers with this parting wish: "So have I crossed him, and so blessed him, your godchild, and your servant; that you may likewise give him your blessing" (a4v).

The explicit plea that readers adopt an orphan text into a generic family was not the most popular method by which early dictionary makers secured their genreness.[8] The first monolingual English dictionaries seem to have construed typification by different means, notably by way of alignment with other widely recognizable (nontextual) types. Because the genre of the dictionary was not yet publicly legible nor likely to become more so by virtue of its similarity to any or all of its antecedent genres, early dictionary makers seem to have turned to another powerful mode of typification: gender. Of the first four monolingual English-language dictionaries, all four specify women as a primary audience (Blount 1656; Bullokar 1616; Cawdrey 1604; Cockeram 1623). It is here worth remembering that, while women were systematically denied formal education in the early modern English-speaking world, they were decidedly *not* the population that had articulated a recurrent need for language education (in the form of a dictionary or otherwise), nor does evidence remain of widespread dictionary popularity among women readers (Russell 2014, 99). In fact, the first four dictionaries all identify women as a primary audience, but they project different needs and wants onto that audience: Cawdrey imagines women to be keepers of the mother tongue and reminders of the motherland to their traveling sons who might otherwise return home speaking "English Italianated" (Cawdrey 1604, A3r–A3v). John Bullokar casts women as eager and worthy pupils who, in receiving the rarified knowledge of English academe, confirm and increase its authority (Bullokar 1616, A2r–A4r). Henry Cockeram situates women as socially ambitious, hungry for the "choice," "vulgar," "curious," "ridiculous," "fustian" terms of the language that will delight and refine (Cockeram 1623, A3r–A5r, A6v–A7r). Thomas Blount locates women as a passive and ignorant audience, witnesses to the erudition of English (as in Bullokar), but more likely to pursue dictionary use for correction than inclusion (1656, A3r–A3v, A4v–A6v). Women are thus actuated in these texts more than they are actual (Brown 2001, 144)—they conjure the potential for typification and, with it, a degree of genreness, even as the genre is only yet proposed and was then, as now, a site of many different kinds of social action.

In this brief discussion of an important dictionary beginning, I hope to have demonstrated that, while dictionary makers existed within systems of other genres and certainly borrowed from prior texts as they produced their own, they nevertheless perceived themselves to be inventors, not just of individual dictionaries but of the dictionary genre. And, as they invented that genre, they were not simply registering societal wants; they were attempting to build expectations and invite repetitions by rhetorical means. Early dictionaries thus register the array of motivated interests articulated in and through the genre. Moreover, I suggest that the somewhat dissimilar portraits of the dictionary these earliest texts produce were not simply artifacts of the past—a fuzzy beginning to a genre that would stabilize—but rather representative of the variety the genre has always permitted.

INVENTION

Why Does Genre Invention Matter?

Genres are continuously and tenuously constituted in time. They are invented and reinvented. And yet, the argument that invention happens only *within* genres often discounts or displaces the invention *of* genres. That is, while individual rhetors may well perceive themselves to be operating within established systems of recognized genres or conditions of genre ideology, they nevertheless often find themselves and their work to be *outside* of particular genres. And this is not strictly the result of imperfect genre knowledge, incomplete genre initiation, or in-progress genre evolution; it is a common and conscientious rhetorical move in which rhetors pointedly and powerfully understand themselves to be departing from extant genres and proposing new confluences of intention and consequence. It is perhaps here, in the conscientious production of textual events as social possibilities, that generic features—of form, content, audience, and exigence—are most visibly orchestrated. Eschewing experiences of beginning runs the risk of concealing these processes of invention.

Notes

1. Michael Adams notes that "'The Dictionary' is a term of convenience for a complex, variegated genre" (Adams 2010, 47). While there are many types of dictionary, the "monolingual general-purpose dictionary" holds pride of place within the genre: "It is the one that every household has, that everyone thinks of first when the word *dictionary* is mentioned, it is the type that is most often bought, most often consulted, and the one that plays the most important role in the society that produces it" (Béjoint 2000, 40).
2. *Wiktionary* editors include people as well as scripts and bots.
3. The phrase "mangle of practice," used by both Paul Prior 1998 and Charles Bazerman 1998, alludes to the work of Andrew Pickering (1995, for example).
4. My interest in beginnings is indebted to feminist thinking. Suspicious of the singular patrilineal narrative that proceeds from "the masculine myth" of origin, feminist work sees beginnings as multiple—"start[ing] on all sides at once, start[ing] twenty times, thirty times, over"—and radical—allowing for productive departures, breaks, separations, and disengagements (Cixous and Kuhn 1981, 53).
5. This history of English dictionaries appears in any number of sources; Murray 1900, which is discussed in some detail here, is largely echoed in subsequent scholarship, such as Henri Béjoint 2000 and Johnathon Green 1996.

6. I here echo other critiques of biological metaphors in genre studies, including Anthony Paré 2002, Risa Applegarth 2012, and Susan Wells 2014.
7. Spelling and punctuation have been modernized for clarity in quotations from early print documents; early print titles appear shorted but otherwise unaltered in the list of references.
8. The metaphor of the dictionary as a vulnerable infant is deployed by other early dictionary makers; Richard Perceval's Spanish–English dictionary is a "silly new born infant" (Perceval 1591, A2r), John Bullokar's monolingual English dictionary is an "unknown Infant" (1616, vA2r).

References

Adams, Michael. 2010. "Historical Dictionaries and the History of Reading." In *Reading in History: New Methodologies from the Anglo-American Tradition*, edited by Bonnie Guzenhauser, 47–62. London: Pickering and Chatto.

Applegarth, Risa. 2012. "Rhetorical Scarcity: Spatial and Economic Inflections on Genre Change." *College Composition and Communication* 63 (3): 453–83.

Bakhtin, M. M. 1986. *Speech Genres and Other Late Essays*. Edited by Caryl Emerson and Michael Holquist. Translated by Vern W. McGee. Austin: University of Texas Press.

Bawarshi, Anis. 2003. *Genre and the Invention of the Writer: Reconsidering the Place of Invention in Composition*. Logan: Utah State University Press.

Bazerman, Charles. 1988. *Shaping Written Knowledge: The Genre and Activity of the Experimental Article in Science*. Madison: University of Wisconsin Press.

Bazerman, Charles. 1998. Editor's introduction to *Writing/Disciplinarity: A Sociohistoric Account of Literate Activity in the Academy*, by Paul A. Prior, vii–viii. New York: Routledge.

Béjoint, Henri. 2000. *Modern Lexicography: An Introduction*. Oxford: Oxford University Press.

Bitzer, Lloyd F. 1968. "The Rhetorical Situation." *Philosophy & Rhetoric* 1 (1): 1–14.

Blair, Carole. 1999. "Contemporary U.S. Memorial Sites as Exemplars of Rhetoric's Materiality." In *Rhetorical Bodies*, edited by Jack Selzer and Sharon Crowley, 16–57. Madison: University of Wisconsin Press.

Blank, Paula. 2012. "The Babel of Renaissance English." In *The Oxford History of English*. Updated ed. Edited by Lynda Mugglestone, 262–97. Oxford: Oxford University Press.

Blount, Thomas. 1656. *Glossographia: Or a Dictionary, Interpreting All ſuch Hard VVords, Whether Hebrew, Greek, Latin, Italian, Spaniſh, French, Teutonick, Belgick, Britiſh or Saxon; as are now vſed in our refined Engliſh Tongue . . . .* London: Tho[mas] Newcomb and Humphrey Moseley.

Brown, Sylvia. 2001. "Women and the Godly Art of Rhetoric: Robert Cawdrey's Puritan Dictionary." *Studies in English Literature* 41 (1): 133–48. http://dx.doi.org/10.2307/1556232.

Bullokar, John. 1616. *An English Expositor: Teaching the Interpretation of the hardeſt words vſed in our Language . . . .* London: John Legatt.

Bullokar, William. 1580. *Bullokars Booke at large, for the Amendment of Orthographie for Engliſh ſpeech . . . .* London: Henrie Denham.

Bullokar, William. 1586. *William Bullokarz Pamphlet for Grammar: Or rather too be ſaied hiz Abbreuiation of hiz Grammar for English . . . .* London: Edmund Bollifant.

Cawdrey, Robert. 1580. *A Shorte and fruitefull treatiſe, of the profite and neceſſitie of Catechiſing: That is, of inſtructing the youth, and ignorant perſons in the principles and groundes of Chriſtian religion . . . .* London: Thomas Dawson.

Cawdrey, Robert. 1604. *A Table Alphabeticall, conteyning and teaching the true vvriting, and vnderſtanding of hard vſuall Engliſh wordes, borrowed from the Hebrew, Greeke, Latine, or French, &c . . . .* London: J. R. for Edmund Weaver.

Cixous, Hélène, and Annette Kuhn. 1981. "Castration or Decapitation?" *Signs* 7 (1): 41–55. http://dx.doi.org/10.1086/493857.

Cockeram, Henry. 1623. *The English Dictionarie: Or, an Interpreter of hard Engliſh Words* . . . . London: [Eliot's Court Press] for Edmund Weaver.

Colie, Rosalie. 1973. "Genre-Systems and the Functions of Literature." In *The Resources of Kind: Genre Theory in the Renaissance*, edited by Barbara K. Lewalski, 1–31. Berkeley: University of California Press.

Coote, Edmund. 1596. *The English schoole-maister teaching all his scholers, the order of distinct reading, and true writing our English tongue.* London: The Widow Orwin for Ralph Jackson and Robert Dextar.

Devitt, Amy. 2004. *Writing Genres*. Carbondale: Southern Illinois University Press.

Elyot, Thomas. 1538. *The Dictionary of syr Thomas Eliot knyght.* London: Thomae Bertheleti.

Florio, John. 1598. *A Worlde of Wordes, Or Moſt copioius, and exact Dictionarie in Italian and Engliſh, collected by Iohn Florio.* London: Arnold Hatfield for Edw[ard] Blount.

Fowler, Alastair. 1982. *Kinds of Literature: An Introduction to the Theory of Genres and Modes.* Oxford: Oxford University Press.

Green, Johnathon. 1996. *Chasing the Sun: Dictionary-Makers and the Dictionaries They Made.* New York: Henry Holt.

Hope, Jonathan. 2000. "Rats, Bats, Sparrows and Dogs: Biology, Linguistics and the Nature of Standard English." In *The Development of Standard English, 1300–1800: Theories, Descriptions, Conflicts*, edited by Laura Wright, 49–56. Cambridge: Cambridge University Press. http://dx.doi.org/10.1017/CBO9780511551758.004.

Jamieson, Kathleen Hall. 1975. "Antecedent Genre as Rhetorical Constraint." *Quarterly Journal of Speech* 61 (4): 406–15. http://dx.doi.org/10.1080/00335637509383303.

Johnson, Samuel. 1755. *A Dictionary of the English Language: In Which the Words are deduced from their Originals, and Illustrated in their Different Significations by Examples from the best Writers* . . . . London: Printed by W[illiam] Strahan for J[ohn] and P[aul] Knapton et al.

Kersey, John [J. K.]. 1702. *A New Engliſh Dictionary: Or, a Compleat Collection Of the Moſt Proper and Significant Words, Commonly uſed in the Language* . . . . London: Henry Bonwicke and Robert Knaplock.

LeFevre, Karen Burke. 1987. *Invention as a Social Act.* Carbondale: Southern Illinois University Press.

Miller, Carolyn R. 1984. "Genre as Social Action." *Quarterly Journal of Speech* 70 (2): 151–67. http://dx.doi.org/10.1080/00335638409383686.

Miller, Carolyn R. 1994. "Rhetorical Community: The Cultural Basis of Genre." In *Genre and the New Rhetoric*, edited by Aviva Freedman and Peter Medway, 67–78. London: Taylor and Francis.

Miller, Carolyn R., and Dawn Shepherd. 2009. "Questions for Genre Theory from the Blogosphere." In *Genres in the Internet*, edited by Janet Giltrow and Dieter Stein, 263–90. Amsterdam: John Benjamins. http://dx.doi.org/10.1075/pbns.188.11mil.

Mulcaster, Richard. 1582. *The First Part of the Elementarie VVhich Entreateth Chefelie of the right writing of our Engliſh tung, ſet furth by Richard Mvlcaster.* London: Thomas Vautroullier.

Murray, James A.H. 1900. *The Evolution of English Lexicography. The Romanes Lecture Delivered in the Sheldonian Theatre, Oxford, June 22, 1900.* Oxford: Clarendon.

Murray, James A.H., Henry Bradley, William A. Craigie, and Charles T. Onions. 1889–1928. *A New English Dictionary on Historical Principles [Oxford English Dictionary].* Oxford: Clarendon.

Nevalainen, Terttu. 2006. *An Introduction to Early Modern English.* Oxford: Oxford University Press.

Paré, Anthony. 2002. "Genre and Identity: Individuals, Institutions, and Ideology." In *The Rhetoric and Ideology of Genre: Strategies for Stability and Change*, edited by Richard Coe, Lorelei Lingard, and Tatiana Teslenko, 57–71. Cresskill, NJ: Hampton.

Perceval, Richard [Richard Percyuall]. 1591. *Bibliotheca Hispanica. Containing a Grammar; with a Dictionarie in Spanish, Englifh, and Latine . . . .* London: John Jackson for Richard Watkins.

Pickering, Andrew. 1995. *The Mangle of Practice: Time, Agency, Science.* Chicago: University of Chicago Press. http://dx.doi.org/10.7208/chicago/9780226668253.001.0001.

Popken, Randall. 1999. "The Pedagogical Dissemination of a Genre: The Resume in American Business Discourse Textbooks, 1914–1939." *Journal of Advanced Composition* 19 (1): 91–116.

Prior, Paul A. 1998. *Writing/Disciplinarity: A Sociohistoric Account of Literate Activity in the Academy.* New York: Routledge.

Prior, Paul A., and Jody Shipka. 2003. "Chronotopic Lamination: Tracing the Contours of Literate Activity." In *Writing Selves/Writing Societies: Research from Activity Perspectives*, edited by Charles Bazerman and David R. Russell, 180–238. Fort Collins, CO: WAC Clearinghouse.

Russell, Lindsay Rose. 2014. "Before Ladies and Gentlewomen Were Unskillful: Honorific Invocations of Learned Women in Early Modern Bilingual Dictionaries." *Dictionaries: Journal of the Dictionary Society of North America* 35:93–120. http://dx.doi .org/10.1353/dic.2014.0022.

Starnes, De Witt T., and Gertrude E. Noyes. 1946. *The English Dictionary from Cawdrey to Johnson 1604–1755.* Chapel Hill: University of North Carolina Press.

Thomas, Thomas. 1587. *Dictionarivm Lingvae Latinae et Anglicanae . . . .* Canterbury: Thomae Thomasii and Richardum Boyle.

Todorov, Tzvetan. 1976. "The Origin of Genres." *New Literary History* 8 (1): 159–70. http://dx.doi.org/10.2307/468619.

Wells, Susan. 2014. "Genres as Species and Spaces: Literary and Rhetorical Genre in *The Anatomy of Melancholy*." *Philosophy & Rhetoric* 47 (2): 113–36. http://dx.doi.org/10 .5325/philrhet.47.2.0113.

Wilson, Thomas. 1553. *The Arte of Rhetorique, for the vfe of all fuche as are ftudious of Eloquence, fette forth in Englifh, by Thomas Wilson.* London: Richardus Graftonus.

5

GEOGRAPHIES OF PUBLIC GENRES
Navigating Rhetorical and Material
Relations of the Public Petition

Mary Jo Reiff

Imagining acts of writing as material—carving text out of time and space, in particular circumstances that differ for each writer—opens up new spaces in which to understand literacy and the construction of meaning.

—Nedra Reynolds

While rhetorical frameworks for understanding publics have primarily focused on the examination of the textual artifacts of public cultures or the discursive interactions that construct publics, there has been a recent movement—in line with Nedra Reynolds's above quotation—to "open up new spaces" for the rhetorical study of publics by grounding discursive inquiry in the material. Drawing on perspectives from cultural geography, Reynolds advances a conceptualization of "geographic rhetorics informed by the material, the visual, and the everyday" (Reynolds 2004, 2), with a focus on the material locations—the spaces and places—of discursive activity. Locating discourse in its material conditions and recognizing the material resources that influence the production, circulation, and reception of discourse in the public sphere magnify our critical lens for studying public discourse. Applying Reynolds's geographic framework to public genre systems (the genre of municipal zoning codes), Dylan Dryer argues that examination of the spatial and material conditions of genre uptake—institutional (and asymmetrical) social relations, economic and political resources, the routes of circulation, technological affordances, and affective and bodily experiences—can draw attention to "the injustices that some genre systems reflect and produce" (Dryer 2008, 504). Similarly, John Ackerman and David Coogan, in *The Public Work of Rhetoric*, also seek to recover the "lost geographies" of public life and to approach public scenes with an awareness of the "cultural and economic forces that have worked . . . to trouble the bonds of

DOI: 10.7330/9781607324430.c005

wealth, health, progress, and community" (Ackerman and Coogan 2010, 9). It is this potential for a materialist perspective to "trouble" our narratives of publics—and to illuminate how public discourse can both enable and limit public participation and change—that makes it an especially useful critical framework for studying publics and public genres.

In what follows, I draw on a materialist lens for studying a distinct public genre, the petition, which functions rhetorically—and has functioned historically—to "seek redress for grievances" (US Const. amend.). In *Origins of Democratic Culture*, David Zaret argues that the study of petitions "provides an unparalleled empirical site for exploring how, long before the Enlightenment, public opinion began to mediate between the state and civil society" (Zaret 2000, 15). This chapter will focus on the historical process of public engagement through petitioning—particularly the material location, production, distribution, and circulation of petitions—moving from an examination of the economic and political factors conditioning early petitions, to the disparity in material resources for women's petitioning in the nineteenth century, to the embodied performances of petitioners, to more contemporary online petitions that occupy virtual spaces and create digital networks that traverse geographical boundaries. Rhetorical genre studies, with its study of genres in more bounded organizational or disciplinary contexts, has primarily focused on genres as typified discursive sites that coordinate social action, often overlooking the more diffuse, varied, and multidirectional actions of public genres and the complex material conditions that genres inhabit and that play an agentive role in mediating genre use and public actions. Grounding an analysis of the petition in a materialist framework can provide insight into how a public genre whose exigency is to bring about change and enable political agency can be shaped by conditions that work to exclude participants and forestall change, thus enabling a more critical, resistant reading of the rhetorical performances of this public genre.

EARLY PETITIONS AND MATERIAL CONDITIONS: LEGAL, POLITICAL, ECONOMIC

Public sphere scholar Robert Asen has emphasized the importance of adding to our study of public discourse "a conception of materiality that places discourse in relation to the material conditions from which it arises and that it engages" (2009, 268), a relationship between the material and discursive illustrated well by the case of the public petition. Indeed, the rhetorical act of petitioning—which seeks a response to cultural, political, and economic injustices—cannot be considered apart from its location in "the constellations of materiality and ideology" and "the ways in which relations of power and symbolic and material resources influenced the production, circulation, and reception of discourse in the public sphere" (Asen 2009, 265). Petitions within the early democratic public sphere functioned within material conditions that could lead to dire material consequences, such as revolution, prison, or even death. For example, with the establishment of the Magna Carta in the early thirteenth century, some of the earliest forms of petitioning had a legal function and were viewed as a means of enforcing the charter: "If the barons thought that the king had failed to comply with the substantive provisions of Magna Carta, they could ask him by petition to remedy the grievance; if he failed to do so, the barons were given what amounts to the legal right of revolution" (Lawson and Seidman 1999, 5). But there were also material consequences—economic and political—for the king, who in turn received assurances that his government would be appropriately financed. In addition to the threat of revolution, the material conditions of petitioning extended to more serious consequences. For example, prior to the 1689 Declaration of Rights in England, one could be sentenced to death for complaining in a petition about the expenses of the king's household. And in early England, James II had bishops confined to the Tower for petitioning against his religious policies (van Voss 2001, 4). As these examples make clear, while individuals had the right to petition—and while the genre of the petition functioned as a tool that mediated between citizens and authorities—the conventional act of petitioning was undercut by uneven power relations and political and socioeconomic conditions that precluded the uptake of this genre. Examining "the specific material conditions through which readers and writers are 'taken up' into social relations when they 'uptake' a genre" (Dryer 2008, 504)—or in this case, how they are often *not* taken up into expected social relations between citizen and authority—can help us better understand how, despite the role of public genres in coordinating public actions, the sociopolitical conditions surrounding the genre may limit public action. This focus on the complex and more diffuse realities within which public genres function reveals the need for further attention to materiality within rhetorical genre studies, which would productively challenge current research on genres as mediational tools within activity systems that primarily facilitate actions or carry out shared goals.

Because the rhetorical purpose of the petition is to seek redress for an injustice, the rhetorical act of petitioning "takes up the spatial and material conditions around it" (Dryer 2008, 505); in other words, the public genre of the petition illustrates how spatial and material conditions seep into and act on the genre's uptake (what Dryer, in chapter 3, refers to as "uptake residue"), with dynamic interplay between the rhetorical purpose and material conditions of petitions—and with structural, institutional, and societal forces providing an exigence or motive to seek redress for grievances. This interplay between what Asen calls "material and cultural disparities and rhetorical practices" (2009, 269) can be seen clearly in early petitions. In medieval England, petitioning emerged at a time when the crown was sovereign and held enormous powers and when English subjects vitally needed the petition as a vehicle for economic and political discourse with the king. The right to petition emerged within these material structures, and the petition was a product of social, legal, and economic conditions unique to the time, with more than sixteen thousand petitions to parliaments from the thirteenth to the fifteenth century (Zaret 2000, 82), most having to do with complaints about the miscarriage of justice or requesting relief from taxes, forest laws, and other regulations.

Early petitions—ranging from requests based on personal, individual circumstances to collective expressions of grievance—all arose in response to specific material conditions, from the mundane (a 1717 petition from German cow farmers requesting a license to keep goats) to the less mundane (a wave of petitioning surrounding the March 1848 German revolution). Petitions emerged both from individual material conditions as well as from material conditions affecting the common good. Andreas Würgler chronicles how individual petitions in sixteenth-century Germany constituted 50 percent to 80 percent of petitions submitted and often contained personal histories or what he calls "lifestories" (Würgler 2001, 25)—materially embodied experiences and daily routines. He cites numerous examples, such as the case of Margaretha Lichtensteiner, who petitioned the Zurich City council in 1583 for a job as a teacher. As part of her petition, she focuses on economic and material conditions, including how she was left a widow eight weeks after giving birth to her child, her husband leaving her nothing but debts. The city council's response to the petition is also expressed in terms of material factors "that signify not through language but through their spatial organization . . . utility . . . and tactility" (Dickson 1999, 297). For example, although her petition was denied, Lichtensteiner was given alms of grain by the city council (petitions for grain support or firewood were common in early-modern shortage societies). In this case, then, the rhetorical actions of the petition are situated materially, with the action "occur[ing] in a material setting, employ[ing] material tools, and result[ing] in material artifacts" (Haas 1996, 4), a perspective that foregrounds critical connections between material resources and rhetorical practices. The importance of considering the material conditions of petitioning is also apparent in the range of grievances throughout the seventeenth century, with complaints about teacher incompetence at local schools, tailors requesting protection from trade violations, and "Puritan aldermen in Norwich complaining that 'spit,' 'shit,' and an occasional chair rained down on them from hostile clerics who sat in an overhead galley" (Zaret 2000, 86), all clear illustrations of how material conditions and materially embodied actions inform individuals' genre performances and serve as exigencies for genre uptake. Bruce McComiskey has noted that material rhetorics insist upon "reality's construction of the social" and not simply "the social construction of reality" (McComiskey 2000, 700). Studying the materiality of public genres, such as the petition, can complicate perspectives on the discursive formation of publics and understandings of genres as discursive sites that coordinate social actions, enabling scholars to account further for how material conditions motivate and limit genre uptake and public performances, the focus of the next section.

MATERIAL UPTAKES AND EXCLUSIONARY GENRE SYSTEMS: NINETEENTH-CENTURY WOMEN'S PETITIONING

The historical case of nineteenth-century women's petitioning, often described as a revolutionary period when women exploited the subversive potential of petitioning, further illustrates the need to ground rhetorical inquiries into public performances in the material. In her historical study of women's nineteenth-century antislavery petitioning, Susan Zaeske seeks to demonstrate how "women seized the radical potential of one of the few civil rights they were understood to possess—the right to petition—to assert substantial political authority" (Zaeske 2003, 1). However, while histories of petitioning, such as Zaeske's history of antislavery petitioning and Alisse Portnoy's (2005) history of Native American antiremoval petitioning, acknowledge how petitioning enabled political participation and contributed to the success of these social movements, it is also important to critically consider the material conditions that complicate narratives of historical progress and political change. Indeed, as women activists worked to negotiate public and private roles and used public petitions as a bridge to political participation, they also had to navigate material conditions—from verbal assaults and threats of physical violence, to geographical obstacles that limited organizing, to legislative bodies that responded to a huge influx of petitions by instituting the gag rule—that worked to undermine their participation and to preclude change. A focus on materiality—informed by an examination of the political and domestic economies of nineteenth-century women's activism—foregrounds issues of access and power, acknowledges the constraints of exclusionary systems of public genres, and contributes to our understanding of the strategic uptakes of genres, thus complicating historical research on public genres and their role in social change.

In his study of the materiality of genre uptakes, Dryer asks us to consider "the specific material conditions through which readers and writers are 'taken up' into social relations when they 'uptake' a genre," and how this can "help us better understand the persistence of exclusionary systems of genres" (2008, 504). The exclusionary nature of the public petition's uptake is clear, particularly for women in the 1830s who took an active role in the antislavery movement and who faced what Dryer describes as "inequities of access to the material and discursive resources for engaging" with public genres (527). Unable to break out of the role in which they were "taken up" by the social relations of petitions (as individuals excluded from public debate), women strategically drew on and appropriated antecedent genres (such as prayer)—genres that reinforced their exclusionary role and maintained their position in the domestic realm. For example, the antiremoval petitions submitted by women in the nineteenth century (and described in Portnoy's historical account) contained many features of the genre of prayer and conventionally began or ended with petitioners affirming their commitment to their moral duty and place in the domestic sphere, which is evident in the following antiremoval petition signed by fifty women of Hallowell, Maine, in January 1830: "To the Honourable Senate and House of Representatives in Congress assembled, we the undersigned, feeling deeply interested in the honour, integrity, and virtue of our country, and considering the questions soon to be presented before you in relation to several tribes of Indians in the western States, as affecting all these, we do most humbly and ardently unite our prayers with those of ten thousand in our land, that your determination may be favourable to these devoted, persecuted, and interesting people" (quoted in Portnoy 2005, 68). The petition reflects a typical opening for female petitioners at this time, noting that the signers are "deeply interested in the honor, integrity, and virtue" of the country, a moral concern they use as a bridge into the political sphere. The women of Hallowell drew on the accepted conventions of discourse as well as their conventional roles in the domestic sphere in order to address the established authorities and begin carving out roles for themselves as citizens. This example illustrates the potential for the study of public genres and their material uptakes to enrich rhetorical genre studies' understanding of genre performances and identities by examining how participants in public genres negotiate multiple roles, draw on these roles strategically, and carry out rhetorical performances that are improvised and that draw on a range of available genres.

While these negotiations, improvisations, and entry points into public discourse are often described in symbolically empowering ways—in terms of how woman constructed "access routes" or "bridges" to public participation—a materialist orientation turns our attention to how petitions worked to exclude users by "sublimating dissatisfaction and desire for change into participation in institutionally sanctioned ways of reading and writing" (Dryer 2008, 518). In the case of nineteenth-century women committed to the abolition movement, they were forced to redirect antislavery political action into moral suasion and to adopt "institutionally sanctioned" roles within the domestic sphere, adopting a humble tone of supplication and an acknowledgment of the superior status of the recipient, as illustrated in the above petition. This deference to authority can also be seen in an antislavery petition submitted by the women of Massachusetts, which "respectfully" addresses the "Honorable Senate and House," and in which the women crossed out "citizens" and wrote in "ladies." Zaeske notes that this common move to replace *citizens* with *women* or *ladies* placed limits on the political agency of women, their authority to instruct elected representatives, and their expectations about whether their requests would be considered by Congress (Zaeske 2003, 25). By focusing on how women gained access to public debate via the public petition, it's possible to view this public genre as a tool of access and empowerment that enabled the "transformation of the political identity" of women (2) and to thereby minimize the material conditions that precluded the full participation of women in the public sphere. The very fact that women—without the legal right to vote, run for office, or participate in public debate as full citizens—were forced to employ strategic uptakes to frame the debate in terms of their moral, Christian duties or in terms of their position in the domestic sphere rather than public sphere reveals the material conditions at work and reveals both the enabling and exclusionary constraints of this public genre.

An inquiry into the material conditions and domestic economies of nineteenth-century women's petitioning—on into "the cultural economies of actual places" (Ackerman and Coogan 2010, 17)—keeps consideration of access and power firmly in view. For instance, women in the early nineteenth century held public fairs to sell needlepoint and other hand-made goods in order to raise money for abolitionist causes. They also used the spaces of literary societies and sewing circles for political organizing and signing of petitions. In addition, as chronicled by historian Beth Salerno in *Sister Societies*, many female societies at this time promoted boycotts of slave-made goods and promoted patronage of free-produce stores. In this way, women sought to use their limited access to economic resources and their limited power—their ordinary household purchases—to promote an antislavery agenda (Salerno 2005, 42). The constraints on full participation in the genre system of antislavery petitioning are also reflected in the economic and geographical limitations women faced, such as the cost of travel to antislavery conventions and the hardship of several days' travel by rail and steamer. Salerno notes the difficult itineraries of those who had to travel several days by rail and steamer, including a delegate from New Hampshire who had a long boat ride to Boston and then a seventeen-hour boat ride from Boston to the conference in Philadelphia (55). Our scholarship on public rhetoric and counterpublics, as Daniel Brouwer notes, should explain "how various qualities and quantities of various resources delimit the available means of persuasion" (Brouwer 2005, 200–201). By focusing only on discursive networks, we risk oversimplifying the material conditions that constrained the formation of public networks.

Focusing on women's discursive actions within the context of material conditions illustrates how, as women participated in public petitioning, they were simultaneously taken up by networks of social relations that forestall change. Women, for instance, participated in all-female petition drives (petitions by men were filed separately) and were not allowed to join male antislavery societies, leading them to form separate female societies or counterpublics; however, while enabling women to organize and create alternate spaces for political agency, there were material consequences to these separate meeting spaces, which resulted in verbal assault or physical violence. In her history of women's organizing, Salerno notes that a group of fifty-five women met in a Concord, New Hampshire, courthouse to form a female antislavery society, while outside a group of men threw rocks at the windows and women ducked rotten eggs being hurled at them (2005, 44)—a reminder of how women's increasing empowerment and construction of counterpublics or alternative spaces for activism must be seen in the context of the material realities and conditions of those actual spaces in which women gathered, along with a recognition of the resource disparities among social actors.

Grounding an inquiry into public genres in materiality and economies of rhetoric can lead to an active, resistant understanding of the material conditions that exclude users and that forestall change, a resistant reading that can enrich historical studies of discourse and complicate our metaphors of the evolution and change of public genres. Rhetorical genre studies (RGS)—as part of its reconceptualization of genres as dynamic actions rather than static classifications—has frequently invoked spatial metaphors for (re)imagining genres. For example, genres have been described as *discursive sites of interaction* or *locations for communication*, as *ecosystems* or *habitats*, as *discursive structures* or *ideological formations*, or as a means of "positioning" writers and readers as they "navigate" or "gain access" to situations. In an oft-cited quotation, Charles Bazerman notes that genres are "locations within which meaning is constructed . . . the familiar places we go to create intelligible communicative action with each other and the guideposts we use to explore the unfamiliar" (Bazerman 1997, 19). While these spatial metaphors are powerful ways to conceptualize the dynamic interactions within genres, these metaphors may also limit our understanding of the more wide-ranging, heterogeneous interactions within public genres. As Nedra Reynolds argues, "Material theories of rhetoric must either reject disembodied ideas—those created through spatial metaphors—or learn how to fold them into corporeal, spatial, and textual efforts to locate rhetorical agency in public life" (Reynolds 2004, 42). The metaphors of public petitions as "conduits" or "alternative routes" to citizenship (Zaeske 2003, 2, 5) or as a means of "crossing into new terrain" (7), "opening doors" (Portnoy 2005, 72) for active political participation, or creating "bridges" (74) to the public sphere are better understood, then, in the context of the cultural, physical, and spatial limitations that nineteenth-century women activists faced. This includes their efforts to overcome very real geographical boundaries, which they did by going door to door and canvassing, forming antislavery societies that reached across regions, attending national conferences to organize and distribute fliers, coordinating mailings, and networking across geographic regions—embodied actions that will be the focus of the next section.

MATERIALITY AND EMBODIED RHETORIC

As described in the previous section, nineteenth-century female antislavery petitioners were "motivated by the embodied practices . . . cultivated in relationship with people in [their] own communities; by a rhetorical labor shared with others" (Ackerman and Coogan 2010, 7) as they canvassed, went door to door, gathered signatures, and talked to women face to face in sewing circles and other gatherings. Petitions, then, are unique sites for studying the interaction of the rhetorical and the material based on their embodied practices, practices that challenge the disembodied ideals of rhetorical agency and focus attention on public actors performing rhetorical acts. As Christina Haas has argued, "ignoring the materiality of literacy, its basis in bodily movements and habits, is no longer possible" (Haas 1996, 227). The place of the body in the history of rhetorical petitioning and the embodied experiences of petitioners can be seen most readily in early petitions, where petitioning bodies engaged in rhetorical action under specific physical and spatial conditions. For example, in prerevolutionary England, in order for citizens to have their petitions recognized and acted upon by authorities, the petitions were physically thrust into the hands of rulers, often by citizens who were able to sneak into the palace via back stairs or who hid behind bushes and sought out a ruler while he was hunting in the royal forest (Zaret 2000, 85).

Moving from individually embodied to collectively embodied action, in *Petitions in Social History*, Lex Heerma van Voss reports that in 1779 Lord George Gordon introduced a petition against the relief of anti-Catholic measures in the British Parliament and took fourteen thousand supporters with him to Parliament to hand deliver the petition (van Voss 2001, 3). Similarly, further demonstrating the locatedness and lived textuality of petitioning, colonists in the late seventeenth and eighteenth centuries, seeking extension of a county road or exemption from local taxes, physically presented their petitions to the county court by taking them each month to a fixed location, where they were collected. An historical account of the circulation of local petitions in the antebellum public further demonstrates these embodied rhetorical actions: "These were your neighbors who sought you out in your home or field or forest, behind your counter, at your desk, with your team—in a time more innocent than ours, before such canvassing was commonplace and at a time when a petition meant something. . . . The woman who approached you with her petition in hand, at Wednesday night prayer meeting, or in your barbershop or at your door, would probably be somebody you knew, or somebody who knew somebody you knew" (Miller 1995, 305). A materialist perspective of public performances as "embodied, emotioned, and localized within conditions of production, circulation, and consumption" (Bawarshi forthcoming, n.p.) enables us to analyze the rhetorical force of petitions once they are no longer "motivated by the embodied practices . . . cultivated in relationship with people in [their] own communities" (Ackerman and Coogan 2010, 7) and once delivery is no longer dependent on groups of people physically assembling to gather petition signatures or hand delivering petitions to authorities. Contemporary petitions, distanced by time and space (mailed petitions or electronic petitions), are more disembodied, relying more on discursive and rhetorical strategies to promote mutuality and connectedness. However, these indirect (or represented) embodiments can be traced back to lived embodiments in the history of the genre.

This embodied rhetoric—and affective and "emotioned" dimension of petitioning—can be seen in a contemporary petition from the United Farm Workers appealing to the Pizza Hut president to boycott Pictsweet mushrooms until Pictsweet workers are given deserved wage increases, health benefits, and decent working conditions. While the petition is sponsored by the UFW, it includes a personal declaration or lifestory of Pictsweet worker Jose Luna, whose testimonial demonstrates the embodied rhetorical actions or lived textuality of petitions: "I am a single parent with two sons living with me, and I'm suffering right now because I can't make ends meet. I can hardly make the rent payment and to feed two growing boys is almost impossible with the little money I am bringing home. Things are so tight that I might have to get a second job just to afford the basic necessities and pay my bills. If things don't change and we don't get a new contract, it could have serious effects on my family. . . . We need this contract and change for the betterment of our families." The rhetorical effect of the petition on behalf of worker's rights is heightened by the account of the worker's experiences, which illustrate a definition of materiality forwarded by Carole Blair: "the lived-in body as condition and consequence of discourse" (Blair 2001, 288). In their critique of the classical bourgeois public sphere—for its failure to recognize the material conditions of everyday life—and their proposal of a counterpublic proletarian sphere, Oscar Negt and Alexander Kluge define this counterpublic space as "embodied" and based on a "horizon of experiences" of working-class lives (Negt and Kluge 1993, 1–2), similar to the ways in which those who see literacy as embodied practice "see rhetoric as enmeshed in the everyday" (Reynolds 2004, 43). Based on his experiential interests and the everyday, informal voice of his experiential linguistic practices, Luna's testimonial invokes the "context of living" (Negt and Kluge 1993, 57) and creates a counterpublic discourse that reaffirms the relational quality of discourse and its material conditions, particularly those conditions that limit power and access to economic resources. As Barbara Dickson explains, "Material rhetoric shares the assumption of cultural materialism that corporeal bodies are socially produced—and therefore shares as well its interest in identifying how rhetorical and literary productions are potentially disruptive of the dominant structures which produce them" (Dickson 1999, 298). A materialist framework, then, can complicate an understanding of how the genre of the petition rhetorically embodies and maintains (within its typifications) motives for action based in lived experience, drawing attention to how rhetorical performances, such as Luna's testimonial, work to disrupt dominant economic structures and illustrating the dynamic interactions between lived experience (the embodied, material conditions of publics) and lived textuality (the rhetorical actions and discursive performances of publics). Such an approach can also enrich our understanding of how participants in public discourse, by "removing their actual bodies from physical spaces" and participating in online communities, can "create another set of problems for geopolitics" (Reynolds 2004, 35), which will be taken up in the next section.

NETWORKED PUBLIC PERFORMANCES

The focus on materiality and embodied rhetoric is especially fruitful for considering the ways in which public petitions are affected by digital networks that influence the circulation of petitions and their intervention in civic actions—how they are taken up as tools of mobilization by citizen petitioners and how they are taken up by authorities who act on the petition. When comparing historical cases of petitioning rooted in the material and physical gathering of petitioners (such as petitions circulated in nineteenth-century women's sewing circles or prerevolutionary petitions hand delivered to the king) to more contemporary online petitions (such as e-mailed petitions from an online advocacy group like MoveOn.org), there's an obvious shift in the tactical dimensions of the interchange as the sequence of uptakes becomes further removed and increasingly mediated. Reynolds notes that "participation in online communities removes people from their geophysical communities—the streets and schools, sidewalks and shops that make up a neighborhood" (Reynolds 2004, 35). And Howard Rheingold has argued that electronic petitions give people "the illusion that they're participating in some meaningful political action" (quoted in Regan 2002, n.p.). Prior to the digital age, the right to petition was closely associated with the right to physically assemble in order to draw up, discuss, and sign petitions or to circulate petitions door to door. But what happens when participation in virtual communities removes people from their geophysical communities and from the material locations of the discursive activity? Will it be more or less likely that petitions will enable intervention and civic action?

Scholars have embraced the potential for the Internet to increase political participation in public discourse and to empower marginalized citizens or groups that previously had no access to the public arena, with a focus on the Internet's potential to "flatten hierarchies of power" (Mitra and Watts 2002, 493) and to "give play to many voices without assimilating them into a single voice" (Warnick 2001, 62–63). However, this view of a more democratic space more open and accessible to multiple voices often fails to consider the politics of digital spaces and the material conditions of issues of access affected by gender, class, and race (Banks 2005; Ito 2008; Nakamura 2002) along with the embodiment of participants within digital spaces (Haas 1996; van Doorn 2011). As networks of petitioners canvassing and going door to door increasingly move to "networked publics," where "the properties of bits—as distinct from atoms—introduce new possibilities for interaction" (boyd 2010, 39), they continue to negotiate a range of material limitations and affordances. In her discussion of the architecture of digital spaces and properties of digital media, danah boyd notes that one of the affordances of digital media is that it enables wider distribution; however, while "the Internet may enable many to broadcast content and create publics . . . it does not guarantee an audience" (boyd 2010, 48). A focus on the materiality of uptakes indicates that while the genre of the petition activates the social relations of those mobilizing to join the petition effort and the list of signatories, the genre may not activate a response from authorities who receive the petition.

For example, the White House recently initiated a new citizen's online petition site We the People, which opens up a space for citizens' voices and political participation; its purpose is "giving all Americans a way to engage their government on the issues that matter to them" (https:// petitions.whitehouse.gov). However, "it does not guarantee an audience" and requires a threshold number of signatures in order to "trigger" genre uptakes: "If a petition meets the signature threshold, it will be reviewed by the Administration and we will issue a response" (We the People). Petitions are submitted electronically by individual citizens but must reach a material threshold for numbers of signatures before receiving a response, a direct correspondence between the material and the rhetorical. To receive a rhetorical response (an official response from the Obama administration), a petition initially had to reach 25,000 signatures within thirty days; however, that threshold has now been increased to100,000 signatures within thirty days. In addition, petitioners must get to 150 signatures in order for the petition to be publicly searchable on the We the People page on WhiteHouse.gov. boyd notes that "searchability," along with "scalability," are affordances that emerge out of the properties of networked technologies.

With this focus on the influence of new communication technologies on petitioning, it is worth noting that as the embodied practices of petitioning (canvassing, meeting face to face, going door to door) become more dispersed and move to online networks, the material conditions from which the grievance arises may become secondary to the material condition of getting X number of signatures or collecting a threshold number of signatures to necessitate the genre's uptake. It might well be that in cases in which there is no official uptake of the petition, the genre performance itself (the act of signing a petition) becomes its own uptake—a performance of citizenship. Political scientist Daniel Carpenter has argued that the rhetorical force of petitions lies not in the rhetorical and material response—the redress of grievances—but in their networking potential, noting that the list of signatories is "a rich political resource" and that in addition to identifying individuals sympathetic to the petition's declaration, the list of signatories "locate[s] individuals in a social structure" (Carpenter 2003, 1). In this case, a materialist, spatial view of rhetorical activity can broaden our understanding of petitions as rhetorical tools of mobilization—of ways of locating supporters and creating networks of support, moving from physical assembling of publics to virtual spaces of networking. Neils van Doorn has examined how "lived social relations extend into digital space, where they are renegotiated within, and made possible by, hybrid assemblages of embodied users, cultural discourses and new media technologies" (van Doorn 2011, 535). Examining the rhetorical practice of petitioning in relation to material traces of social structures and material conditions for gathering signatures can lead to a more critical understanding of how petitions both enable and limit social action, particularly as public actors move from the physical right to assembly when exercising the right to petition to participation in actor networks composed of dispersed and diverse assemblages of people, artifacts, and practices (Spinuzzi 2008). Studying these interactions within a material framework—particularly a framework of how genres circulate and build networks of activity—gives us insight into the complex, unpredictable, heterogeneous connections among public actors and the ways in which their actions are collectively coordinated.

CONCLUSION

Carpenter calls petitioning "one of the most consequential yet least analyzed institutions of republican government" (Carpenter 2003, 1). This
chapter's analysis of the public petition has demonstrated how an understanding of the material conditions of public genre uptakes produces a
more critical understanding of the exclusionary nature of publics and the
complex and interagentive nature of public participation. As Reynolds
argues, "To begin with the material means grounding an inquiry into
taken-for-granted spatial metaphors and geographical practices that
affect reading and writing, living and learning. An inquiry . . . into space
and place can offer insights into the connections between locatedness
and moving through the world; between travel and dwelling; between
public and private" (Reynolds 2004, 12). By focusing on movement in
addition to dwelling, we can move beyond focusing primarily on how
individuals inhabit genres to an examination of how individuals perform genres in space, place, and time—from petitions against the power
of the monarchy in the early democratic sphere, to petitions as a means
of gaining access to public debate for women in the nineteenth century,
to contemporary online petitions and the negotiation of technological
constraints and affordances. As this chapter has examined, a materialist perspective enables critical insights into the petition and its uses that
would otherwise be overlooked in traditional rhetorical genre studies
approaches or public rhetoric approaches. Acknowledging the ways in
which material conditions (economic, political, cultural, embodied, and
affective factors) influence genre performances or uptakes, leading to
reinscriptions of certain roles but also of strategic uptakes, helps us see
how agency is much more complex and multifaceted, residing in much
more than the genre itself and its affordances.

Exploring the interagentive nature of genre performances within
material conditions and the interplay of generic constraints and the particular historical and cultural situations out of which rhetorical genres
evolve and operate also allows us to see how the genre of the public petition both enables and limits intervention and public/political change.
While it may be tempting to focus solely on how the public genre of
the petition, by seeking redress for grievances, enables rhetorical action
and promotes social change, grounding an inquiry in the material can
increase critical attention to the material conditions that can exclude
genre users and can impede social change—for instance, by drawing
attention to the inequity of access to resources on the part of petitioners
in monarchal England or on the part of women in the nineteenth century who participated in publicly sanctioned and "normalized" forms of

communication (like the petition) while existing outside the "normal" political activities (and legal rights) of their male counterparts. A material approach to genre uptake makes it possible to imagine discourse through both dwelling, or the normalized interactions within systems of genre, and movement, the active, resistant understanding of the material conditions that exclude users and that forestall change, a resistant reading that has the potential to complicate our understanding of the evolution and change of public genres and to enrich studies of public discourse and public performances.

References

Ackerman, John M., and David Coogan. 2010. *The Public Work of Rhetoric: Citizen-Scholars and Civic Engagement*. Columbia: University of South Carolina Press.

Asen, Robert. 2009. "Ideology, Materiality, and Counterpublicity: William E. Simon and the Rise of a Conservative Counterintelligentisia." *Quarterly Journal of Speech* 95 (3): 263–88. http://dx.doi.org/10.1080/00335630903140630.

Banks, Adam. 2005. *Race, Rhetoric, and Technology: Searching for Higher Ground*. Mahwah, NJ: Erlbaum.

Bawarshi, Anis. Forthcoming. "Accounting for Genre Performances: Why Uptake Matters." In *Trends and Traditions in Genre Studies*, edited by Natasha Artemeva and Aviva Freedman. Edmonton: Inkshed.

Bazerman, Charles. 1997. "The Life of Genre, the Life in the Classroom." In *Genre and Writing: Issues, Arguments, Alternatives*, edited by Wendy Bishop and Hans Ostrom, 19–26. Portsmouth, NH: Boynton/Cook.

Blair, Carole. 2001. "Reflections on Criticisms and Bodies: Parables from Public Places." *Western Journal of Communication* 65 (3): 271–94. http://dx.doi.org/10.1080/10570310109374706.

boyd, danah. 2010. "Social Network Sites as Networked Publics: Affordances, Dynamics, and Implications." In *A Networked Self: Identity, Community, and Culture on Social Network Sites*, edited by Zizi Papacharissi, 39–58. New York: Routledge.

Brouwer, Daniel C. 2005. "Communication as Counterpublic." In *Communication as . . .: Perspectives on Theory*, edited by Gregory J. Shepherd, Jeffrey St. John, and Ted Striphas, 195–208. Thousand Oaks, CA: SAGE.

Carpenter, Daniel. 2003. "The Petition as a Tool of Recruitment: Evidence from the Abolitionist Congressional Campaign." Prepared for the Yale Conference on Crafting and Operating Institutions, New Haven, CT, April.

Dickson, Barbara. 1999. "Reading Maternity Materially: The Case of Demi Moore." In *Rhetorical Bodies*, edited by Jack Selzer and Sharon Crowley, 297–313. Madison: University of Wisconsin Press.

Dryer, Dylan B. 2008. "Taking Up Space: On Genre Systems as Geographies of the Possible." *JAC* 28 (3/4): 503–34.

Haas, Christina. 1996. *Writing Technology: Studies on the Materiality of Literacy*. Mahwah, NJ: Erlbaum.

Ito, Mizuko. 2008. Introduction to *Networked Publics*, edited by Kazys Varnelis, 1–13. Cambridge: MIT Press. http://dx.doi.org/10.7551/mitpress/9780262220859.003.0001.

Lawson, Gary, and Guy Seidman. 1999. "Downsizing the Right to Petition." *Northwestern University Law Review* (93) 3: 1–27.

McComiskey, Bruce. 2000. "Rev. of *Rhetorical Bodies*, ed. Jack Selzer and Sharon Crowley." *JAC* 20 (3): 699–703.

Miller, William Lee. 1995. *Arguing About Slavery: John Quincy Adams and the Great Battle in the United States Congress.* New York: Vintage.

Mitra, Ananda, and Eric Watts. 2002. "Theorizing Cyberspace: The Idea of Voice Applied to the Internet Discourse." *New Media & Society* 4 (4): 479–98. http://dx.doi.org /10.1177/146144402321466778.

Nakamura, Lisa. 2002. *Cybertypes: Race, Ethnicity, and Identity on the Internet.* New York: Routledge.

Negt, Oscar, and Alexander Kluge. 1993. *Public Sphere and Experience: Toward an Analysis of the Bourgeois and Proletarian Public Sphere.* Minneapolis: University of Minnesota Press.

Portnoy, Alisse. 2005. *Their Right to Speak: Women's Activism in the Indian and Slave Debates.* Cambridge, MA: Harvard University Press. http://dx.doi.org/10.4159/9780674042223.

Regan, Michael P. 2002. "Online Activism _ A Lot More Than Just Petitions." http:// www.greenday.net/activism.html.

Reynolds, Nedra. 2004. *Geographies of Writing: Inhabiting Places and Encountering Differences.* Carbondale: Southern Illinois University Press.

Salerno, Beth. 2005. *Sister Societies: Women's Antislavery Organizations in Antebellum America.* DeKalb: Northern Illinois University Press.

Spinuzzi, Clay. 2008. *Network: Theorizing Knowledge Work in Telecommunications.* Cambridge: Cambridge University Press. http://dx.doi.org/10.1017/CBO9780511509605.

van Doorn, Niels. 2011. "Digital Spaces, Material Traces: How Matter Comes to Matter in Online Performances of Gender, Sexuality, and Embodiment." *Media Culture & Society* 33 (4): 531–47. http://dx.doi.org/10.1177/0163443711398692.

van Voss, Lex Heerma. 2001. *Petitions in Social History.* Cambridge: Cambridge University Press.

Warnick, Barbara. 2001. "Rhetorical Criticism in New Media Environments." *Rhetoric Review* 20 (1/2): 60–65.

Würgler, Andreas. 2001. "Voices from Among the Silent Masses: Humble Petitions and Social Conflicts in Early Modern Central Europe." In *Petitions in Social History*, edited by Lex Heerma van Voss, 11–34. Cambridge: Cambridge University Press. http:// dx.doi.org/10.1017/S0020859001000311.

Zaeske, Susan. 2003. *Signatures of Citizenship: Petitioning, Antislavery, and Women's Political Identity.* Chapel Hill: University of North Carolina Press.

Zaret, David. 2000. *Origins of Democratic Culture: Printing, Petitions, and the Public Sphere in Early-Modern England.* Princeton, NJ: Princeton University Press.

6

BODILY SCRIPTS, UNRULY WORKERS, AND PUBLIC ANXIETY
Scripting Professional Embodiment in Interwar Vocational Guides

Risa Applegarth

Among successful business women nowadays there is a certain accepted way of dressing which is restrained yet smart. . . . In general you can be fairly sure that any employer will favor well-brushed clothes, polished well-kept shoes, clean gloves, neat stockings, conservative makeup, well-groomed hair.

—Hazel Cades 1930

The space between genres is the space where actual human bodies house historic dispositions.

—Dylan Dryer 2012

Like numerous vocational guides for women workers published during the interwar period, Hazel Cades's 1930 guide, *Jobs for Girls*, advises readers to adopt "a certain accepted way of dressing," portraying such dress as the settled preference of both "successful business women" and employers (19). Such a depiction clearly aims to naturalize "well-brushed clothes, polished well-kept shoes, clean gloves, neat stockings, conservative makeup, [and] well-groomed hair" as the uncontroversial, rational preferences of "any employer," yet including such advice belies its obviousness. Just as Janet Giltrow (2012) has argued that genre scholars must attend closely to "what goes without saying"—what is shared so fully by a genre's users that it remains unsaid—I want to suggest, conversely, that repeated injunctions like those voiced by Cades can alert scholars to the presence of anxiety, of public norms undergoing renegotiation. In this case, for instance, repeated advice focused on the embodied behaviors of women as potential professionals makes legible a significant public anxiety surrounding the intrusion of women's bodies into professional spaces during the revolution in white-collar work that took place in the 1920s and 1930s.

DOI: 10.7330/9781607324430.c006

This chapter assesses the proliferation of advice discourse in vocational guides governing the behavior, dress, and comportment of women professionals, reading these repeated injunctions not as evidence that "a certain accepted way of dressing" had become the settled preference but proceeding instead under the assumption that what is *said*, and said repeatedly, is *not* held sufficiently in common that it can remain *unsaid*. Instead, I read the repetitive, body-focused advice offered to women through this genre as soliciting women's participation in the policing of their own embodied performances of professional competence. I argue that this advice discourse enacts a set of highly constrained norms governing gendered embodiment, sediments these norms through performative repetition, and consequently undermines the potentially disruptive quality of women's incursions into the powerful public spaces of professional employment during this period. Drawing from feminist historiographic work that seeks to excavate the rhetorical practices through which bodies and spaces become gendered, this chapter investigates how genre-based repetition helps to generate and sediment bodily dispositions and to govern embodied performances in the public sphere. Consequently, I suggest that public genres function as sites of constitutive repetition, sites where crucial public discursive work can remain visible to scholars even as the bodies that materialized those public norms—that, in Dylan Dryer's (2012, n.p.) words, "house[d] historic dispositions"—no longer remain. Through historical work that attends to the anxious repetitions of genre, rhetorical scholars can denaturalize bodily dispositions and the material-semiotic systems that elicited and maintained them, revealing the centrality of genre in shaping and stabilizing social, rhetorical, and gendered spaces of public life.

The vocational-guide genre is able to manage women's performances of professional competence in part because this genre is public not only in its circulation but also in its function as a source of vocational advice—advice that aims to move women readers from domestic spaces into the public arena of paid employment outside the home.[1] This genre, typically written by women professionals to other women seeking work, seeks to maneuver women's bodies into the public spaces of professional employment—offices, newsrooms, secretarial and managerial positions, and so on. Yet the presence of those bodies disrupted the smooth functioning of these newly powerful professional sites. Public anxiety surrounding these economic and cultural shifts was manifested on women's bodies in part because those bodies—unlike men's—were seen as bearers of gender; as the analyses below demonstrate, the bodies of women workers were viewed as *bodies* in a way that male professionals could largely avoid, and the presence of these bodies shifted the dynamics of professional workplaces understood previously as free from such considerations. The anxious, repeated advice found in vocational guides reveals the intensity of discursive efforts to govern women's bodies in order to manage this labor transition and to minimize the disruption women's bodies posed to the workplace as a public—rather than private—arena. Against the backdrop of this labor transition—and particularly in the context of the Great Depression, which generated strong public opposition to women's employment—how did public genres such as the vocational guide enable women workers to navigate such anxious conditions? How, too, did genre-based repetition contribute to the discursive conditions that made certain embodied performances legible as appropriate and "professional" while marking off other performances as *unruly* or *ungoverned?* How did the numerous vocational guides for women published between World War I and World War II shape the bodily dispositions women took up in their entrance into professional workplaces?

In attending to the forms of embodiment crafted and sedimented in these guides, I rely upon the insights of feminist historiographers who have investigated the rhetorical practices by which specific forms of gendered embodiment have been generated, maintained, and transformed. As they investigate gendered dress, gendered spaces such as schools and pulpits, and embodied practices such as bicycle riding and medical dissection, these studies underscore embodiment as historically contingent (see Enoch 2008; Hallenbeck 2010; Mattingly 2002; Mountford 2001; Suter 2013; Wells 1999). Preferred bodily performances are subject to change over time and thus require rhetorical maintenance or renovation through the discursive practices and material environments that together constitute public and private space.

Feminist research into gendered histories of rhetoric often insists upon the mutuality of material environments, embodied behaviors, and discursive practices—upon what Nathan Stormer has called the "exquisite, even infernal, imbrication of meaning, matter, and action" (Stormer 2004, 262). For instance, Jordynn Jack (2009) has analyzed World War II–era rhetorics recruiting women into wartime work, making use of Pierre Bourdieu's concept of "acts of institution," which argues that language acts performatively to produce the object or order it designates. The 1920s and 1930s were likewise a period when economic and cultural changes prompted major revisions to the material-symbolic system of gender, changes worked out, I argue, in part through women's uptake of public genres such as the vocational guide.

Although repetition is crucial to feminist historians investigating the practices that accomplish gendering, scholars focusing on embodiment have tended not to make use of genre as a framework for such investigations. The concept of uptake, so crucial to contemporary genre studies, represents a form of constitutive repetition similar to the acts of institution and other performative theories of embodiment that have been so fruitful for feminist scholars in their efforts to historicize forms of embodiment. Uptakes, like the performances that collectively both stabilize and undermine gendered embodiment, are imperfect, contingent, and shared among bodies and writers, sedimented through the dispersed performances of numerous actors. That is, gendered embodiment and genred rhetorical activity both rely upon a form of recurrence that is always only partial and is both stabilized through repetition and rendered contingent through the imperfect nature of that repetition. In his contribution to this volume (chapter 3), Dylan Dryer suggests that uptake can be understood as bearing five dimensions: *uptake affordances* inscribed within a text, wherein a text invites or induces certain kinds of response; *uptake artifacts* that result from a text as actual, concrete responses; *uptake enactments* that constitute what writers and readers *do* in response to a text, and conversely *uptake captures* that identify what uptakes themselves *do to* readers and writers; and *uptake residues*, the sedimented ways uptakes become materialized into social formations as habits, inclinations, conventions, and desires. As Dryer explains, "any instance of any of these dimensions of uptake is an incremental contribution to social formations: uptake affordances, artifacts, enactments, and captures all help maintain, modify, and destabilize cultural institutions" (chapter 3, 66). A similar investment in the role of genre-based repetition in the work of revising or maintaining social institutions—including embodied experiences such as illness—motivates Kimberly Emmons's reformulation of uptake as "the disposition(s) assumed through the use of genres" (Emmons 2009, 139). Emmons writes that "to account for the power, particularly the intimate, embodied power, of uptake, we must redefine uptake not as the relation between two (or more) genres, but as the disposition of subjects that results from that relation" (Emmons 2009, 137). In other words, the work of genres in maintaining or destabilizing gendered systems of embodiment relies upon this "intimate, embodied power" wherein subjects find themselves "tak[ing] on" certain "subjective dispositions" when they "*take up* particular genres and discourses" (138).

Drawing on Dryer's and Emmons's work, I regard the gendered bodily dispositions of the professional woman as *uptake residues*—that is, as formidable social formations enacted and maintained in part through the *uptake affordances* of vocational guides. This genre is not, of course, alone in crafting the cultural institution of the gendered professional body. An intricate system of bodily surveillance elicits and maintains the gendered form of professionalism that developed so powerfully (and persistently) during this period, involving images, advertisements, department-store window displays, magazine profiles, subtle verbal comments on women's dress, and so on. But the numerous guides produced during this period explicitly to offer advice and guidance to women workers form a powerful node in that system, in part because they reveal through their repetitions the unsettled nature of this emerging public norm. Discursive and embodied performances sediment through repetition into convention, comportment, and conduct, making the body a site that materializes discursive prescriptions and preferences like those I trace in this chapter. In particular, I suggest, the public need this genre meets is unannounced yet implicit in the repetitious nature of the advice it circulates; the genre emerges to meet public anxiety over transformations in the gendered labor system and resolves that public anxiety within gendered bodies. Analyzing the *uptake affordances* this genre repeats, we see how genre can transform a broad public affect into gendered bodily dispositions; in this way, we can historicize—and perhaps unsettle—the serene but still tightly governed professional body that persists as a legacy of bodily scripts enacted and sedimented during this period of public transformation.

SHIFTING GENDER AND LABOR RELATIONS IN THE INTERWAR PERIOD

Massive economic and cultural shifts after World War I brought unprecedented numbers of women into the formal labor force in the United States, creating new labor conditions and also generating a proliferation of texts: reports, narratives, labor surveys, news features, government bulletins, anecdotes, and cautionary tales by which Americans debated and accommodated the new status quo of the working woman. Publishers, both commercial and governmental, presented girls and women with a burgeoning assortment of books and pamphlets designed to advise them on a somewhat dizzying array of new career options. Such texts included career-focused feature stories in women's magazines such as *Cosmopolitan* and *Independent Woman*, research-based surveys routinely published by the Women's Bureau of the US Department of Labor, and a growing slate of occupational guides explicitly identifying young women as their target audience. Scores of these texts were published in the 1920s and 1930s, such as Emmett Leroy Shannon's 1920 guide *Money for the Woman Who Wants It* and Catherine Filene's 1934 guide *Careers for Women: New Ideas, New Methods, New Opportunities to Fit a New World.*

In relation to this broader public discourse, vocational guides position their readers as facing a newly accessible yet dauntingly complex vocational landscape. For instance, Doris Fleischman's 1928 guide, *An Outline of Careers for Women*, opens with this assertion: "It is not long since the feminist movement broke down the barriers that kept women from occupational fields which men had regarded as exclusively their own. Today there are few pursuits which women do not follow with more or less success. The opportunities are almost unlimited, and for this reason it is difficult for the young woman to make her choice of a career" (Fleischman 1928, xi). After the onset of the Depression, writers point to changed economic conditions as creating an urgent need for career guidance for women; Miriam Simons Leuck, for instance, writes in her 1938 guide, *Fields of Work for Women*, that "in the face of the recent sentiment against the employment of women, combined with their greater need to earn under difficult economic conditions, the proper choices of a profession and adequate training therefore have become more important to girls than ever" (Leuck 1938, ix). Vocational guides collectively invoke an audience of women and girls who recognize their career options as newly open and who likewise recognize the authority of experts to help them take advantage of new workplace opportunities. Orie Latham Hatcher, for instance, addresses the guide she compiled and edited for the Southern Woman's Educational Alliance in 1927

> to all interested in occupations for women: to girls and women who need help in choosing an occupation, or for progressing in one already chosen; to any interested in helping girls or women to such ends, [especially] . . . to school superintendents and principals, to deans of girls, counselors, and teacher-counselors; college deans, deans of women, advisers of women, directors of student personnel, appointment bureau secretaries, alumnae secretaries, . . . mothers and fathers, high school graduates, and thoughtful high school seniors; girls' welfare workers; employers; business and professional women, and organizations of such women; and such organizations as parent-teacher associations, and other educational and civic groups interested in the guidance of girls. (1927, vii)

This extensive list of people positioned as advisers conveys something of the scope of the changing labor landscape that vocational guides seek to help women navigate—and evokes, furthermore, a world of workplace possibilities too dauntingly complex for women to navigate without the aid of vocational experts.

While most vocational guides try to encompass this new occupational environment, others focus their advice on gaining access to a specific profession, such as Beatrice Doerschuk's 1920 *Women in the Law* or the 1938 guide *How the Fashion World Works: Fit Yourself for a Fashion Future.* Many guides assemble the guidance of numerous individuals who have already successfully established themselves in various fields; Catherine Filene's (1934) *Careers for Women* includes, for instance, more than 150 chapters, each devoted to a particular career, ranging from familiar fields such as "The Dietician" and "The Advertising Copy Writer" to less typical entries such as "The Congresswoman," "The Taxidermist," and "Railroad Work for Women," with each entry authored by a different individual with expertise and experience in that occupation. As Wendy Sharer (2003) and others have noted, this period privileged the ethos of expert authority with a particular fervor, and numerous realms of activity that were not previously understood as professional became so during the early twentieth century.

The proliferation of vocational guides in this period signaled the enormity of the economic shift underway. In the 1920s, more US women held paying jobs than at any point previously. By 1930, 10 million women participated in the paid workforce, and the next decade added another 2.5 million women. The most dramatic increase in female employment in the early twentieth century came from women's movement into white-collar clerical and sales fields. From 1890 to 1920, the "number of women typists, stenographers, sales people, and others in related occupations grew from a little over 171,000 to almost two million, from 5.3 percent to 25.6 percent of all gainfully employed women" (Scharf 1980, 10). Economic historian Claudia Goldin (1992) has identified only two episodes in US history when the ratio of female to male earnings *rose*: the early nineteenth-century Industrial Revolution, and the early twentieth-century bureaucratic, professional revolution that marked the enormous growth of clerical and white-collar work. The rise in bureaucratic institutions during this period, accompanied by specific technological changes and a widespread embrace of professionalization, offset even the dampening effects of the Depression on women's earnings and women's labor-force participation. Over these decades, across races, classes, and nativity groups, women pursued paid employment in a greater variety of fields and in greater numbers than ever before, casting up, in the words of historians Penina Glazer and Miriam Slater, "a spectrum of professionally trained women whose

numbers and variety would not be matched for another half century"
(Glazer and Slater 1987, 11).[2]

This shifting labor context generated substantial public resistance to
women's employment. For instance, widespread public discourse during the Depression asked whether married women should be barred
from employment; a 1936 Gallup poll found that 82 percent of respondents opposed the employment of married women (Amott and Matthaei
1996, 128). Many employers justified keeping women in low-paying and
entry-level positions through the commonplace argument that women
would quit once they married, and some critics called for working
women to "solve" the unemployment problem during the Depression
by voluntarily leaving the workforce. Vocational guides both register and
respond to the public anxieties that attended women's participation in
a changing national economy. Although these texts categorically assert
the acceptability of women working, they often reference—in order to
rebut—concerns raised in other public forums. For instance, Hatcher
devotes considerable space in her 1927 *Occupations for Women* to countering numerous points of opposition against women working. These
include the fear that higher education develops in young women ambi-
tions for work that lead fewer of them to marry; the strong belief that
married women have no compelling financial reason to pursue paid
employment; and numerous concerns that mothers, by working outside the home, are undermining their children's well-being (Hatcher
1927, xii–xxxiii). Hatcher, who earned a PhD in English literature from
the University of Chicago in 1903 and who founded the Department
of Comparative Literature at Bryn Mawr and the Southern Woman's
Educational Alliance, marshals labor statistics, findings from sociologi-
cal and educational research studies, and long quotations from published essays by women professionals, both married and single, to counter each of these concerns. She also advises her readers that, however
unsound might be the arguments in opposition to their professional
work, they can successfully navigate these oppositional forces only by
attending assiduously to expert advice to fit themselves as competently
as possible to take up the work for which they are most suited.

Many guides likewise register a widespread public anxiety that women
would compete with men for jobs. Hatcher and others promote a strategy of overqualification as a response to the opposition women workers
are likely to face, advising women to prepare to be "twice as good" as
a man applying for a similar position. For example, Catharine Oglesby,
in her 1937 *Business Opportunities for Women,* justifies her book's emphasis on higher education by remarking that a "woman must be twice as

able as a man and do twice as much work to get and hold the same job"
(Oglesby 1937, 8–9); consequently, "every girl who goes into business
should strain every resource to obtain the equipment which will advance
her beyond the army of ordinary workers to the vanguard of outstand-
ing ones. Even then," she warns her readers, "the way will be hard" (9).
Hatcher, too, concedes that "women must usually present better prepa-
ration, if not also more unusual personal qualifications than is required
of men, in order to secure the same opportunity" (1927, xxxiv), though
she hesitates to name this practice "sex prejudice" and advocates that
women respond by "acquir[ing] the experience which will ultimately
solve the difficulty" (xxxiv). The genre in this way registers broad public
concerns and offers strategic advice, though that advice legitimates discriminatory hiring practices born from such anxieties.

If the prospect of women competing for positions with men was
threatening, the specter of women serving in positions of power within
professional workplaces was even more so, leading numerous guides to
devote chapters specifically to the challenges faced by women in executive
positions. These discussions reveal a collective concern *among* women
professionals that their own authority and ethos may be strengthened or
undermined by other women's successful or unsuccessful performances
of professional competence. Rebecca Lingenfelter and Harry Kitson's
1939 *Vocations for Girls*, for instance, contains a chapter titled "The Lady
Boss" that begins by rehearsing the opposition women are likely to meet
in positions of authority. The authors advise women, "If you are a fore-
lady in a factory, a section manager in a department store, or a supervi-
sor for a telephone company it will be up to you to make yourself the
best boss you can possibly be . . . if for no better reason than to keep
people from saying—and men are not the only ones who say it—that
women are no good as executives. They do say it" (Lingenfelter and
Kitson 1939, 302). Lingenfelter and Kitson "refuse to admit that women
get power-drunk any more than men when they're given authority, but
how quickly people pounce on the few women who do become tyranni-
cal, condescending, or just plain high hat. 'Isn't that just like a woman?'
they shout, gleefully. That's one of the reasons why it's important for you
to start right now to train yourself for being a good executive" (302).
Similar passages across vocational guides reveal another dimension of
the work this genre performs in relation to anxiety: that is, as a genre
written primarily *by* women professionals *to* other women seeking to
become professional workers, it registers women's shared anxiety that
they will be judged collectively for other women's professional short-
comings and workplace failures. In these ways, the vocational guide

genre can be read as a measure of women's determination to work—and to guide other women into professional positions—despite considerable public opposition and, at the same time, as a measure of the anxiety prompted by the movement of women's bodies into new—and newly professionalizing—workplaces.

BODILY SCRIPTS IN VOCATIONAL GUIDES

The anxious context described above frames the embodied advice vocational guides circulate. As the analyses that follow demonstrate, this genre translates public anxiety into discursive scripts, revealing the repertoire of embodied behaviors women were advised to adopt in order to be *taken as* competent professionals, to have their bodies read as employable. The anxieties prompted by their movement into professional workplaces help to explain the striking amount of attention vocational guides devote to women's bodies. These texts describe postures, suggest behaviors, and advocate routines for maintaining bodily health; they advise women workers on matters ranging from the purchasing of a pair of stockings to the selection of living quarters and roommates; and they repeat this advice in ways that sediment, I argue, into scripts for embodied performance. These advice scripts function as "textual phenomena that illuminate the subjectivities available and contestable within processes of uptake" (Emmons 2009, 139)—that is, they reveal the kinds of bodily dispositions a reader might either take up or counter through her participation in the gendered genre system through which these bodily dispositions gained legibility. Such scripts consequently help scholars today to see the public discursive work required to shepherd women into new positions in professional life as well as the role of genre in dispersing and concretizing that work. Public anxiety over women's changing social and material position is translated into discursive practices, organized by genre, and materialized through uptake in the form of embodied dispositions via the constitutive repetition upon which both genre and gendered embodiment depend. As Emmons has argued, "The problem of uptake is the problem of what is *taken on* when an individual *takes up* particular genres and discourses" (2009, 138); in this case, I suggest, vocational guides invited women professionals to take on sharp constraints on embodiment in the act of taking up, via their embodied behaviors, the postures and practices that marked them as suitable for professional employment. Scripts for professional embodiment, detailed in the examples below, work together to naturalize certain behaviors, to legitimate an intense degree of scrutiny, and to recruit women's participation in self-scrutiny. Ultimately, they invite women professionals to perform a paradoxical kind of embodiment: they demand bodily denial by requiring women to govern, minimize, and aggressively constrain their disruptive and unruly bodies, yet they also elevate the body as a primary site upon which women who seek employment must be willing to lavish their attention and effort.

POSTURE AND COMPORTMENT

Posture and comportment are extensively prescribed in vocational guides, which solicit women into dispositions that imply restraint, subordination, and bodily scrutiny. To secure a job and to keep the job once hired, women are advised strongly against engaging in any irritating embodied behaviors. One 1932 guide, *The Girl and Her Future*, advises women "to look at the man or woman who is interviewing her, to speak clearly and distinctly, and not to cover her mouth with her hands; to fold her ankles one upon the other, not to cross her knees, and to let her hands lie quietly in her lap . . . don't giggle, and don't twist around and coil yourself about the chair or lean on the desk. Look at the interviewer and answer plainly, sitting as still as you can" (Hoerle 1932, 38–39). A 1933 guide, *The Girl and Her Job*, reminds readers that "the way in which you cross the room, the way in which you sit down, and whether you do so before or after being asked; whether your legs are crossed, your hands in your lap or your elbows on your prospective employer's desk, all contribute toward arresting favorable or unfavorable attention" (Brooke 1933, 36). Another guide forbids women workers to sulk if their boss snaps at them and warns against "whin[ing] and complain[ing] about small indispositions, of headaches and overfatigue"—instead, women are advised to "look fresh, vital, healthy, interested and enthusiastic" (Maule 1935, 48). This attention to posture and comportment collectively suggests that a woman's every embodied behavior must be calculated toward creating the right impression on an employer. For instance, a 1941 vocational guide, *She's Off to Work*, reminds women that a smile "is not merely a way of arranging the muscles about the mouth, or of contrived lines in a face; a smile is a heartfelt thing. Otherwise it remains a grimace and is repellent and artificial and does something quite terrible to the pleasantness of an expression" (Alsop and McBride 1941, 37–38). During an interview, they write, "though the mouth should smile, the eyes should be serious. And the eyes should look directly at the person to whom one is talking" (Alsop and McBride 1941, 38). Such descriptions advise women to arrange their facial expressions with great care in order to mitigate any impression of artificiality, inviting women to maintain a bodily disposition that renders them pleasant adornments to their workplaces.

A bodily disposition toward restraint, in order to "arrest favorable [rather than] unfavorable attention," is evident in numerous injunctions against engaging in any unnecessary movement. Oglesby's 1937 guide warns against squirming or fidgeting during an interview, advocating that women "wear comfortable clothes. You can't expect to interest man or woman in your ideas if you are tugging at a too-tight hat, tucking in stray hair-ends and pulling up slippery shoulder-straps" (1937, 20). Frances Maule, who wrote several extremely popular vocational guides, advises her readers to inventory whether they are "victims of the fidgets" (Maule 1935, 153). Maule prompts women to engage in self-scrutiny in order to *still* their bodies as much as possible, asking, "Do we fuss with our hair, fiddle with our rings or beads or bracelets, nervously adjust our collars or cuffs or belts? Are we sufficiently on guard against such annoying habits as scratching, picking at the face, biting or picking at or polishing the fingernails, swinging the foot, chewing gum, flourishing the handkerchief about, or drawing meaningless curlycues in the notebook?" (153). Such admonitions ask women to understand their bodies as perpetually inviting scrutiny and solicit women into a vigilant disposition toward their own bodies.

In this way, vocational guides invite readers to understand female embodiment as a project, one that women must pursue scrupulously in order to be taken as competent professionals. For instance, Loire Brophy's 1936 guide, *If Women Must Work*, presents the example of a now-successful businesswoman whom Brophy observed years earlier; although the woman was then only a receptionist, she was "vitally interested in everything and everybody. She walked forward lightly, eagerly, when the elevator disgorged various persons. She sorted them out with ease. Her manner was friendly but decisive. Many of them she greeted and instantly shunted here and there" (Brophy 1936, 51). This receptionist "contrived to appear good-looking, although an impartial survey by trained eyes revealed, as the source of this impression, good points made much of and poor points covered" (52). Lingenfelter and Kitson's guide offers a similar description of an ideal female worker, who "was never afraid to do more than she was paid to do—she kept little records of the customers, studied books and magazine articles on her occupation, and nothing was ever too much trouble for her if it helped the sales in her department. Her appearance was attractive, even though she was not a beauty, and she kept herself physically fit and keen" (Lingenfelter and Kitson 1939, 11). Both of these model workers, "attractive" although not pretty, demonstrate their competence not only through their work but also through their active efforts on behalf of their appearance. The receptionist generates the kind of attention that singles her out for success—that signals her competence to her ever-observant employer—not only by embodying alacrity and vigor in her interactions with customers but also by *working* on her appearance, "covering" her "poor points" and "making much of" her good ones, "contriving" to be pleasing as a woman and a worker at the same time. Such accounts invite readers to view their embodiment as a project, one crucial to their professional advancement.

NOISES AND SCENTS

The necessity of using their embodied behaviors to cultivate positive attention from their employers is made more challenging for women professionals by a parallel script that advises women to pursue a kind of bodily denial in the workplace. Vocational guides strongly admonish women to eschew producing noises and scents that draw attention to the presence of their bodies. For instance, Lingenfelter and Kitson advise women to adopt "a gentle voice" and to pursue courses in speaking and elocution, "especially if your voice rasps" (Lingenfelter and Kitson 1939, 16–17); Hoerle's guide advises women not to be too talkative, warning that speaking "to try to make an impression" is unwise (Hoerle 1932, 27). Maule objects to an extensive litany of sounds women's bodies might make, advising women workers to "examine ourselves carefully to ascertain whether we: Drum or tap with fingers or toes or pencils, hum or whistle under our breath, sniff, snuffle, breathe noisily, snort when we mean merely to laugh, chew gum audibly, blow the nose with a stentorian blast, clear the throat with a raucous rasp, or cough or sneeze . . . oftener, or louder, than is absolutely unavoidable" (Maule 1935, 152). The implication of these scripts prohibiting any noise not strictly necessary is stated outright by Maule: "The ideal woman employee is noiseless" (152).

The scents that might accompany—and draw attention to—women's bodies likewise require the vigilant surveillance of the woman worker. Oglesby (1937), for instance, writes that "halitosis and bromidrosis have cost many women their jobs" (48) and advises women to "shun exotic perfumes" (21) and to wear perfumes "pianissimo rather than fortissimo" in the office (48). Maule devotes many pages to the problem of unpleasant breath, including advice about which medical specialists should be consulted to discover the source of the problem. If a woman has ensured that her teeth, gums, throat, and digestion are all healthy, she must then govern her appetites to ensure she does not produce unpleasant bodily smells: "In regard to the eating of onions and garlic, your conscience and your common sense must be your guide. If thorough gargling and tooth-brushing with a mouth antiseptic would remove all traces of their odor—that would be one thing. But the trouble is, they don't. The odor is absorbed into the blood stream, and comes out all over the body in the perspiration. It gets into your clothing, and there you are—simply reeking—a day or even two days after your indulgence. To eat onions or garlic in the middle of the day is simply courting disaster" (Maule 1935, 151). The exaggerated language that treats the scent of garlic as a "disaster" brought on by the triumph of "indulgence" over "common sense" asks women professionals to engage in rather strenuous efforts of bodily denial. Soliciting readers into embodied uptakes focused on exercising the control their bodies demand, vocational guides collectively craft an ideal woman employee who, through her vigilance, maintains a presence that is quiet, unscented, and still. Maule (1935), in fact, characterizes "poise" as "being quiet physically," being "able to sit still in a natural, easy and relaxed attitude" while resisting the impulse to "fuss with their hair . . . drum on their desk with their finger or tap the floor with their toes" (72). The pursuit of this "physical quietness" (72) requires an enormous effort on the part of the woman worker.

CLOTHING

The script inviting women to take up a disposition toward their bodies as projects extends to the selection of clothing, a subject upon which vocational guides lavish attention. A maxim for female employment reported in Oglesby's guide runs, "To get a job and a better one a woman must be mentally capable, emotionally stable and *sartorially smart*" (Oglesby 1937, 25; emphasis in original). To demonstrate sartorial smartness, women are asked to view their clothing selection as simultaneously confirming their status as *female* and yet reassuring colleagues, clients, and employers of their competence as workers. Reflecting the public anxiety over women competing with men for positions, for instance, vocational guides advise women against adopting the clothes that professional men wear for work. Maule explains that "masculine clothes for the business woman" are unacceptable because "men hate them," conveying as they do "the impression that a woman is competing with him on his own ground instead of supplementing his masculine abilities with her distinctly feminine gifts" (Maule 1935, 128). In their 1941 guide, *She's Off to Work*, Gulielma Fell Alsop and Mary Frances McBride distinguish between the disregard male workers may display toward their clothing and the attention women should demonstrate; unlike men's work wardrobes, which function uniformly to mask men's individuality, women's clothing must convey something of a woman's personality while "hint[ing] at a universal femininity" (Alsop and McBride 1941, 37). Readers taking up this advice come to embody an attitude that undermines their legitimacy in the workplace; displacing public concerns over women as workplace competitors, this script instead invites women to take up bodily behaviors that position women professionals as "supplementing," in decorative fashion, the properly masculine spaces of professional work.

Furthermore, such advice legitimates employers' practice of reading women's capabilities from their clothing selections. A woman professional must select smartly because such choices are interpreted as evidence either for or against her suitability for employment. For instance, Alsop and McBride describe a successful woman professional on her first day of work: "She has probably selected some kind of dark blue dress with white trim and she looks very well and neat in it. Her shoes should be polished, her gloves clean, her hair smooth but not too smooth, and her hat should bespeak a readiness, nay even a willingness or an eagerness, to be smart" (Alsop and McBride 1941, 37). Maule cautions her readers that wearing a brown hat with a black coat conveys "merely that you happen to possess a brown hat and a black coat. But a red hat with a black coat—ah, that suggests deep and artful planning" (Maule 1935, 133). Women are advised to communicate through their clothing that they have *selected* that clothing deliberately—through "artful planning"—and to communicate furthermore their familiarity with the proper markers of expense and quality that characterize "good" selections. Employable women must convey, in short, their willingness to conform to clothing requirements and their ability to discriminate among options to communicate their suitability for professional spaces.

Advice about clothing further reinforces the restrained bodily dispositions that vocational guides elsewhere advise women to take up. To embody professional suitability, women must not only still their fidgety hands, quiet their noisy voices, and control their appetites but must also select clothing that bespeaks their capacity to avoid extremes. Maule's guide, for instance, argues that the "ideal costume for the business woman is navy blue or black with touches of white at the neck and wrists. Simple in line, but feminine. . . . Well-fitting, but not too revealing.

With not too deep a V at the neck-line, not too tight or too short a skirt, and with long sleeves" (Maule 1935, 128). Oglesby warns, "Don't go in for giddy polka-dots, wild stripes, checks or plaids" (Oglesby 1937, 20). Such outlandish choices can be read as telling evidence of unsuitability for a professional workplace; as Maule reminds her readers, "Sleeveless and short-sleeved dresses . . . may never cause you to *lose* your job, but they may prevent you from getting a coveted advancement" (1935, 130). Shoes should be chosen with a similar attention to moderation; Hoerle specifies "moderately high heels, not sport shoes, not old-lady heels, not spikes, nor wedgees, but medium high heels" (Hoerle 1932, 41). Clothing, then, must reinforce the perception created by a woman's comportment; as her postures and voice must create an impression of cultivated stillness and restraint, her clothing must communicate both thoughtfulness and subservience, an acceptance of employment conditions that permit her into professional workplaces on sufferance rather than by rights.

CONCLUSION

Collectively, vocational guides argue that women should make their bodies the object of considerable attention in order to secure professional employment; they ask women to expect significant scrutiny and to subject *themselves* to scrutiny in order to cultivate bodily behaviors that will garner a specific kind of positive attention from employers and coworkers. To minimize the distractions their bodies threaten in the workplace, women are advised to maintain bodily stillness, noiselessness, odorlessness, and to govern their impulses—yet they also must use their bodies to demonstrate their alertness, eagerness, and capacity for advancement. The body-focused advice organized by this genre reminds women repeatedly that one of the most crucial things they must signal to others—through their postures, their clothes, their movements, even their chosen foods—is that they are making an effort, engaging always in deliberate acts, aimed toward securing and retaining employment.

In these ways, vocational guides legitimate the special scrutiny women's bodies are subject to and legitimate the evaluation of women workers in these terms, treating bodily conformity as an acceptable mechanism for determining a woman worker's worth, intellect, character, and employability. That is, these bodily scripts imply a close analogy between the control and deliberateness a woman is meant to demonstrate by governing her behaviors and dress and the qualities she might demonstrate through the completion of her work. Many vocational guides assert this analogy explicitly. Hoerle, for example, writes that "personal neatness, employers have learned, is in direct ratio to the precision and perfection of work. A girl who is careless of her own appearance usually does sloppy work" (Hoerle 1932, 29). Other texts posit this link implicitly by inviting women to follow these scripts so as to fit themselves for the professional workplace—soliciting their participation in sedimenting and naturalizing these embodied performances of professional suitability.

Taking up such advice in their embodied performances of professional competence, I suggest, women workers also take *on*—take into their bodies—the diffuse public anxieties that attend their workplace advancements. Anxieties surrounding a changing material-symbolic system of gender and labor become translated in vocational guides into directives for women to follow; the anxiety itself becomes something for women not to reject, confront, or argue with but to *manage* through their embodied performances, which should themselves be anything but anxious. These scripts allocate the *consciousness* of effort entirely to the woman worker while soliciting performances that render the *result* of all that effort only barely legible to those around her, who find her "inconspicuously agreeable." Such advice discourse reminds readers that anxious embodied performances are ineffective. Professional women's embodied performances must take up public anxiety in order to take it *away*—out of circulation, into their own bodies, where it is refashioned into effortless and pleasing competence. Women are asked through this discourse to take up in their embodied behaviors a set of practices that rationalize scrutiny as a response to women's presence, to take anxiety into their own bodies and dispel it through managed, efficient, productive, and pleasing behaviors.

At the same time, such scripts construct a specter that looms behind this ideal: an ungoverned, unruly female body. Reading genre-based repetition of bodily scripts reveals, I suggest, a public anxiety that understands female embodiment as a threatening encroachment into professional workspaces. Even as vocational guides craft and sediment the ideal of a noiseless, odorless, decorous female employee, the analysis I have offered here should help to make evident the *fragility* of this norm, its dependence upon the embodied performances that materialize it. The repetition of these scripts aims to secure a still-fragile ideal, soliciting women into embodied performances and professional spaces that, it seems, could be undermined through any number of tiny intrusions: through the tapping of a foot, the disruption of a scent, the flash of exposed skin on an uncovered arm.

Ultimately, examining the kind of performative repetition that genres organize can alert scholars to the presence of a not-yet-settled public norm, making historical genres potentially valuable sites for scholars to exploit in order to contribute to the feminist project of historicizing—and thus denaturalizing—various forms of gendered, raced, and classed embodiment. Historicizing the material and discursive practices that make bodies legible as *professional* is especially important, I suggest, because the legacy of these practices persists—in the excessive, repetitive demand that the "unruly" hair of black men and women be governed to suit professional environments, for instance, or in the repeated admonition to academic job seekers that their clothing must make them legible as part of a professional class, even when their income makes that status an impossibility. Historical studies such as this one can undertake not only to reveal the processes by which *uptake residues* sediment over time into bodily dispositions but also to unsettle those dispositions, opening rhetorical space for new kinds of embodied performances.

Notes

1.   Although viewing the professional realm *as* public might seem counterintuitive now, when these terms often sit in opposition (for instance, in writing teachers' choice to emphasize "public" genres such as editorials and PSAs or "professional" genres such as memos and business letters), the relation between these terms was configured differently during the rise in the early twentieth century of a professional class, whose status as experts and specialists protected their practices from outsider scrutiny even as members of this class were identified as uniquely positioned to comment on traditionally civic matters of public policy and governmental action. See Clark and Halloran (1993); Sharer (2003).

2.   Women's labor-force participation increased broadly during this period, even as the percentages of participation continued to vary significantly by race, marital status, and nativity. For instance, in 1900, 20.6 percent of American women participated in the paid labor force, but this average covers substantial variation: 3.2 percent of married white women, 26 percent of married nonwhite women, 41.5 percent of single white women, and 60.5 percent of single nonwhite women. By 1930, these numbers shifted to 6.5 percent of married white women, 33.2 percent of married nonwhite women, 48.7 percent of single white women, and 52.1 percent of single nonwhite women (see Goldin 1992, 17). The vocational guides I examine in this chapter generally assume an audience of white women of a poor, working-class, or middle-class background whose professional aspirations connect to their pursuit of social mobility. Although nonwhite women and foreign-born women worked disproportionately in service and industry sectors, the labor profiles of these groups were also affected by the burgeoning professional context of the 1920s and 1930s. For instance, professional employment for women of color also expanded during this period, prompting the formation of numerous local Negro business and professional women's clubs and the organization of a national association of NBPW clubs in 1936.

References

Alsop, Gulielma Fell, and Mary F. McBride. 1941. *She's Off to Work: A Guide to Successful Earning and Living.* New York: Vanguard.

Amott, Theresa, and Julie Matthaei. 1996. *Race, Gender, and Work: A Multicultural Economic History of Women in the United States.* Boston, MA: South End.

Brooke, Esther Eberstadt. 1933. *The Girl and Her Job: A Handbook for Beginners.* New York: D. Appleton.

Brophy, Loire. 1936. *If Women Must Work.* New York: D. Appleton-Century.

Cades, Hazel Rawson. 1930. *Jobs for Girls.* New York: Harcourt, Brace.

Clark, Gregory, and S. Michael Halloran. 1993. "Transformations of Public Discourse in Nineteenth-Century America." In *Oratorical Culture in Nineteenth-Century America,* edited by Gregory Clark and S. Michael Halloran, 1–28. Carbondale: Southern Illinois University Press.

"CNN Transcript: George Zimmerman Juror Speaks." 2013. *Orlando Sentinel* Accessed December 4, 2013.

Dryer, Dylan. 2012. "Central Problems in Uptake Studies: An Assessment and Two Proposals." Paper presented at the Genre 2012 Conference, Ottawa, ON.

Emmons, Kimberly K. 2009. "Uptake and the Biomedical Subject." In *Genre in a Changing World,* edited by Charles Bazerman, Adair Bonini, and Debora Figueiredo, 134–57. Fort Collins, CO: WAC Clearinghouse and Parlor.

Enoch, Jessica. 2008. "A Woman's Place Is in the School: Rhetorics of Gendered Space in Nineteenth-Century America." *College English* 70 (3): 275–95.

Filene, Catherine. 1934. *Careers for Women: New Ideas, New Methods, New Opportunities to Fit a New World.* New York: Houghton Mifflin.

Fleischman, Doris E. 1928. *An Outline of Careers for Women: A Practical Guide to Achievement.* Garden City, NY: Doubleday.

Giltrow, Janet. 2012. "Form Alone: Historical Genres in Canadian Supreme Court Decisions." Paper presented at the Genre 2012 Conference, Ottawa, ON.

Glazer, Penina Migdal, and Miriam Slater. 1987. *Unequal Colleagues: The Entrance of Women into the Professions, 1890–1940.* New Brunswick, NJ: Rutgers University Press.

Goldin, Claudia. 1992. *Understanding the Gender Gap: An Economic History of American Women.* Oxford: Oxford University Press.

Hallenbeck, Sarah. 2010. "Riding Out of Bounds: Women Bicyclists' Embodied Medical Authority." *Rhetoric Review* 29 (4): 327–45. http://dx.doi.org/10.1080/07350198.2010.510054.

Hatcher, Orie Latham. 1927. *Occupations for Women.* Richmond, VA: Southern Women's Educational Alliance.

Hoerle, Helen. 1932. *The Girl and Her Future.* New York: Harrison Smith and Robert Haas.

Jack, Jordynn. 2009. "Acts of Institution: Embodying Feminist Rhetorical Methodologies in Space and Time." *Rhetoric Review* 28 (3): 285–303. http://dx.doi.org/10.1080/07350190902958909.

Leuck, Miriam Simons. 1938. *Fields of Work for Women.* 3rd ed. New York: D. Appleton-Century.

Lingenfelter, Mary Rebecca, and Harry Dexter Kitson. 1939. *Vocations for Girls.* New York: Harcourt, Brace.

Mattingly, Carol. 2002. *Appropriate[ing] Dress: Women's Rhetorical Style in Nineteenth Century America.* Carbondale: Southern Illinois University Press.

Maule, Frances. 1935. *She Strives to Conquer.* New York: Funk & Wagnalls.

Mountford, Roxanne. 2001. "On Gender and Rhetorical Space." *Rhetoric Society Quarterly* 31 (1): 41–71. http://dx.doi.org/10.1080/02773940109391194.

Oglesby, Catharine. 1937. *Business Opportunities for Women.* 3rd ed. New York: Harper & Brothers.

Scharf, Lois. 1980. *To Work and to Wed: Female Employment, Feminism, and the Great Depression.* Westport, CT: Greenwood.

Sharer, Wendy B. 2003. "Genre Work: Expertise and Advocacy in the Early Bulletins of the U.S. Women's Bureau." *Rhetoric Society Quarterly* 33 (1): 5–32. http://dx.doi.org/10.1080/02773940309391244.

Stormer, Nathan. 2004. "Articulation: A Working Paper on Rhetoric and *Taxis*." *Quarterly Journal of Speech* 90 (3): 257–84. http://dx.doi.org/10.1080/0033563042000255516.

Suter, Lisa. 2013. "The Arguments They Wore: The Role of the Neoclassical Toga in American Delsartism." In *Rhetoric, History, and Women's Oratorical Education: American Women Learn to Speak*, edited by David Gold and Catherine L. Hobbs, 134–53. New York: Routledge.

Wells, Susan. 1999. "Legible Bodies: Nineteenth-Century Women Physicians and the Rhetoric of Dissection." In *Rhetorical Bodies*, edited by Jack Selzer and Sharon Crowley, 58–74. Madison: University of Wisconsin Press.

PART III

Intermediary Public Genres

Mobilizing Knowledge across Genre Boundaries

7
UNCOVERING OCCLUDED PUBLICS
Untangling Public, Personal, and Technical Spheres in Jury Deliberations

Amy J. Devitt

After a highly public and controversial trial in 2013 of George Zimmerman for killing Trayvon Martin, reactions to the jury verdict of not guilty involved many elements, including race and justice most significantly. One less apparently controversial element that received attention was the nature of a genre, the instructions to the jury. The jury was obligated to make its decision based on this genre, yet the particular text was so technically complicated that one juror, Maddy (Juror B29) reported in a later interview that she was "confused" by it, and some believe she may have acted on a misunderstanding of the law. Similar technical complexity dominates other jury instructions as well, including those for capital murder cases, with the extraordinarily high stakes of the death penalty. Analyzing jury instructions and juror interviews from these situations reveals that not only must such public actions—verdicts—derive from a high level of technical expertise, but jurors during jury deliberations also must both draw from and deny any personal beliefs or values. This unrecognized mixing of public, technical, and personal spheres creates a rhetorical situation for jurors stepping into a jury room that is highly complex and may be untenable.[1]

To complicate matters further, the action that results from this difficult situation is hidden from public observation and hence rhetorical analysis and critique. Jury deliberations—the oral discussions of a defendant's guilt toward the purpose of deciding on a verdict—occur in a closed jury room, with no written record, and can be reconstructed only from potentially unreliable post hoc self-reported interviews. Thus, jury deliberations seem to constitute what John Swales has called an "occluded" genre. Occluded genres are ones whose exemplars are "hidden, 'out of sight' or 'occluded' from the public gaze by a veil of confidentiality" (Swales 1996, 46)—like letters of recommendation,

DOI: 10.7330/9781607324430.c007

submission cover letters, and reviewers' reports. In fact, many people never see a single exemplar of jury deliberations outside fictional representations unless they serve on a jury themselves, and then they see only that particular instance. Even those people seemingly most involved in the situation—lawyers, judges, and defendants—do not have access to exemplars of jury deliberations. Most important, unlike the occluded genres mentioned by Swales, the genre of jury deliberations has consequences well beyond the immediate participants, as I will discuss in the next section. Jury deliberations represent public participation and have public consequences.

Fortunately, occluded genres do not exist in isolation. Surrounding them are entire sets of visible genres whose exemplars we can see, and these surrounding genre sets can give us access to the situation, if not to the genre itself. In the case of jury deliberations, the surrounding visible genre set includes the trial itself (constituted by multiple genres) and the genres most directly shaping jury deliberations—the instructions to the jury, questions to the judge, and verdict form. This visible genre set partially constructs the situation that shapes the hidden jury deliberations and can be used to infer the occluded situation underlying the occluded genre. Scholarship in rhetorical genre theory has established that genres derive from recurrent rhetorical situations, not arhetorical formulas, and that those genres are therefore rhetorically and culturally meaningful. We can, then, not only use situations to reveal genres but also use genres to reveal situations. Scholarship in public sphere theory (by such scholars as Gerald Hauser 1999 and others) examines publics and public participation through the discourse that constructs them. We can, then, use the genres surrounding publics to reveal and critique them. Although jury deliberations themselves may constitute an invisible center to the trial, all of those surrounding, visible genres give us insight into that publicly significant yet occluded situation.

In this chapter, I use the genres of jury deliberations and jury instructions, supplemented by juror interviews, to examine how genre analysis can reveal hidden situations and open those situations to critique. The critique is especially important for such publicly consequential acts as jury deliberations. For acts in the public sphere to change, they must be visible. Jury instructions, with their complex mix of legal expertise and moral judgment, reveal some of the dysfunction of jury deliberations and the current jury system. Although I explore in the end whether revising or adding intermediary genres to the existing genre set might improve the system, I offer no quick fix but rather movement toward awareness and dialogue. The case of jury service represents larger issues of the occluded nature of some publicly important work and of how genres can help tease out the intricacies and difficulties of these significant public yet unobservable acts.

My argument in this chapter is twofold, methodological and theoretical. Methodologically, I demonstrate how we might use rhetorical genre studies to gain access to occluded actions, examining the material evidence of surrounding genres and reports of how those genres are taken up. Theoretically, I demonstrate the difficulties genres have dealing with tangled technical, public, and personal spheres and consider how sets of intermediary genres might be necessary to unravel those tangled threads and preserve public participation.

PUBLIC ACTS PERFORMED PRIVATELY

Interaction in a jury room appears to be a model of a public sphere, a space where all are eligible to participate and all have a voice in debating important public matters. What better act than jury deliberations to fit Gerald Hauser's rhetorical model of a public sphere: "a discursive space in which individuals and groups associate to discuss matters of mutual interest and, where possible, to reach a common judgment about them. It is the locus of emergence for rhetorically salient meanings" (Hauser 1999, 61). Jury deliberation fits, as well, Hauser's revision of Jürgen Habermas's public space: "Whenever private citizens exchange views on a public concern, some portion of the Public Sphere is made manifest in their conversation" (64). Jury deliberations also fit G. Thomas Goodnight's requirement within argument theory that acts in a public sphere "extend the stakes of argument beyond private needs and the needs of special communities to the interests of the entire community" (Goodnight 2012, 202). With the discourse that constitutes the group of jurors and their acts as a public occluded from public view, though, the public becomes unavailable to the rhetorician's analysis and critique.

Simply making jury deliberations public, however, is probably not the answer. The privacy of the jury room prevents a greater dominance of popular opinion over fact-based judgment. Instead, the goal may be to improve the quality of the acts that happen privately, to make it less likely that jurors will act out of ignorance or misunderstanding. Examining the genres surrounding jury deliberations enables us to inspect their "rhetorical environment," in Hauser's (1999, 80–81) terms, and reveals some potential sources of jury difficulties. Examining juror interviews as well confirms the textual evidence and offers glimpses of how those surrounding genres are taken up. Together, these sources suggest what might need to happen for the quality of jury deliberations to improve, even as they remain hidden.

THE DIFFICULT TANGLE OF PUBLIC, TECHNICAL, AND PERSONAL

Although jury deliberations operate in a public sphere, their surrounding genre set demonstrates a tangle of public, personal, and technical spheres that creates a difficult rhetorical situation for jurors during jury deliberations. In distinguishing those three spheres, I am drawing first from G. Thomas Goodnight's long-standing distinctions within argument theory. Goodnight characterizes spheres as "vast, and not altogether coherent superstructures which invite [people] to channel doubts through prevailing discourse practices" (Goodnight 2012, 200). "'Sphere,'" he continues, "denotes branches of activity—the grounds upon which arguments are built and the authorities to which arguers appeal" (200). He captures the differences among the three spheres of personal, technical, and public by illustrating "the standards for arguments among friends versus those for judgments of academic arguments versus those for judging political disputes" (200). In the special issue of *Argumentation and Advocacy* that reprints Goodnight's original 1982 article, David Zarefsky points out that Goodnight later offered four criteria for distinguishing among the spheres: "who is affected by the discourse, who is eligible to participate in the deliberations, what expertise and training are required, and what evaluative norms apply" (Zarefsky 2012, 212). Later scholarship has clearly established that these three spheres overlap and do not remain distinct in action (see Barbara Couture and Thomas Kent's collection on the blurring of the private and public, for example [Couture and Kent 2004]). Hauser also notes the blurring boundaries of the public and private spheres in particular and the many who have rejected such a distinction (Hauser 1999, 269–70), though he argues that we need a distinction between "public issues, publics, and the publicness of public life" and "our private, intimate existence" (270). The overlapping of all three spheres, in fact, makes jurors' deliberations especially complex.

Of course, Hauser and other scholars in public sphere theory like Nancy Fraser (1992) and Frank Farmer (2013) have already pointed out the unreality of a Habermasian ideal of the public sphere itself and the impossibility of bracketing personal identities. In fact, from the moment of selecting those called to report for jury duty (based on voter rolls, in some cases, even though citizens are not required to vote), juries do not include everyone in the public equally. Once in the jury room, inequities of gender, class, and other identities are surely exaggerated by the fact that these are former strangers who must debate facts and argue the case. That difficult rhetorical situation jurors face when they enter the juror room appears in more detail through examining one of the surrounding genres—jury instructions, in which the public, personal, and technical spheres meet.

At the conclusion of a trial, when courtroom testimony and statements from both the prosecution and defense (or plaintiff and defendant)[2] have concluded, the judge instructs the jury about the decision they must make, the relevant legal distinctions they must consider, and the processes they must follow. (The next section will offer examples of what might be instructed.) Though first read aloud to the jurors in court, these jury instructions are written documents whose details the attorneys and judge negotiate, and written copies may be supplied to the jury as well. In many cases, those instructions originate in templates of standard instructions, sometimes called *model* or *pattern* instructions, used in similar types of cases. Those standard instructions are then modified for the details of the particular case or through the strength of an attorney's argument. The pattern instructions and standard instructions are published and are frequently available on state websites.[3] Although the text of the jury instructions in a specific trial might not be made public without a public-records request, jury instructions as a genre are visible to the public. The ways those instructions shape hidden jury deliberations are open for analysis.

As the analysis in the next section demonstrates, jury instructions—and jurors in jury deliberations—operate often in an untenable rhetorical situation. At first glance, jury instructions might seem to have a straightforward rhetorical situation: for the judge to tell jurors the laws they must apply and the tasks they must complete. But analyzing examples of this genre in the sections below reveals that jurors must shift among public, personal, and technical spheres without identifying those shifts and while constantly privileging the technical.

The personal sphere complicates the situation not only through the identities and roles of jurors in voir dire (the process of selecting which citizens will serve on a particular jury) but also, as jury instructions reveal, because the debate often involves highly private and emotionally laden concepts—including evil for example, as I will discuss in the next sections. Yet jurors are told to set aside many of their judgments and personal beliefs to focus instead on facts and unstated public values. The jury instructions reveal that another element also enters the jury room, intruding its presence even though not humanly represented: the legal system and the specialized knowledge of attorneys. This technical sphere dominates the jurors' deliberation as the judge and both attorneys negotiate the text of the jury instructions, selecting content and wording that subtly balances both sides of the case while upholding legal distinctions and following historical traditions in case law. The rhetorical task at hand is not simply helping jurors render a just verdict, as difficult as that task must be, but also, among other things, assuring the verdict's being upheld on appeal. The resulting rhetorical situation—in which nonspecialists are asked to act on specialist technical knowledge they do not have and asked to ignore many of the personal instincts and first-hand knowledge they do have in order to make a public judgment that affects another individual not present in the room and, in its repercussions, society at large—is a mishmash of deliberation. Jury instructions do not create this messy situation; they merely make it evident.

THE CASE OF CAPITAL MURDER CASES

The stakes in such messy jury deliberations are especially high in capital murder cases, where the technical, personal, and public spheres appear most tangled. In capital murder cases, a separate sentencing trial requires a jury to decide whether the crime merits sentencing the convicted defendant to death. In the state of Kansas, the instructions to the jury start from a set of pattern instructions that have been used and tested legally in past cases (Pattern Instructions for Kansas PIK-Criminal-3d Sect. 56.00-B-H 2000). My first encounter with those pattern jury instructions came when the Death Penalty Defense Unit, a group of state-funded attorneys charged with defending all capital murder cases, asked me to examine the pattern instructions for potential bias. As I consulted with the attorneys to check my rhetorical and linguistic analyses, I found that potential sources of bias were clouded by potential sources of misunderstanding. Behind what seemed like simple instructions or clarifications lay presumptions and background knowledge the attorneys had but jurors did not. After being asked to revise the pattern instructions for clarity, I worked to state those presumptions explicitly and to provide the missing background, but the attorneys objected at times that I was dropping important distinctions captured in the original language or introducing new legal complications through the new wording. As I wrote in my first account of this work, "No matter how much I elaborated, no matter how many assumptions I made explicit, I could not capture in those instructions all the information that the lawyers considered relevant to the jury's task" (Devitt 2003, 545). The problem was not primarily the complexity of the language but rather the complexity of the jury's rhetorical situation: "Clarifying for the jury's purposes clashed with adhering to legal purposes" (Devitt 2003, 545). Analyzing the genre reveals the difficult rhetorical situation hidden in that deliberation room, including not only a clash of purposes but also a clash of spheres.

Consider an instruction at the heart of the decision to sentence the defendant to death: the jury must determine that "there are one or more aggravating circumstances and that they are not outweighed by any mitigating circumstances" (*PIK 3d* 56.00-E). The highly technical meaning of this exact wording is not evident to the nonspecialist jury, but it is meant to direct how jurors deliberate. Jurors are meant first to decide which if any aggravating circumstances exist, which if any mitigating circumstances exist, and then how those balance out. In a later instruction (56.00-F), the jurors are cautioned not to decide "solely by the number of aggravating or mitigating circumstances that are shown to exist." They are being asked not to simply tally the two sides, but an alternative process for making that judgment remains unspecified. Presumably, jurors are to draw on what they consider most important, to make a value-laden judgment of which circumstances matter more—an issue resolved in the personal and, in their deliberation, the public spheres rather than the technical. Yet the weighing of aggravating and mitigating circumstances is highly circumscribed by the technical sphere. The complex syntax of that initial instruction—that "there are one or more aggravating circumstances and that they are not outweighed by any mitigating circumstances"—represents the critical burden of proof, as I learned from the attorneys' objections when I revised to more easily comprehended syntax. The defense does *not* have to prove that mitigating circumstances outweigh aggravating circumstances, though that wording would be easier to comprehend. Instead, the state must prove to the jury that the aggravating circumstances exist and must prove that those aggravating circumstances are not outweighed by mitigating ones.[4] Already, then, in that initial instruction, the jury must act on personal values, public morality, and highly technical knowledge. Although the jury instructions are meant to explain that knowledge and negotiate those three spheres, they in fact entail such complex syntax and unstated background knowledge that they fail to construct the jury's deliberations as fully as they seem to propose.

Not only are jurors required to process complex legal concepts like burden of proof and understand nuances of acceptable ways of deliberating, they also must make highly subjective and value-laden judgments

that can come only from their personal experiences while pretending those judgments come only from the evidence. The weighing of
aggravating alongside mitigating circumstances is one such judgment.
So too is the judgment of whether a circumstance is aggravating. The
circumstances cannot aggravate the jurors in the most commonly used
sense. Rather, according to this set of jury instructions, they must be
aggravating in one of potentially eight specified ways. Those include,
in my somewhat simplified form, that the defendant "knowingly or
purposely" killed more than one person, "authorized" someone else to
commit the crime, or was in prison for a felony at the time. Most revealing of the jurors' difficult rhetorical situation is potential aggravating
circumstance number six: "That the defendant committed the crime
in an especially heinous, atrocious or cruel manner." To clarify for the
jurors, the pattern instructions go on to define those terms: "The term
'heinous' means extremely wicked or shockingly evil; 'atrocious' means
outrageously wicked and vile; and 'cruel' means pitiless or designed to
inflict a high degree of pain, utter indifference to, or enjoyment of the
sufferings of others" (56.00-C 6). Imagine the jurors now in that jury
room, a group of former strangers discussing whether any aggravating circumstances exist. They must come to a consensus on whether
an act was "wicked" or "shockingly evil" or "vile." The technical sphere
makes their situation even more difficult by asserting that those aggravating circumstances must be "shown from the evidence" (56.00-C). In
fact, though, the technical sphere must step aside at this point, having
defined its terms not from factual evidence or specialized knowledge but
from moral judgments. What constitutes evil? How bad must something
be to be wicked? What is the threshold for vile? This technical sphere
offers no answer. As representatives of society and constituents of a public sphere, the jurors will deliberate to a public judgment, and their conclusion may reflect a broader society's notion of good and evil, wicked-
ness and vileness. But this public sphere also offers no answer, no clear
agreement about the nature of these judgments. Juries will have to reach
that judgment through their personal experiences and values, sharing
individual judgments and collaborating to some common decision. The
jury's consensus will be public, and it will be grounded in technical evidence and distinctions, but the route to that consensus must begin in
the personal.

The jurors in sentencing trials of capital murder cases thus must
enact a rhetorical situation that interweaves the personal, technical, and
public, an interweaving common to juries in most trials, both criminal
and civil. The fact that they enact these situations behind closed doors

delays the discovery that the recurrent rhetorical situation is problematic. Jurors during deliberation may not recognize the sources of their difficulties—may not recognize that they are confusing a technical point, or that they are disagreeing over individual value systems. Most juries do come to a consensus and render a verdict, but analyzing the genre of jury instructions suggests that the hidden process of jury deliberations may be more like making sausage than the ideal of making rational decisions in the public sphere. The genre meant to direct that tangle of spheres proves inadequate to the task.

THE CASE OF THE GEORGE ZIMMERMAN JURY

Interviews with jurors after the fact confirm that they do not necessarily recognize the sources of their difficulties and that the jury instructions do not necessarily clear up that confusion. Juror interviews allow us glimpses of how the genre of jury instructions is taken up during the occluded act of jury deliberations (for more on uptake among genres, see Anne Freadman 2002; see also Anis Bawarshi and Dylan Dryer in this volume). The case of the trial of George Zimmerman for the killing of Trayvon Martin, a trial that ended in 2013 with a verdict of not guilty, reveals the same complications of technical and personal spheres necessarily intruding into public jury decisions. Both the analysis of those jury instructions and the reports of jurors after the fact confirm that the jurors struggled with their rhetorical situation: they struggled to meet the technical requirements of the law in the face of their personal beliefs and experiences while attempting to represent the public will. Faced with such a difficult rhetorical situation, the jurors also reveal in their interviews that they allowed a technical sphere, as they interpreted it, to dominate the personal. My purpose in this section is not to review the Zimmerman case or the ample legal analyses of it, nor to join the debate about the correctness of the verdict and its cultural significance, though these are all important topics. Rather, I examine the jurors' interviews for evidence of their perception of their rhetorical situation and their uptake of the jury instructions, and I examine the jury instructions for evidence of how this genre reflected and affected that rhetorical situation.

In the case of the Zimmerman trial, the text of these particular jury instructions makes explicit the usual requirement that jurors repress the personal in favor of the technical sphere. On the twenty-second page of the (unnumbered) twenty-seven-page jury instructions (Final Jury Instructions 2012), the Rules for Deliberation require the jurors to find a verdict that "follow[s] the law as it is set out in these instructions" and that is "decided only upon the evidence that you have heard from the testimony of the witnesses and have seen in the form of the exhibits in evidence and these instructions." Other requirements caution against deciding on a verdict "because you feel sorry for anyone, or are angry at anyone" or letting feelings about the lawyers influence the decision. The final rule sums up the balance of the legal over the personal: "Your verdict should not be influenced by feelings of prejudice, bias or sympathy. Your verdict must be based on the evidence, and on the law contained in these instructions." This final rule also encapsulates the reason the technical legal sphere must be privileged over the personal. Laws may represent public will at some point and on some level, but they are embedded in specialist expertise and presumptions, as seen in the last section. There are, then, many reasons for failing to follow the law in a case, including misunderstanding it.

That the jurors in the Zimmerman case took the Rules for Deliberation seriously and attempted to follow the law seems apparent in their interviews after the conclusion of the case.[5] Their struggle to take up that technical sphere, and its domination over the personal, is also evident. According to an interview with Juror B37 afterward, the jurors initially were split on Zimmerman's guilt, but in the end some voted against their own judgment: "Juror B37: There was a couple of them in there that wanted to find him guilty of something and after hours and hours and hours of deliberating over the law, and reading it over and over and over again, we decided there's just no way, other place to go" (Ford 2013). Some jurors thus personally believed Zimmerman was guilty but could not find basis for that guilt in the technical description of the law. One of those is Juror B29, Maddy, who revealed her position in an interview with ABC's Robin Roberts afterward: "I know I went the right way because the law and the way it's followed, is the way it went. But if I would have used my heart, I probably would have went a hung jury" ("CNN Transcript: George Zimmerman Juror Speaks," *Orlando Sentinel,* July 13, 2013). Maddy describes the conflict between her personal understanding of the evidence and the technical distinctions in the law:

> MADDY: In between the nine hours, it was hard. A lot of us had wanted to find something that was bad, something that we could connect to the law. Because, for myself, he's guilty. Because the evidence shows he's guilty.
>
> ROBERTS: He's guilty of?
>
> MADDY: Killing Trayvon Martin. But as the law was read to me, if you have no proof that he killed him intentionally, you can't say he's guilty.

Both jurors here refer directly to the jury instructions and their efforts to take up those instructions: "the law" that "was read" and read "over and over again." This genre, then, played a critical role in constructing jurors' deliberations.

The conception of intent Maddy based her verdict on, for a particular example, must have come from her interpretation of intent as used in the jury instructions, a genre which, as I have indicated, relies heavily on technical expertise. Looking only at how this twenty-seven-page set of instructions used the words *intent* and *intention* reveals the complexity of what Maddy and the other jurors had to discern. Just a few instances make the difficulty obvious (I have emphasized the word *intent* in each instruction below).

- The instructions to the jury on "Excusable Homicide" state that "the killing of a human being is excusable, and therefore lawful" under particular circumstances, including that the killing happens "without any unlawful *intent*."
- The instruction on "Second Degree Murder" requires jurors to put together items in two lists: first one of three required circumstances is "an act imminently dangerous to another and demonstrating a depraved mind without regard for human life"; then, in the second of another list of three elements, the value-laden term "depraved" is defined as an act "done from ill will, hatred, spite or an evil *intent*."
- The instructions assert, "In order to convict of Second Degree Murder, it is not necessary for the State to prove George Zimmerman had an *intent* to cause death."
- After instructions on other issues, the section on "Manslaughter" specifies that the state must prove that Zimmerman "*intentionally* committed an act or acts that caused the death of Trayvon Martin" and that an act is "merely negligent" if it is done "without any conscious *intention* to harm."
- On page 11, the instructions repeat the statement of page 6 that the state does not have to prove "an *intent* to cause death," but this time the instructions add that the state has to prove "only an *intent* to commit an act that was not merely negligent, justified, or excusable and which caused death."

From these instances alone, the legally complex nature of *intent* is obvious.

These jurors had other complex legal terms to interpret as well in their efforts to take up the jury instructions. Juror B37 reported, "The law became very confusing" ("CNN Transcript: George Zimmerman Juror Speaks," *Orlando Sentinel,* July 13, 2013). "We had stuff thrown at us. We had the second-degree murder charge, the manslaughter charge, then we had self-defense, stand your ground, and I think there was one other one" ("CNN Transcript"). In response to a question from Anderson Cooper about the instructions being "tough to follow," Juror B37 agrees and says, "And that was our problem." They came to a verdict eventually, she says, "Through going through the law." Maddy also reports being "confused" by the legal definitions of self-defense, a part of the jury instructions meant to clarify the state's so-called Stand Your Ground law and included in the instructions under "Justifiable Use of Deadly Force." Given that these jurors had multiple legal concepts to consider, their task seems enormous and the likelihood of their interpreting the law as a judge would do seems low. In spite of the fact that the instructions on "Weighing the Evidence" instruct the jurors to "use your common sense" in weighing the evidence, it is clear that common sense would not get jurors far in coming to a legally supported conclusion.

The distance between the ideal jury deliberation and the real rhetorical situation seems great. For jurors to carry out the public will as the law represents it, these nonspecialist jurors must not only understand but also then apply technical specialist distinctions. For jurors to act as a public sphere rather than personal judges, each individual must repress inappropriate bias and sympathy but then evaluate actions by such moral terms as *depraved* and *evil*. Jurors may want to perform their duty as public citizens responsibly, but they confront what may be an untenable situation. Jury instructions may reveal these difficulties, but the genre may be unable to resolve them.

A NOT-SO-MODEST PROPOSAL: CHANGE THE SURROUNDING GENRE SET TO IMPROVE THE OCCLUDED PUBLIC

As is evident from both the Zimmerman and the capital murder cases, the genre meant to clarify the situation of jury deliberation—jury instructions—does not adequately fulfill its purposes. That fact is not surprising since this genre, too, has a complex and difficult rhetorical situation. In addition, this genre reflects the intertwined spheres of public, private, and technical that the jury's situation—and our entire jury system—encompasses. The law has become a specialized, highly technical body of distinctions that have been tested in previous court cases, appeals, and rulings, a complex web of case law that requires interpretation by highly trained attorneys and judges, who still disagree on its meaning. Yet those distinctions are based at least partly on prior actions in public spheres, prior jury decisions, and public opinion that gains enough consensus or power to lead to being codified in the law. And those public actions emerge from individual experiences in the personal as well as public spheres. Hence we get laws that protect private property, that allow individuals to stand their ground, and that punish people differently depending on how evil or heinous are the crimes they commit.

This complex web of spheres cannot be managed by jury instructions alone since jury instructions necessarily privilege the technical sphere. They originate in case law and legal documents, and the particular texts develop from legally based arguments among attorneys and a judge about the precise legal implications of carefully chosen wording. This genre has all the problems of genres written by experts for nonspecialist readers, but no amount of plain-language revising will unpack all the background knowledge and assumptions needed for those nonspecialist readers to use the genre on its own. This genre also has all the problems of mixed purposes with its goal both of enabling jurors to enact the public will and of upholding decisions in future court appeals, a goal that introduces another set of readers in future attorneys and judges. And this genre is limited to logical appeals only as part of a technical trial system that has defined itself as governed by facts and logical evidence, even in realms beyond logical argument, like the nature of evil.

One solution to the difficulty of jury deliberations might be to hand the problem back to the courts. With the sources of the problems rhetorically detailed, perhaps the courts could act to address the needs of the jurors in some ways that make sense to those in the system. Yet, even though this difficult situation has recurred repeatedly over decades, no solution has emerged, in part perhaps because those trying to solve it have stayed within the world they know, the technical sphere. Another solution might be to eliminate jury instructions altogether, or drastically reduce them. Perhaps the instruction for all trials could simply be to draw a conclusion based on the evidence presented and the collaborative common sense of the jurors. In the end, though, this problematic genre may be necessary. Jury instructions attempt to regulate individual biases and reactions, focus attention on relevant versus irrelevant information, and share with jurors what we have learned from many decades of dealing with similar situations. Our current system needs jury instructions.

But our system also needs something more: a way to give jurors a voice after they have been isolated in the deliberation room, a way to have dialogue (trialogue?) among the three spheres. The jurors bring their personal values into a discussion meant to create public action, but the technical knowledge is represented by documents only, not by interactive communication. Analyzing the genre of jury instructions makes abundantly clear that documents alone cannot enable jurors to apply the law. The jurors are left with no adequate way to take up the technical sphere. The jurors need to be able to have dialogue with the technical, not just one-way communication. Perhaps that dialogue could occur through adding to or revising other genres in the surrounding genre set so multiple genres together could manage the complexity of this occluded and publicly significant situation.

One possibility is to exploit the capabilities of other intermediary genres. An intermediary genre is defined by Tosh Tachino as "a genre that facilitates the 'uptake' . . . of a genre by another genre" (Tachino 2012, 456). It is a genre used "to connect and mobilize two otherwise unconnected genres to make uptake possible" (456). Tachino applies the concept to intermediary genres that connect scientific research to the judicial system. In many ways, jury instructions seem already to be an intermediary genre. They are meant to connect the genres of the law to the jury deliberations. Yet, as I have demonstrated, they fail at enabling jurors to take up the law reliably. Another existing intermediary genre is the attorneys' closing arguments, which are meant to connect the law to the details of the particular case in ways jurors will understand. Unfortunately, not all attorneys are equally adept at explaining how the law applies, and one side might be a more effective persuader than the other, leaving the system at the mercy of individual abilities in an adversarial context. Another intermediary genre that already exists in the genre set surrounding jury deliberations is questions to the judge. While the jury is deliberating, in addition to asking to see evidence again, they may send through the bailiff written questions for the judge to answer. Those questions might, for example, ask the judge to clarify a definition they received, ask whether they can consider something they think relevant, or otherwise ask for clearer instructions. The judge confers with the attorneys and then responds to these questions in writing. Questions to the judge do not occur in every trial, of course, and there are no standard patterns of those questions. This intermediary genre, though, potentially could help jurors take up jury instructions.

In addition to asking for a list of all the evidence, the foreperson in the Zimmerman jury sent one question to the judge, a note that asked, "May we please have clarification on instructions regarding manslaughter?" (Schneider and Lush 2013). After consulting with the attorneys, the judge returned this written reply: "The court can't engage in general discussion but may be able to address a specific question regarding clarification of the instructions regarding manslaughter. If you have a specific question, please submit it" (Schneider and Lush 2013). That was the end of the exchange between the judge and the jury until the verdict was decided. The jurors were clearly indicating to the judge their confusion over the legal requirements for manslaughter, but they may not have understood the basis of their confusion enough to be able to offer a more specific question, as the judge demanded. When Juror B37 tried to articulate her understanding of the judge's response to their question in an interview, she struggled: "So they sent it back saying that if we could narrow it down to a question asking us if—what exactly—not what about the law and how to handle it, but if they could just have— I guess—I don't know" ("CNN Transcript: George Zimmerman Juror Speaks," *Orlando Sentinel,* July 13, 2013). In the discussion at the bench, the knowledgeable lawyers and judge crafted their response based on the case law over providing jury clarification, not based on the most effective way to help the jury out of their confusion.

The jury instructions currently limit the intermediary role of the genre of questions to the judge. When the Zimmerman jury instructions raise the option of asking the judge questions, they include more hedges and obstacles than invited dialogue: "If you need to communicate with me, send a note though [sic] the bailiff, signed by the foreperson. If you have questions, I will talk with the attorneys before I answer, so it may take some time. You may continue your deliberations while you wait for my answer. I will answer any questions, if I can, in writing or orally here in open court." The judge will answer questions only if they "need to communicate with" her, and then not directly but through the bailiff. Even then, the judge will answer the questions only "if [she] can," leaving the jurors, once again, on their own to interpret the jury instructions into their jury deliberations. The clash of purposes and privileging of the technical appear again.

If questions to the judge are to work as an intermediary genre more successfully than do jury instructions, then, they must be seen not as a genre in the technical sphere but rather as a genre bridging the technical and the jurors' personal/public realms. Instead of treating questions to the judge as identical in rhetorical situation to jury instructions, an effective judge (and not all would be capable) might consider the surrounding genre set by responding to a different rhetorical situation: the jurors need help understanding an area of the law in which they have already been instructed; the judge has the expertise they need; dialogue about the confusion and the law could help clear it up and improve the chances of a technically accurate verdict. If questions to the judge cannot serve that purpose, the courts might devise a new genre to add to the existing genre set that will serve as an intermediary between the technical jury instructions and the public act of jury deliberations. Or change the jury instructions to allow them to be an intermediary between the law and the jury deliberations. Or teach all attorneys how to be effective intermediaries in their closing arguments.

If none of that is possible because of fear the resulting verdict will be overturned on appeal, we may need to acknowledge that verdicts are no longer public acts but rather technical decisions—and moreover that such technical decisions cannot be made by a group of public citizens in a public sphere but must be made by a specialist, the judge. Many legal scholars have debated the efficacy of the jury system in our highly technical legal system (see Ellen Sward [2001] for one example). My argument here is that the instructions to the jury and the questions to the judge demonstrate the nature of the problem in new ways. Examining the whole set of genres surrounding the jurors' deliberation reveals how heavily weighted that set is in favor of the lawyers' needs and the technical sphere. Without help from other genres that prioritize their needs in the public sphere, juries are in untenable rhetorical situations.

CONCLUSION

Analyzing the genres surrounding jury deliberations allows us to examine and critique the situation, even though the essential act of deliberating is hidden from public view. In the public sphere, where actions affect society, hidden situations can be dangerous. In opening such hidden situations, the surrounding genre set also reveals dysfunction. The genres of jury service reflect the rhetorical situations out of which they derive: not a debate about and resolution of important public issues based on shared and conflicting values and perspectives on a particular case, but rather a highly constrained, technical, and yet underspecified debate about legal meanings, a near guessing game by well-intentioned citizens who are asked to meet the needs of well-intentioned attorneys and judges. While the interaction of personal and public spheres can be messy, that tangle of spheres can still serve well, in Hauser's terms, if the subjective joins in an "intersubjectivity" to create a public (Hauser 1999, 66–67)—what would seem the very nature of jury deliberations. Individual jurors bring their personal experiences to help develop a collective determination of broader significance. But to the extent that the technical sphere dominates without adequate intermediaries, the effectiveness of jury deliberations as a public sphere is challenged. As

Hauser writes, "A well-functioning public sphere requires that its discursive arenas contextualize public problems in ways that foster clear apprehension of the issues" (1999, 78). The dysfunctional genre set reveals a dysfunctional jury system that requires a level of specialized knowledge that removes it from the realm of the public and places it squarely in the realm of the technical. Although Hauser describes radical efforts at reform as "quixotic adventure" (273), the practices that have developed historically in the jury system have remained in a technical sphere. To repair the jury system might require repairing the genre set. Since genres define and delimit the actions we can take, changing the genre sets may be a practical rather than quixotic way to improve these dysfunctional public situations.

Speaking especially of democratic deliberation, Hauser argues that "before we can rehabilitate public life, we first must understand the way actually occurring discourse shapes it" (1999, 273). Similarly, before we can rehabilitate our jury system, we first must understand how discourse is shaping it, including the discourse occluded in the jury room. Hauser emphasizes the need for rhetoricians, in trying to understand public actions, to see how a text was taken up, "to discover how it was understood and responded to by those who were paying attention and responding to what was being communicated. This is especially necessary if we wish to understand more fully the way in which discourse is related to the quality of public judgment" (279). In the case of occluded publics, that process can be observed only indirectly. That indirect observation can come from examining the genre sets surrounding an occluded genre. Interviews, though limited in reliability, can confirm textual evidence, as Hauser desires (276–77) and suggest how people take up an occluded genre. Together, the information gives us access to public acts performed privately and allows us to offer critique and perhaps even the quixotic adventure of change.

Notes

1. I am grateful to several colleagues who read earlier drafts of this chapter and offered valuable advice and insight: David Brown, Marta Caminero-Santangelo, Frank Farmer, James Hartman, Jonathan Lamb, Laura Mielke, and Mary Jo Reiff. Without the helpful suggestions, pithy phrasings, and perceptive questions, this chapter might have been considerably neater and considerably less truthful.

2. I use the terms and processes from criminal cases, like *prosecution* and *defense*, both because they are the ones with which I am most familiar and because the examples I analyze are all from criminal cases. The same method could be used fruitfully to examine the genres surrounding civil cases, where the jury instructions, for example, are arguably considerably more dense and complex.

3. See, for example, California's website http://www.courts.ca.gov/partners/juryinst
    ructions.htm, Washington state's http://www.courts.wa.gov/index.cfm?fa=home
    .contentDisplay&location=PatternJuryInstructions, Florida's http://www.florida
    supremecourt.org/jury_instructions/instructions.shtml, or Massachusetts's http://
    www.mass.gov/courts/court-info/trial-court/dc/dc-crim-model-jury-inst-gen.html.
4. Confirming my sense of this statement's syntactic complexity, Word's grammar-
    check program highlighted it in my text and suggested changing from passive to
    active voice.
5. My analysis of the juror interviews comes from complete transcripts of all interviews
    with both jurors B29 and B37, listed in the References.

References

Couture, Barbara, and Thomas Kent, eds. 2004. *The Private, the Public, and the Published: Reconciling Private Lives and Public Rhetoric.* Logan: Utah State University Press.

Devitt, Amy J. 2003. "Where Communities Collide: Exploring a Legal Genre." *College English* 65 (5): 543–49.

Farmer, Frank. 2013. *After the Public Turn: Composition, Counterpublics, and the Citizen Bricoleur.* Logan: Utah State University Press.

Final Jury Instructions. 2012. State v. Zimmerman (2012-CF-001083-A).

Ford, Dana. 2013. "Juror: 'No Doubt' That George Zimmerman Feared for His Life." *CNN.* Accessed December 4, 2013. http://www.cnn.com/2013/07/15/justice/zimmerman-juror-book/index.html.

Fraser, Nancy. 1992. "Rethinking the Public Sphere: A Contribution to the Critique of Actually Existing Democracy." In *Habermas and the Public Sphere,* edited by Craig Calhoun, 109–45. Cambridge: MIT Press.

Freadman, Anne. 2002. "Uptake." In *The Rhetoric and Ideology of Genre: Strategies for Stability and Change,* edited by Richard M. Coe, Lorelei Lingard, and Tatiana Teslenko, 39–53. Cresskill, NJ: Hampton.

Goodnight, G. Thomas. 2012. "The Personal, Technical, and Public Spheres of Argument: A Speculative Inquiry into the Art of Public Deliberation." *Argumentation and Advocacy* 48 (4): 198–210.

Hauser, Gerard A. 1999. *Vernacular Voices: The Rhetoric of Publics and Public Spheres.* Columbia: University of South Carolina Press.

Pattern Instructions for Kansas PIK-Criminal-3d Sect. 56.00-B-H. 2000.

Schneider, Mike, and Tamara Lush. 2013. "Jurors in Zimmerman Trial Have Question." *AP The Big Story.* July 14. http://bigstory.ap.org/article/court-groups-gather-await-zimmerman-verdict.

Swales, John M. 1996. "Occluded Genres in the Academy: The Case of the Submission Letter." In *Academic Writing: Intercultural and Textual Issues,* edited by Eija Ventola and Anna Mauranen, 45–58. Amsterdam: John Benjamins. http://dx.doi.org/10.1075/pbns.41.06swa.

Sward, Ellen E. 2001. *The Decline of the Civil Jury.* Durham, NC: Carolina Academic Press.

Tachino, Tosh. 2012. "Theorizing Uptake as Knowledge Mobilization: A Case for Intermediary Genre." *Written Communication* 29 (4): 455–76. http://dx.doi.org/10.1177/0741088312457908.

Zarefsky, David. 2012. "Goodnight's 'Speculative Inquiry' in its Intellectual Context." *Argumentation and Advocacy* 48 (4): 211–15.

8

DISCOURSE COALITIONS, SCIENCE BLOGS, AND THE PUBLIC DEBATE OVER GLOBAL CLIMATE CHANGE

Graham Smart

INTRODUCTION

The research presented in this chapter extends a long-term study of discourses and argumentation in the ongoing public debate over global climate change as this debate continues to unfold day by day in a multiplicity of texts circulated on the web. Within this intertextually intraconnected field of recurrently patterned discourse, or genre system, my research has focused on argumentative texts—in this case, texts communicating a clear claim regarding the nature, causes, and implications of climate change—produced by social actors actively engaged in the climate-change controversy. In the present study I draw on three sources of theory to form a conceptual framework for further investigating discourses and argumentation in the climate-change debate: contemporary theorizing of the public sphere, particularly as this research relates to the public understanding of science; scholarship on collective argumentation in public spaces, with a focus on the notion of the "discourse coalition" (Hajer 1995), a cluster of social actors—individuals, organizations, institutions—who, within the context of a major social debate, are attracted to a common set of arguments, or "macro-argument" (Toulmin 1959); and theory in genre studies, specifically the concepts of genre set, genre system, and genre uptake.

In earlier research (Smart 2012, 2011), I described the formation and continuous reproduction of two opposing discourse coalitions extremely active within the climate-change debate, the "climate-change crisis discourse coalition" (hereafter the Advocates) and the "climate-crisis skepticism coalition" (hereafter the Skeptics), each with its collectively held argumentative position on climate change. In the study presented here, I identify a third discourse coalition, the Eco-optimists.

DOI: 10.7330/9781607324430.c008

I also investigate how discursive interaction between the three discourse coalitions—Advocates, Skeptics, and Eco-optimists—creates opportunities for communicating knowledge about climate science to their respective publics, albeit in ways that reflect entrenched adversarial positions and a limited view of audience rather than potentially contributing to a fuller public understanding of climate science and greater public engagement within the climate-change debate. The present study also explores the primary role that science blogs, with their affordance of immediate circulation on the web, play in facilitating discursive interaction among the three discourse coalitions. I then describe the blog of one climate scientist, a glaciologist, who has created a space for herself in public discussion of climate change outside the constraints of the hegemony-seeking discursive struggle among the Advocates, Skeptics, and Eco-optimists.

Exploring the ways knowledge about climate science is made available to different publics and examining the nature of this knowledge are high-stakes pursuits given that the views of these publics have the potential to influence the actions (or inaction) of policymakers at different levels of democratic governance. At the same time, combining genre theory with theories of publics and collective argumentation in the public sphere can create a conceptual synergy for such investigations. In addition, the concept of the discourse coalition adds usefully to a category of conceptual metaphors—including the "discourse community" (Swales 1990), the "rhetorical community" (Miller 1994), and the "activity system" (Cole and Engeström 1993)—that have been used by scholars in genre studies in theorizing and empirically investigating the contexts in which genres are situated and function. Adding the discourse coalition to this category of conceptual metaphors provides researchers with another distinctive way of thinking about the activity of social actors linked discursively through their joint use of a set of genres—in this case specifically within the agonistic context of major public debates. Polarizing disagreement over issues such as assisted dying, marriage equality, abortion, radical disparities of income in society, militaristic foreign policies, and the threat of climate change call for innovative methods of rhetorical inquiry. Further, in bringing the notions of the genre sets, genre systems, and genre uptakes associated with discourse coalitions into play, we can better understand the sociopolitical actions performed by these discourse coalitions as well the effects of these actions on genre users. In what follows, I first provide some historical background on the science and politics of climate change as well as research and theory relevant to the present study. Then I describe the study and findings before concluding with a brief discussion of their implications for public agency within the discursive dynamics of major public debates.

THE SCIENCE AND POLITICS OF CLIMATE CHANGE

The climate-change controversy of the twenty-first century is rooted in nineteenth-century European science in the research of Joseph Fourier, John Tyndall, and Svante Arrhenius. The cumulative outcome of this research was the theory that certain atmospheric gases, including carbon dioxide (CO_2), combine to produce a *greenhouse effect* (a term conceived by Arrhenius) that could potentially raise the surface temperature of the earth. In the following years, a line of climate scientists, including Guy Callendar, Charles Keeling, and Stephen Schneider—the latter coining the term *global warming*—provided empirical evidence for three claims, respectively: that rising levels of atmospheric CO_2 were a consequence of the mounting use of fossil fuels, particularly coal; that growing levels of atmospheric CO_2 were leading to higher annual temperatures; and that higher concentrations of atmospheric CO_2 could eventually result in an extremely dangerous increase in the earth's average surface temperature. Subsequently, the 1980s saw growing concern among climate scientists around the world that global warming could lead to climate change—severe disruptions in global weather patterns such as heat waves, droughts, severe storms, and widespread coastal flooding (Weart 2003).

An international political response to the scientific reports of human-caused climate change emerged in the late 1980s. A landmark event was the founding in 1988 of the United Nation's Intergovernmental Panel on Climate Change. The IPCC was given responsibility for monitoring peer-reviewed scientific publications on various aspects of climate change, evaluating the risks for the biosphere and humankind, and reporting regularly on its work to policymakers from the 194 member countries of the IPCC. The IPCC released major assessment reports in 1990, 1995, 2001, and 2007. The IPCC's *Fifth Assessment Report* was published in three installments from September 2013 to April 2014. Each of the assessment reports has evoked animated public debate over the reality, causes, impacts, and need for mitigation of climate change through worldwide reductions in CO_2 emissions from fossil fuels.

RELATED RESEARCH AND THEORY

The Public and Publics

To trace the origins of contemporary theorizing on the public sphere, we can do no better than to begin with John Dewey's (1929) *The Public and Its Problems*, a rejoinder to Walter Lippmann's (1925) assertion that there is no such thing as "the public." In the course of defending the idea of the public as a valid and useful concept, Dewey also pointed to the existence of multiple publics, to the permeable boundaries between public and private domains, and to the role of communication in the formation of publics. Here Dewey anticipated themes later taken up by scholars such as Jürgen Habermas (1989), G. Thomas Goodnight (1982), and Charles Taylor (1992). Much of this contemporary scholarship follows Dewey in linking conceptualizations of the public and publics to the ideal of enhancing deliberative discourse within democratic societies.

Narrowing our focus to an area of scholarship known as the *public understanding of science*, we will next consider three representations of the public and its relationship to science and scientific knowledge, discussed here in a sequence of increasingly complex and sophisticated perceptions of the public's ability to take an interest in, comprehend, and contribute to science: the deficit model, the knowledge coproduction model, and the concept of public reasoning. Both scientists themselves and scholars who study science have been criticized for holding a deficit model (Wynne 1995) of the public's relationship with science—that is, for assuming that nonexpert audiences are scientifically nonliterate, not only lacking knowledge about science but also limited by a cognitive inability to understand its complexities. This negative characterization of a scientifically nonliterate general public is often coupled with a naive view of science communication as the direct transfer of simplified knowledge from scientific expert to lay person, with the expert taking on the paternalistic role of lecturer (Bucchi 2008). Further, as Greg Myers (2003) points out, the transfer notion of science communication assumes that the public is a *tabula rasa*—a unitary collective mind without cultural schemas or individual competencies and motives for interpreting scientific knowledge.

In contrast to the deficit model of public audiences, the knowledge coproduction model assumes that certain members of the public, in possessing relevant lay knowledge and competencies in areas of science of particular interest to them, are capable of engaging with professional scientists in setting priorities for research, interpreting the significance of findings, and applying the resulting knowledge in the best interests of society (Bucchi 2008). From this perspective on the relationship between the public and science, the social responsibility of the scientist shifts from attempting to educate a scientifically deficient public to engaging dialogically with interested and competent citizens in "hybrid forums" (Callon 1999) in which lay and expert knowledge can be productively combined.

A final conceptualization of the public and its relationship to science of relevance here is Sheila Jasanoff's (2012) notion of "public reasoning." Jasanoff argues that every modern democratic state, over time, coconstructs with its citizens a distinctive political culture and unique form of public reasoning—that is, the use of sanctioned forms of evidence and modes of argumentation in making and justifying decisions for which the government is accountable to its citizenry. According to Jasanoff (2012), public acceptance of government decisions in areas of public concern, often involving science and technology, depends both on the government's use of technocratic practices such as risk assessment, cost-benefit analysis, and reference to constitutional law and on the government's performance of its "rituals of rationality [in] . . . forums ranging from the high courts to the blogosphere" (9).

Collective Argumentation in the Public Sphere

Much contemporary scholarship on argumentation has focused on interactions between individuals (Fahnestock 2009). For a discussion of scholarship looking at argumentation on a broader social plane—and there is little of this—we can begin with Stephen Toulmin's (1959) concept of the "argument field," which assumes that some features of arguments are field specific while other features are common across all fields. G. Thomas Goodnight (1982) elaborated on this idea with his notion of "argument spheres"—Goodnight identifies three: personal, technical, and public—with each sphere marked by certain topics and particular standards for legitimate evidence and valid argument. For Goodnight, the public sphere should ideally be a site for deliberative discourse among members of a society where issues involving conflicting interests, uncertainty, provisional knowledge, and concern for the future are taken up and resolved.

Maarten Hajer's (1995) concept of the "discourse coalition," part of his "argumentative discourse analysis" approach, provides another way of theorizing occurrences of collective argumentation in the public sphere. A discourse coalition is a cluster of social actors—individuals, organizations, institutions—who, within the context of a major social debate, are attracted to a common set of arguments, or "macro-argument" (Toulmin 1959). A defining feature of the discourse coalition is that it necessarily exists in opposition to other discourse coalitions in a struggle for "discursive hegemony," defined as success in influencing the public and policymakers regarding the issue in question—and performed publicly through genre sets, systems, and uptakes.

Genre Sets, Systems, and Uptake

Researchers guided by a social theory of genre have recognized that genres found in academic, workplace, and public settings often perform in sets, with each genre set operating as an integrated rhetorical/epistemic site within a particular field of activity (Bazerman 1988; Devitt 1991). While providing users with a certain discursive stability and continuity, genre sets also typically display flexibility and continual evolution in their forms and functions. Moving beyond the scale of a single intragroup genre set, Charles Bazerman (1994) identifies a broader intergroup pattern of discourse—the "genre system," which encompasses genre sets used by two or more social groups as these groups interact in pursuing mutually intelligible purposes.

Within the context of this dialogical interaction between genres, Anne Freadman introduced the concept of uptake, occurring when a text in one genre elicits a responding text in another genre. Freadman (2002; 2012) later extended this notion of uptake to include not only one text responding to another but also a situation in which the use of a genre may prompt subsequent, though not necessarily immediate, semiotic events and related human actions. Anis Bawarshi and Kimberley Emmons have further expanded the concept of uptake in empirical studies of genres. Bawarshi (2006) points to how conventionalized relationships between genres can serve to organize different recurrent social actions within a field of human activity. Emmons (2009) has guided our attention beyond the value of uptake as a "necessary heuristic for understanding the ways texts and genres cohere within systems of social activity" (140) to recognize how uptake can also contribute to our understanding of human agency and the formation of individual subjectivities. According to Emmons, "If we are to account for the power . . . of uptake, we must redefine uptake not as the relation between two (or more) genres, but as the disposition of subjects that results from that relation" (140).

Genre Studies and Blogs

In their studies of the interaction between public actions and individual dispositions within the genre of the weblog, Carolyn Miller and Dawn Shepherd note the "astonishing uptake of blogs" (Miller and Shepherd 2009, 263) and the rapid pace of the blog's differentiation into different types. Miller and Shepherd (2004) describe the emergence of personal blogs as a response to "a recurrent rhetorical exigence [arising in] a particular cultural moment . . . a *kairos* of mediated voyeurism, widely dispersed by relentless celebrity, unsettled boundaries between public and private, and new technology" (1, 11). They observe that the blog, seen as an online diary, serves two fundamental purposes, one individual (personal self-expression) and the other social (cultivating relationships within an online community of bloggers), with both purposes related to discursive identity formation. In concluding their study, however, Miller and Shepherd signal their awareness of the rapid differentiation in the types and purposes of blogs, made possible by continuous technological advances afforded by new blogging software, and they raise the question of whether it is still reasonable to see the blog as a single unitary genre. Later, they point to striking changes in the blogging landscape: "Blogs [have begun] to change and adapt, to speciate, as it were. . . . The forms and features of the blog that had initially fused around the unfolding display of personal identity were rapidly put to use for . . . political advocacy, corporate tech support, classroom interaction, and public deliberation" (Miller and Shepherd 2009, 263), and I would add, given their centrality here, for discussion of science.

The Science Blogosphere

John Wilkins (2008) characterizes science blogs as "blogs whose main focus or intent is disseminating or commenting upon science" (411). With respect to the social importance of science blogs, Wilkins asserts that "blogs are highly idiosyncratic, personal and ephemeral means of public expression, and yet they contribute to the current practice and reputation of science as much as, if not more than, any popular scientific work or visual presentation" (411). According to Bora Zivkovic (cited in Bonetta 2007, 443, 444), science blogs emerged in the late 1990s and early 2000s. In 2007, Zivkovic reported that the number of blogs with the word *science* as one of their hashtags was 19,881. As he pointed out, however, many of these blogs were "pseudoscience blogs, new age blogs, creationist blogs, or computer technology blogs," concluding that the number of "actual science blogs"—blogs authored by "graduate students, postdocs, and young faculty [in the sciences]"—was 1,000 to 1,200. (Later in the chapter, I employ the term *science blog* to refer to a broader category of bloggers than Zivkovic does here.)

THE STUDY

This study addresses two sets of research questions. The first set of questions relates to the discursive formation of collective argumentation in the debate over global climate change: (1) What discourse coalitions can we identify within the web-based discourse of the climate-change controversy? and (2) What can an investigation of discursive interactions between discourse coalitions reveal about how climate-science knowledge is presented to different publics and about the nature of this knowledge? The second set of research questions focuses on the subgenre of the science blog and is taken in part from Miller and Shepherd's 2004 study: "What rhetorical work do blogs perform—and for whom? And how do blogs perform this work?" (1). To these questions, I will add others: What role do science blogs play in the formation of the discourse coalitions examined here? And to what extent do these blogs offer their publics a balanced view of climate science?

I have reanalyzed a corpus of some fourteen thousand texts used in my 2011 and 2012 studies, in addition to analyzing approximately four hundred posts to science blogs gathered since 2012. The corpus used for the two earlier studies includes a range of genres, including blogs, news stories from newspaper and magazine websites, as well as online reports, press releases, and other texts from environmental NGOs, think tanks, research institutes, and government agencies—with each text presenting a clear position on one or more aspects of human-caused climate change. The majority of these texts were collected using Google Alerts, with a smaller number of texts collected through subscriptions to organizations' websites or through other electronic texts received via e-mail.

In analyzing this body of texts, I employed Maarten Hajer's (1995) "argumentative discourse analysis" approach, founded on a neo-Foucauldian notion of discourse—one that is quite apposite for examining the discourses of environmental debates: "[A discourse is] an ensemble of ideas, concepts and categorizations through which meaning is given to social and physical phenomena, and which is produced, reproduced, and transformed in a particular set of practices" (447). Hajer offers the discourse analyst a conceptual schema for recognizing broad discursive patterns across multiple texts within a corpus with the aim of identifying macroarguments shared by groups of social actors—or "discourse coalitions"—as they fight for "discursive hegemony" in the context of a major social debate.

As a research method, I have appropriated Miller and Shepherd's (2004) approach in scrutinizing two sources of data: my own corpus of texts, which I examined using content analysis, and published commentaries by professional scientists (Schmidt 2008; Varner 2014). I have also included in my data published work by academics who study the field of science, such as scholars in sociology, communication, organizational studies, and science education (Bonetta 2007; Kouper 2010; Trench 2012; Wilkins 2008).

THREE DISCOURSE COALITIONS AND THEIR ADVERSARIAL INTERACTION

In previous research (Smart 2011, 2012) identifying discourse coalitions in the climate-change debate, I labeled one of these clusters of actors the *Advocates* and another the *Skeptics*. Further, I was able to infer from the corpus of texts a set of logically ordered claims comprising the respective argumentative positions of these two discourse coalitions (Smart 2011, 371–78). These positions can be compressed into the following statements:

> Advocates: Human-caused climate change threatens us with an impending global catastrophe, and policymakers around the world must act without delay to counteract this danger.

> Skeptics: The theory of human-caused climate change is at best uncertain, and we must resist misguided remedial government policies that would undermine our economies and way of life.

My 2011 study also pointed to the intense interactivity in the relationship between the Advocates and the Skeptics: "While these two clusters of [social actors] are diametrically opposed in their positions on climate change and clearly not attempting to establish mutual understanding through an authentic deliberative dialogue, they are nevertheless highly engaged with one another discursively . . . in that each of the coalitions appears very aware of the other's evolving position, or macro-argument, regarding climate change, and highly alert to any emerging claims" (376). In what follows, I use the concepts of genre set, genre system, and uptake to explore this paradox of the intense mutual engagement and yet unremitting contestation characterizing the discursive relationship between Advocates and Skeptics. First, though, who are the social actors comprising these two adversarial discourse coalitions? Examples on the Advocates side are the authors of climate-science blogging sites (RealClimate), environmental NGOs (Sierra Club), international political organizations (United Nations Environment Programme), organized groups of scientists (Union of Concerned Scientists), media organizations (*Guardian*), policy think tanks (Pembina Institute), and religious organizations (Evangelical Climate Initiative). On the Skeptics side, there are are the authors of climate-science blogging sites (What's Up With That?), business corporations (Peabody Energy), industry associations (Canadian Association of Petroleum Producers), organized groups of scientists (Friends of Science), media organizations (*Financial Post*), policy think tanks (Competitive Enterprise Institute), and religious organizations (Cornwall Alliance).

For each cluster of actors, the Advocates and the Skeptics, a set of frequently employed web-circulated genres serves as a vehicle for both the engagement and the contestation between discourse coalitions. Genres used by both sides—which form part of their respective genre sets—include blog posts, press releases, reports, newsletters, documentaries, opinion pieces in newspapers, and books, with the blog appearing to be the most frequently used genre on the part of both discourse coalitions. We can further conceptualize the continuous discursive interplay between the discourse coalitions, performed in the public sphere through their respective web-circulated genre sets, by viewing these two genre sets as comprising a larger genre system, an intertextually intraconnected field of discourse. Ironically, while the two discourse coalitions are diametrically opposed to one another on a range of issues related to climate change, the tension between the two coalitions serves to animate and motivate both of them.

Another useful way of conceptualizing the intense mutual engagement/contestation between the Advocates and the Skeptics is to think of this engagement/contestation as a continuous series of genre uptakes performed by the two sides. One side publishes an instance of a genre on the web, and the other side responds with a countering text, often within days, or even hours in the case of blogs. In Freadman's (1994) terms, we might see this interaction, metaphorically, as a relentless sequence of tennis shots and returns, a rapid-fire exchange primarily performed through the genre of the blog. Within the genre sets employed by the social actors comprising the two discourse coalitions, blogs are the most commonly used, and by a considerable margin—presumably because of the immediacy of web circulation that blogs afford their authors. Unfortunately, I think, the Advocates and the Skeptics use their blogs almost exclusively to pursue discursive hegemony in the climate-change debate, declining any meaningful dialogue with their counterparts in the other discourse coalition. One consequence of this situation is that the climate-science knowledge offered to their respective publics, as a form of genre uptake, is consistently slanted toward the fixed argumentative position of the discourse coalition.

A further concern is that contestation between the Advocates and the Skeptics, each wielding its own version of climate science, could potentially impair the quality of what Jasanoff (2012) terms "public reasoning"—the distinctive form of rationality and evidence-based argumentation sanctioned as acceptable for making and justifying decisions for which a government is accountable to its citizenry. A related danger here is that such contestation could undermine the potential for deliberative discourse among members of a society with respect to a major social issue such as climate change. For each of the three discourse coalitions, an examination of the comments posted by readers in response to blog authors' original posts certainly supports this view in that readers' comments almost always reflect, rather than probe, the blog author's version of climate science.

Below is an example of the regrettable (I would argue) epistemic bias seen in exchanges between Advocates and Skeptics concerning climate science. On March 10, 2008, physicists Knud Jahnke and Rasmus Benestad authored a post on an Advocate blog site called *RealClimate*. As we see below, Jahnke and Benestad's blog post is intended, as an uptake, to undermine the credibility of a Skeptic documentary on climate change by challenging an academic publication by physicist Nir Shaviv that was cited in the documentary.

A Galactic glitch
10 March 2008
[By] Knud Jahnke and Rasmus Benestad

After having watched a new [Skeptic] documentary called the "Cloud Mystery" . . . we realized that a very interesting point has been missed [regarding] climate: galactic cosmic rays and the evolution of the Milky Way galaxy. It is claimed in "The Cloud Mystery" . . . and related articles that our solar system takes about 250 million years to circle the Milky Way galaxy and that our solar system crosses one of the spiral arms [of the galaxy] about every ~150 million years (Shaviv 2003).

But is this true? Most likely not. . . . This claim is seriously at odds with astrophysical data. . . . So it seems that Shaviv's 'periodicity' estimate for crossing of spiral arms by the sun does not hold up under scrutiny when using current astronomical results as the work by Kranz et al. . . . [This undermines] Shaviv's remarkable press-release claims that "the operative significance of our research is that a significant reduction of the release of greenhouse gases will not significantly lower the global temperature."

Remarkably, the poor scientific basis of the galactic cosmic ray hypothesis seems to be inversely related to the amount of media backing it is getting. At least 3 documentaries ("The Climate Conflict", the "Global Warming Swindle", and now "The Cloud Mystery") have been shown on television—all with a strong thrust of wanting to cast doubt on the human causes of global warming.

Two days later, a countering post by Nir Shaviv (see below) appeared on his blog in which Shaviv defends his work from Jahnke and Benestad's attack. In an interesting rhetorical move, Shaviv rewrites the final paragraph from Jahnke and Benestad's earlier blog post, completely reversing its meaning, an unusual instance of uptake.

More slurs from realclimate.org
By Nir Shaviv, Wed, 2008-03-12 11:36

Realclimate.org continues with its same line of attack. Wishfulclimate.org writers try again and again to concoct what appears to be deep critiques against skeptic arguments, but end up doing a very shallow job. . . . According to realclimate.org, everything my 'skeptic' friends and I say about the effect of cosmic rays and climate is wrong. In particular, all [our] evidence is, well, a figment in the wild imagination of my colleagues and I. The truth is that the many arguments trying to discredit this evidence simply don't hold water. The main motivation of these attacks is simply to oppose the theory which would remove the gist out of the arguments of the greenhouse gas global warming protagonists. . . .

To summarize, using the final paragraph of Jahnke and Benestad, we can say that

Remarkably, the poor scientific basis of the attacks against *the galactic cosmic ray hypothesis seems to be inversely related to the* tenacity of the devout global warming protagonists—*all with a strong thrust of wanting to cast doubt on the* possibility that natural climate drivers may have been important to 20th century temperature change. (Italics in the original)

The two blog posts reproduced above illustrate Emmons's (2009) description of genre uptake as "a necessary heuristic for understanding the ways texts and genres cohere within systems of social activity" (140). We can see how the ongoing interaction realized in pairs of blog posts such as the two above serves to organize the discourse in a way readers can recognize as meaningfully connected. Further, if we were to assume the two blog posts were intended not only for a public comprising social actors in the authors' own discourse coalition but also as a performance intended for a nonpartisan public as well, we could—prompted by Emmons (and recalling Bakhtin's [1986] notion of "addressivity")—see uptake occurring here in the form of the authors' intended effects on the thinking and possible future actions of the individuals reading the blog posts. Unfortunately, however, from my observations of readers' comments posted in response to blog authors' initial posts, the Advocates and the Skeptics each appear to elicit their own discrete public, with little or no evidence of readers seeking out different views from a range of science blogs.

The exchange of blog posts reproduced above reveals how both the Advocates and the Skeptics, exploiting the immediacy afforded by blogs, maintain entrenched hegemony-seeking positions on climate change. And while the Advocates and Skeptics each offer their particular public instances of climate-science knowledge, the knowledges offered are incommensurate (Kuhn 1962) with one another, thereby limiting the possibilities for fuller understanding on the part of a broader public. Further, implicit in the pair of blog posts above are deficit-model assumptions regarding a general public's relationship with science, assumptions that are a far cry from an invitation to participate in the coproduction of scientific knowledge and to engage productively in the climate-change debate.

In reanalyzing the corpus used in my 2011 and 2012 studies as well as approximately four hundred blog posts gathered since 2012, I identified a third discourse coalition in addition to the Advocates and the Skeptics—an Eco-optimist discourse coalition (hereafter the Eco-optimists). The position of the Eco-optimists can be abridged as follows: while the human use of fossil-fuel emissions and the consequent rise in atmospheric CO2 have almost certainly been the primary cause of climate change, warnings of a looming ecological catastrophe are misguided since human societies will use their increasing wealth and proven ingenuity to develop new technologies for bringing the earth's climate back into balance. Space does not permit a fuller examination of Eco-optimists' discursive interactions with both the Advocates and the Skeptics. However, the same kind of agonistic relationship between the Advocates and the Skeptics also characterizes the relationship between the Eco-optimists and each of the other two discourse coalitions. An exchange of blogs between Andrew Revkin, an Eco-optimist who authors a blog for the *New York Times*, and Clive Hamilton, an Advocate author of *Requiem for a Species: Why We Resist the Truth About Climate Change*, represents this agonistic relationship.

The exchange began in mid-June 2014 with Revkin's reference on his blog to using the phrase "paths to a 'good' anthropocene" during a conference talk he gave earlier that month (*Dot Earth*, February 8, 2016).

The term *anthropocene* is employed, typically by Advocates and in a negative sense, to denote the twelve thousand-year period since the last ice age, when human activities are seen to have significantly damaged the earth's ecosystems. Revkin's main theme in his conference talk had been that, while it is certainly conceivable that climate change could cause catastrophic disruptions to the global climate, humankind has the collective intelligence, systems of governance, and technologies needed to change paths very quickly and avoid the worst consequences of climate change. Revkin further argued that the best way to encourage the global public to embrace this course of action is to accentuate the possibilities for progress in dealing with climate change rather than presenting the public with scare tactics and apocalyptic visions of future devastation.

Hamilton responded to Revkin's notion of a possible path to "the 'good' anthropocene" with a forceful riposte in his own blog on June 17, 2014. The excerpts from Hamilton's blog post that follow convey the sense and spirit of his response

> Thanks for sending the link to your talk on "Charting Paths to a 'Good' Anthropocene." Since you ask for responses let me express my view bluntly. In short, I think those who argue for the "good Anthropocene" are unscientific and live in a fantasy world of their own construction. . . .
>
> [Individuals like you] do not attempt to repudiate the mass of scientific evidence; instead they choose to reframe it. As you declare so disarmingly, "You can look at it and go 'Oh my God', or you can look at it and go 'Wow, what an amazing time to be alive!' . . . You believe that "with work . . . we can have a successful journey this century. . . . We are going to do OK." Personally, when I think about those toiling, vulnerable masses who are going to suffer the worst consequences of a warming world, I find it offensive to hear a comfortable, white American say "We are going to do OK." (*Clive Hamilton*, June 17, 2014)

In Hamilton's blog post, we have another illustration of how the three discourse coalitions employ blogs, with their affordance of immediacy of circulation on the web, to maintain entrenched hegemony-seeking argumentative positions. Again, we see all three sides, in striving for discursive dominance, offer their public biased instances of climate-science knowledge, which if compared would be seen as incommensurate (Kuhn 2000). Each side's offerings of climate-science knowledge are rooted in particular theoretical assumptions and reflect a particular ideology, with the result that, as Randy Harris (2005) points out, "the lack of a common standard for taking the measure of two systems [of knowledge] with respect to each other . . . disabl[es] progress. If one can't measure sure theories with respect to each other, how can one choose which is best?" (3, 4).

One dimension of the incommensurability among the different climate-science knowledges proffered by the Advocates, Skeptics, and Ecooptimists is linguistic. Even terms used in common by the Advocates, Skeptics, and Eco-optimists, such as *uncertainty, scientific skepticism,* and *climate modeling* are infused with different meanings by each group. Howard Margolis (1996; cited in Harris 2005) describes a scenario that matches up well with the agonistic interaction of the three discourse coalitions: "Arguments [based on climate science] that seem powerful to one side seem unimportant to the other. What looks like striking insight to one side looks like perverse illusion to the other" (20). A key consequence of this incommensurability of climate-science knowledges is that blog readers are left without the opportunity they might otherwise have to make comparative judgements regarding the climatescience-supported claims advanced by the Advocates, Skeptics, and Eco-optimists, even when these claims involve empirical evidence—a situation that obstructs the possibilities for fuller public understanding and for informed political engagement on the part of the blogs' readers. To be fair to Andrew Revkin, his response in his blog to Hamilton's attack was to propose that the two men look at views they hold in common rather than at their differences of opinion and go forward from there. Here Revkin, in the interests of prompting new thinking about climate change, was clearly opting to step outside the constraints of the discourse coalition in which I have placed him.

THE SCIENCE BLOGOSPHERE: BLOGGERS AND THEIR PURPOSES

In this section I take up two of Miller and Shepherd's (2004) research questions—"What rhetorical work do blogs perform—and for whom?" (1)—and apply these questions in examining the genre of the science blog. When we turn to professional scientists who author blogs—and these include scientists in universities and industry as well as graduate students and postdocs in the sciences—I have identified a number of the purposes pursued in these blogs by scrutinizing the three sources of data mentioned earlier: approximately four hundred blog posts I have collected since 2012, commentaries posted by professional scientists themselves on their use of science blogs, and published work by scholars who study science.

One set of purposes is enacted by scientist bloggers, with fellow scientists as the intended audience. Here we see purposes such as sharing one's prepublication findings with other scientists; attracting collaborators for research projects from among specialists in one's own field or in adjacent fields; expanding on one's own published work for fellow experts; and training graduate students in one's field of scientific expertise and preparing them for job searches by creating a forum for discussion and networking. A second set of purposes can be ascribed to scientist bloggers intending to communicate with public audiences. Given their salience to the study presented here, these purposes are listed below:

- engaging with the public regarding topics in one's scientific discipline, particularly topics that are complex and/or contested;

- striving to influence opinion leaders such as journalists, educators, and public intellectuals;

- satisfying the obligation for public outreach that comes with many institutional grants;

- providing a window onto the backstage science-in-the-making activities of one's field;

- writing autobiographically about one's life as a scientist;

- conveying views on science-informed government policies, in the role of a civic scientist.

What is particularly noteworthy about the second set of purposes involving scientists and public audiences is that they appear to hold at least the promise of realizing the "knowledge co-production model" of communication in a way that could allow for Goodnight's (1982) ideal of a public sphere with deliberative discourse among citizens on issues of import. In the next section we will see an example of full-fledged knowledge coproduction involving a climate scientist and her public as mediated through the climate scientist's blog.

A CLIMATE-SCIENTIST BLOGGER ENGAGING WITH HER PUBLIC

I conclude these findings with a detailed look at a blog, *Antarctic Glaciers*, authored by glaciologist Bethan Davies. A journal article coauthored by Davies and a glaciologist colleague, in which the two scientists evaluate Davies's experience with her blog (Davies and Glasser 2014), provide insights into her blogging practices. (While Davies refers to characteristics common to both her blog and the website in which the blog is embedded, I focus here primarily on the blog.)

Davies's website describes her as "a glaciologist specializing in reconstructing glacier dynamics over multiple timescales, from both field and remotely sensed data, particularly in the Antarctic Peninsula, Britain and Patagonia. . . . [who] wrote and developed the Antarctic Glaciers website as part of an ongoing commitment to outreach, education and research impact" (*Antarctic Glaciers*, June 26, 2015). And here is Davies describing the rhetorical work accomplished through her blog as it functions within the larger context of the website: "It delivers peer-reviewed science to the public, [senior high-school] and undergraduate students [and it] underpins and supports my university teaching, increases the visibility and impact of my research, and broadens my professional network" (*Antarctic Glaciers*, June 26, 2015).

As reflected in the design of her website, with its embedded blog and Twitter feed, Davies's rhetorical sophistication is impressive. As one example of her rhetorical savvy, as a guest contributor on a blog called *Bogology*, Davies includes an explicit description of the deficit model of science communication.

> The belief that the simple conveyance of information from scientists to [an ill-informed] public is known as the "Knowledge Deficit Model." . . . The idea [is] that, once citizens [are] up to speed, they [will] judge the issue as the scientists did. [This] decades-old Knowledge Deficit Model [involves] the transmission of information, where the facts . . . speak for themselves and everyone . . . interpret[s] them in the same way. Why doesn't it work? . . . We know that knowledge is only one factor that shapes how individuals make judgements on scientific issues. Ideology, politics, trust, social identity, religion can all have equally strong impacts. (*Bogology*, March 10, 2014)

Davies contrasts the knowledge-deficit model with what she calls the "public engagement model," which has clear parallels to the knowledge coproduction model discussed earlier in the chapter:

> In order to be more successful at science communication, scientists need to have a better understanding of what factors might shape an individual's beliefs and [perspectives]. They must research and understand their audience . . . and listen to and connect with their audience on their terms. [Scientists] need to understand what their audience needs, and to be able to evaluate and evolve in response to these needs. . . . The "Public Engagement" model therefore has deliberative contexts and dialogue at its core. Any [message] should be as interactive as possible. [Public audiences] are encouraged to participate in a dialogue, informing research . . . priorities with an emphasis on participation and feedback. (*Bogology*, March 10, 2014)

To "challenge the deficit knowledge model, with interactive features and a good understanding of the audience" and thereby engage with her public, Davies uses a number of strategies, among which are (1) including a continuing survey of readers on the website and using information from respondents to make ongoing design adjustments to the blog and website; (2) identifying different types of individuals in her intended public and carefully considering how best to engage with each type of person; and (3) creating a synergy within a genre set comprising the blog, the website in which the blog is embedded, Twitter, YouTube and an Ask the Scientist feature by employing each genre according to its particular communicative affordances.

We might take the fact that Davies's website, begun in 2012, has recently been receiving up to five thousand visits a month as evidence that Davies has been successful in engaging with her public. Indeed, we might credit her with having created, together with this public, a "hybrid forum" (Callon 1999) combining lay and expert insights to produce new knowledge in the field of glaciology. And I argue that it is Davies's approach to communicating with her public, positioning herself outside the closed discursive world of adversarial uptakes created by the Advocates, Skeptics, and Eco-optimists, that enables her to join her readers in the coproduction of climate-science knowledge.

CONCLUSION

This chapter has investigated interaction among three discourse coalitions—Advocates, Skeptics, and Eco-optimists—as they compete for discursive hegemony in the debate over global climate change. The study shows that although each of the three discourse coalitions offers its public a version of climate-science knowledge, these versions are incommensurate, with the consequence that individuals are denied the possibility of developing, through dialogue, greater scientific understanding, a gain that could in turn lead to more informed public engagement in the climate-change debate. Further, recognizing the central role that science blogs play in this debate, the study identifies people, audiences, and purposes associated with science blogs, with particular attention given to blogs authored by climate scientists. A significant finding of the research is that climate scientists and other social actors possess sufficient agency to create a space for themselves in public discussions of climate change outside the narrow adversarial exchanges of the Advocates, Skeptics, and Eco-optimists.

In bringing together genre theory, scholarship on the public sphere, and the idea of the discourse coalition, the study offers a heuristic to researchers wishing to explore the discursive dynamics of major public debates. In addition, beyond academia, I hope the study might enhance our ability to approach environmental controversies with additional insight, enabling us to play a more effective part in environmental debates.

References

Bakhtin, M. M. 1986. *Speech Genres and Other Late Essays.* Austin: University of Texas Press.

Bawarshi, Anis. 2006. "Response: Taking Up Language Differences in Composition." *College English* 68 (6): 652–56.

Bazerman, Charles. 1988. *Shaping Written Knowledge: The Genre and Activity of the Experimental Article in Science.* Madison: University of Wisconsin Press.

Bazerman, Charles. 1994. "Systems of Genres and the Enactment of Social Intentions." In *Genre and the New Rhetoric,* edited by Aviva Freedman and Peter Medway, 79–101. Bristol, PA: Taylor and Francis.

Bonetta, Laura. 2007. "Scientists Enter the Blogosphere." *Cell* 129 (3): 443–45. http://dx.doi.org/10.1016/j.cell.2007.04.032.

Bucchi, Massimiano. 2008. "Of Deficits, Deviations and Dialogues: Theories of Public Communication of Science." In *Handbook of Public Communication of Science and Technology,* edited by Massimiano Bucchi and Brian Trench, 57–76. New York: Routledge.

Callon, Michel. 1999. "Actor-Network Theory: The Market Test." In *Actor Network theory and After,* edited by John Law and John Hassard, 181–95. Oxford: Blackwell.

Cole, Michael, and Yrjo Engeström. 1993. "A Cultural-Historical Approach to Distributed Cognition." In *Distributed Cognitions: Psychological and Educational Considerations,* edited by Gavriel Salomon, 1–46. New York: Cambridge University Press.

Davies, Bethan. 2014. "Why Is Communicating Climate Change Science Hard?" *Bogology,* March 10. http://bogology.org/2014/03/10/why-is-communicating-climate-change-science-hard/.

Davies, Bethan. 2015. "Biography." *Antarctic Glaciers,* June 26. http://www.antarctic glaciers.org/about-2/bethan-davies-2/bethan-davies/#SECTION_1.

Davies, Bethan, and Neil Glasser. 2014. "Analysis of www.AntarcticGlaciers.org as a Tool for Online Science Communication." *Journal of Glaciology* 60 (220): 399–406. http://dx.doi.org/10.3189/2014JoG13J194.

Devitt, Amy. 1991. "Intertextuality in Tax Accounting: Generic, Referential, and Functional." In *Textual Dynamics of the Professions: Historical and Contemporary Studies of Writing in Professional Communities,* edited by Charles Bazerman and James Paradis, 335–57. Madison: University of Wisconsin Press.

Dewey, John. 1929. *The Public and Its Problems.* New York: Henry Holt.

Emmons, Kimberly. 2009. "Uptake and the Biomedical Subject." In *Genre in a Changing World,* edited by Charles Bazerman, Adair Bonini, and Débora Figueiredo, 134–57. Fort Collins, CO: WAC Clearinghouse and Parlor.

Fahnestock, Jean. 2009. "Quid Pro Nobis: Rhetorical Stylistics for Argument Analysis." In *Examining Argumentation in Context: Fifteen Studies on Strategic Maneuvering,* edited by Frans van Eemeren, 191–220. Amsterdam: John Benjamins. http://dx.doi.org/10.1075/aic.1.12fah.

Freadman, Anne. 1994. "Anyone for Tennis?" In *Genre and the New Rhetoric,* edited by Aviva Freedman and Peter Medway, 43–66. Bristol, PA: Taylor and Francis.

Freadman, Anne. 2002. "Uptake." In *The Rhetoric and Ideology of Genre: Strategies for Stability and Change,* edited by Richard Coe, Lorelei Lingard, and Tatiana Teslenko, 39–53. Cresskill, NJ: Hampton.

Freadman, Anne. 2012. "The Traps and Trappings of Genre Theory." *Applied Linguistics* 33 (5): 544–63. http://dx.doi.org/10.1093/applin/ams050.

Goodnight, G. Thomas. 1982. "The Personal, Technical, and Public Spheres of Argument: A Speculative Inquiry into the Art of Public Deliberation." *Journal of the American Forensic Association* 18: 214–27.

Habermas, Jürgen. 1989. *The Structural Transformation of the Public Sphere: An Inquiry into a Category of Bourgeois Society.* Translated by Thomas Burger and Frederick Lawrence. Cambridge: MIT Press.

Hajer, Maarten. 1995. *The Politics of Environmental Discourse: Ecological Modernization and the Policy Process.* Oxford: Oxford University Press.

Hamilton, Clive. 2014. "The Delusion of the 'Good Anthropocene': Reply to Andrew Revkin." *Clive Hamilton,* June 17. http://clivehamilton.com/the-delusion-of-the -good-anthropocene-reply-to-andrew-revkin.

Harris, Randy. 2005. Introduction to *Rhetoric and Incommensurability,* edited by Randy Harris, 1–150. West Lafayette, IN: Parlor.

Jahnke, Knud, and Rasmus Benestad. 2008. "A Galactic Glitch." http://www.realclimate .org/index.php/archives/2008/03/a-galactic-glitch.

Jasanoff, Sheila. 2012. *Science and Public Reason.* New York: Routledge.

Kouper, Inna. 2010. "Science Blogs and Public Engagement with Science: Practices, Challenges, and Opportunities." *Journal of Science Communication* 9 (1): 1–10.

Kuhn, Thomas. 1962. *The Structure of Scientific Revolutions.* Chicago: University of Chicago.

Kuhn, Thomas. 2000. "Commensurability, Comparability, Communicability." In *The Road since Structure,* edited by James Conant and John Haugeland, 33–57. Chicago: University of Chicago Press.

Lippmann, Walter. 1925. *The Phantom Public.* New York: Harcourt, Brace.

Margolis, Howard. 1996. *Dealing with Risk: Why the Public and the Experts Disagree on Environmental Issues.* University of Chicago Press.

Miller, Carolyn. 1994. "Rhetorical Community: The Cultural Basis for Genre." In *Genre and the New Rhetoric,* edited by Aviva Freedman and Peter Medway, 67–78. Bristol, PA: Taylor and Francis.

Miller, Carolyn, and Dawn Shepherd. 2004. "Blogging as Social Action: A Genre Analysis of the Weblog." In *Into the Blogosphere: Rhetoric, Community, and Culture of Weblogs,* edited by Laura Gurak, Smiljana Antonijevic, Laurie Johnson, Clancy Ratliff, and Jessica Reyman. http://conservancy.umn.edu/handle/11299/172275.

Miller, Carolyn, and Dawn Shepherd. 2009. "Questions for Genre Theory from the Blogosphere." In *Genres in the Internet: Issues in the Theory of Genre,* edited by Janet Giltrow and Dieter Stein, 263–90. Amsterdam: John Benjamins. http://dx.doi.org /10.1075/pbns.188.11mil.

Myers, Greg. 2003. "Discourse Studies of Scientific Popularization: Questioning the Boundaries." *Discourse Studies* 5 (2): 265–79. http://dx.doi.org/10.1177/1461445603 005002006.

Revkin, Andrew C. 2016. "What's Missing at the U.N. Climate Panel's Meeting on Climate Change Communication." *Dot Earth,* February 8. http://dotearth.blogs .nytimes.com/.

Schmidt, Gavin. 2008. "To Blog or Not to Blog?" *Nature Geoscience* 1 (4): 208. http:// dx.doi.org/10.1038/ngeo170.

Shaviv, Nir J. 2003. "The Spiral Structure of the Milky Way, Cosmic Rays and Ice Age Epochs on Earth." *New Astronomy* 8 (1): 39–77.

Smart, Graham. 2011. "Argumentation across Web-Based Organizational Discourses: The Case of Climate Change." In *Handbook of Communication in Organisations and Professions,* edited by Srikant Sarangi and Chris Candlin, 363–86. Berlin: Mouton De Gruyter. http://dx.doi.org/10.1515/9783110214222.363.

Smart, Graham. 2012. "The Discursive Production and Impairment of Public Trust through Rhetorical Representations of Science: The Case of Global Climate Change." In *Discourses of Trust: The Discursive Construction of "Trust" within Applied Linguistic*

Research, edited by Chris Candlin and Jonathan Crichton, 252–68. Basingstoke, UK: Palgrave Macmillan.

Swales, John. 1990. *Genre Analysis: English in Academic and Research Settings*. Cambridge: Cambridge University Press.

Taylor, Charles. 1992. *The Ethics of Authenticity*. Cambridge, MA: Harvard University Press.

Toulmin, Stephen. 1959. *The Uses of Argument*. Cambridge: Cambridge University Press.

Trench, Brian. 2012. "Scientists' Blogs: Glimpses behind the Scenes." In *The Sciences Media Connection—Public Communication and its Repercussions*, edited by Simone Rödder, Martina Franzen, and Peter Weingart, 273–90. New York: Springer.

Varner, Johanna. 2014. "Scientific Outreach: Toward Effective Public Engagement with Biological Science." *Bioscience* 64 (4): 333–40. http://dx.doi.org/10.1093/biosci/biu021.

Weart, Spenser. 2003. *The Discovery of Global Warming*. Cambridge, MA: Harvard University Press.

Wilkins, John. 2008. "The Roles, Reasons and Restrictions of Science Blogs." *Trends in Ecology & Evolution* 23 (8): 411–13. http://dx.doi.org/10.1016/j.tree.2008.05.004.

Wynne, Brian. 1995. "Public Understanding of Science." In *Handbook of Science and Technology Studies*, edited by Sheila Jasanoff, Gerald Markle, James Petersen, and Trevor Pinch, 361–388. Thousand Oaks, CA: SAGE.

9
MULTIPLE INTERTEXTUAL THREADS AND (UN)LIKELY UPTAKES
An Analysis of a Canadian Public Inquiry

Tosh Tachino

Since Charles Bazerman theorized genre systems as enacting social intentions in 1994, genre scholars have increasingly shifted their attention from single genres to the relationships among multiple genres. With this shift came a number of new issues, such as how genres relate to one another, how they function collectively, and what happens at genre boundaries. Concepts like "genre set" (Devitt 1991), "genre system" (Bazerman 1994), "genre repertoire" (Orlikowski and Yates 1994), "genre assemblage" (Spinuzzi 2003), and "genre ecology" (Spinuzzi 2003; Spinuzzi and Zachry 2000) all attempt to specify some logical groupings of genres (for an overview, see Bawarshi and Reiff 2010). Among these, genre ecology, in particular, captures the multiple, interconnected, and extended/distant relationship among genres, and it highlights the contingent and improvisational aspect of genre by including, for example, technology users' Post-It notes, which restructure the relationship among texts and genres in the textual network and mediate activities. In addition to these broad terms, other relational terms also emerged, such as "meta-genre" (Giltrow 2002) and various interpretations of "uptake" (Freadman 2002), the former referring to a genre that regulates other genres, the latter referring to how a genre responds to—takes up—the rhetorical act of another genre.

Most studies of multiple, interconnected genres have been conducted on academic and workplace genres. While these genres do sometimes interact with external genres, the interactions are typically confined within the genre system of a single disciplinary or workplace community. By comparison, public genres tend to draw from more diverse genres across more boundaries, thus affording greater opportunities for examining the kinds of questions that interest genre scholars: By what rhetorical means and by whom is public knowledge created and circulated?

DOI: 10.7330/9781607324430.c009

What rhetorical resources may the less powerful employ to disrupt the generic stability of the more powerful? These questions and many others are often amenable to rhetorical genre analyses of specific public genres in large networks, where genres and uptakes are multiplied exponentially, and have led me to study public genres so I could examine a particular type of boundary crossing, known as *knowledge mobilization*—the process of moving knowledge from formal research into active use, a key value in the social and natural sciences in relation to public discourse.

Political scientists have long observed that this process is far from linear or direct (Caplan 1979). Not only is the role of research indirect in policymaking (Weiss 1977), but it is also complicated by many factors, such as the policy context (Carden 2005; Kingdon 1984), political actors (Grindle and Thomas 1991), and the relationship between the researchers and policymakers (Haas 1991), as well as the strength and usefulness of the research itself and the credibility of the researchers (Court, Hovland, and Young 2005; Crewe and Young 2002; Stone 2001). Many of these political scientists have also noted the importance of language in knowledge mobilization, and they have suggested that the language directed to policymakers must be simple and clear and that the communication should be bidirectional (Court et al. 2005; Crewe and Young 2002; Figueroa, et al. 2002). Yet their conceptualization of language is limited largely to social-science models of communication. Rhetorical genre studies (RGS) (e.g., Artemeva and Freedman 2006; Bawarshi and Reiff 2010; Coe, Lingard, and Teslenko 2002; Miller 1984; Freedman and Medway 1994) is a perspective, as Dylan Dryer (chapter 3, this volume) points out, that is largely unfamiliar outside of writing studies. Yet it can shed a different light on the problem of knowledge mobilization with its more rhetorical understanding of language.

The concept from RGS I find most relevant to knowledge mobilization is Anne Freadman's (2002) "uptake." In "Anyone for Tennis?" Freadman (1994) emphasized the relational aspect of a discursive event by likening it to a tennis shot. Unlike a ball that can exist without being played, a shot is possible and meaningful only in the context of successive shots, opposing players, a tennis match, the rules of playing, and so on. Similarly we cannot understand a discursive event unless we understand the ways in which it is taken up and represented, the manner in which it acquires meaning from its discursive chain, and the collective social action performed by that discursive chain.

That's why uptake is crucial for understanding circulation and mobilization of knowledge as well as boundary crossing. This aspect is illustrated by Freadman (2002), who uses as an example the fate of the last man hanged in Australia, in 1967, to examine how a death sentence was taken up as an execution. At first glance, this uptake seems unproblematic: the executive branch was legislatively authorized to carry out the decision by the judicial branch. But this case was complicated because execution was routinely suspended in practice in Australia in the 1960s, and the sentencing judge opposed the execution even though he had been forced to pass a death sentence because he had been legislatively deprived of his discretionary power to give any other sentence. Under these circumstances, the premier (analogous to a US state governor), who did not legally have to justify the uptake (i.e., execution), held an irregular meeting with the sentencing judge and compelled him to agree with his own original sentence as if he were a prosecution witness—and to repeat the death sentence. This repetition, Freadman argues, was what crossed the jurisdictional boundary and secured the uptake.

Freadman's proposal to locate uptake as the defining feature of genre provoked many uptakes itself among genre scholars and raised many issues about the nature of uptake. The most prominent of these issues is the problem of rhetorical agency, as some theorists see in uptake an opportunity to undo the failure—as they perceive it—to account for agency in RGS proper (for an overview, see Bawarshi and Reiff [2010]). For this reason, Kimberly K. Emmons (2009) defines uptake as "the dispositions assumed through the uses of genres" (139), thus assigning uptake as a property of an individual. Dylan B. Dryer (2008) takes a similar position with a similar definition—"readers' and writers' enactment of acquired dispositions toward recurrent textual form" (503)—but he is more vocal about using uptake as a site of resistance: "I ask those interested in genre uptake and the spatial turn [in RGS] to help fashion physical and discursive spaces where people can work together to develop resistant knowledge of generic knowledge" (527).

In a recent article, Freadman (2012) herself gives due attention to agency but not to that of a single rhetor. Instead she focuses on the agency of all participants because any discursive event is an interaction made meaningful by its uptake by other agents. Thus, she argues, there is a difference between "calculating one's rhetoric in order to maximize the chances of securing a desirable uptake" and delivering a "'returning serve' in order to turn the play to one's advantage" (559). Any discursive event, she argues, is constitutive of its sociohistorical context, and genre, as the nexus between the discursive event and the context, simultaneously asserts its power and becomes destabilized through uptake (560).

The second issue is the typology of uptake. Emmons (2009) distinguishes discursive uptake from generic uptake, and within this discursive uptake, one can isolate various linguistic and rhetorical elements, such as clause, phrase, grammatical subject, and rhetorical emphasis (Tachino 2010). Dryer (in this volume) makes the following five distinctions:

- *uptake affordances*: opportunities and constraints that precede and shape the encounter;
- *uptake artifact*: a text produced in response to other texts;
- *uptake enactment*: the act of producing an utterance or text in response to uptake affordances;
- *uptake capture*: lingering effects of what writers see;
- *uptake residues*: incremental contribution to social formations.

As Dryer's analysis demonstrates, the term/concept *uptake* serves different pragmatic ends—even within RGS. Emmons's distinction and other typologies may be useful in conducting certain kinds of analysis but not others. In writing this chapter, I appeal to some of these distinctions and introduce my own modifiers.

Given this interest in uptake and agency, this chapter offers a network approach to explore the mechanism of uptake at a nexus of multiple (and possibly competing) intertextual threads with multiple rhetorical expectations, such as those often found in policy deliberations, political exchange, and other public discourse. How do genres enable or disable or resist certain uptakes in various ways for various agents? The approach I offer shows the multiplicity and complexity of the relationship among genres through analyzing multiple intertextual threads. Under this model, uptake is influenced by the relative strength of these threads and the configuration of the network. This process is illustrated through knowledge mobilization in my historical and linguistic study of a Canadian public inquiry.

INTERTEXTUAL NETWORK AND MULTIPLE RHETORICAL EXPECTATIONS

The idea of examining rhetorical expectation is not new. The idea has been theorized by many scholars, from Lloyd Bitzer (1968) with "exigence," Kenneth Burke (1945) with "motive," and Mikhail Bakhtin (1981; 1986) with "rejoinder" and "addressivity" to Freadman (1994; 2002) with her tennis metaphor of uptake. In Bitzer and Burke, exigence (in the external situation) and motive (within the rhetor) in the immediate context prompt the rhetor to act in certain ways. In Bakhtin's rejoinder and addressivity, we gain the temporal dimension, looking back and forward. A text contains echoes of the text it responds to; it also contains words (and other elements) that anticipate future utterances. Freadman's tennis metaphor and uptake can explain a long series of related discursive events, and it is this semiotic context that gives meaning to an individual text: just as the same tennis shot has different meanings depending on whether it is delivered in a neighborhood park or in the Wimbledon final, the same utterance (e.g., "I sentence you to death") means something different if uttered by the judge to a defendant at a sentencing hearing or by some teenager among friends in a competitive video-game session.

In order to advance the theory of uptake intertextuality—and increase its relevance for understanding public discourse—I turn to a recent spatial metaphor in RGS, especially Spinuzzi and Zachry's (2000) genre ecology, which includes "an interrelated group of genres (artifact types and interpretive habits that have developed around them) used to jointly mediate the activities that allow people to accomplish complex objectives" (172). Their framework seems most suitable for exploring uptake and agency because it emphasizes contingency and its network model can accommodate complex and multiple connections. In this metaphorical space, discursive events and genres exist neither singly nor only sequentially but in multiples and everywhere so that multiple intertextual and intergeneric relationships are possible. In other words, I want to take Freadman's tennis metaphor and multiply it so that at any given point there are multiple tennis shots, each with different and possibly—although not necessarily—competing expectations, such as one finds in, for example, the political arena.

As seen in Figure 9.1, any given text belongs not only to one but to many intertextual threads, and the significance and the outcome of the discursive event are influenced by the rhetorical expectations from other texts in all intertextual threads. Let us consider, for example, a political candidate who puts together a campaign that makes certain textual threads salient (e.g., policy statements, voting records, supporters' signatures and endorsements). From this candidate's perspective, they must populate this intertextual space with their texts and Bakhtinian addressivity, anticipating a particular response to the campaign. If everything goes as well as this candidate hopes, the voters will let those utterances cross generic boundaries to be repeated in the subsequent utterance that constitutes a favorable uptake for that candidate (i.e., being elected).

However, this intertextual space is filled by not just one candidate. Other candidates are also preparing their campaigns to compete for the favorable uptake. Thus, the election becomes a node in the intertextual

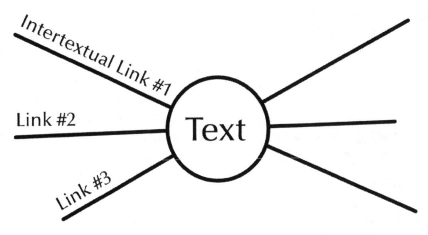

Figure 9.1. Multiple intertextual links.

network with multiple intertextual threads with competing rhetorical expectations. If the multiple candidates introduce a multiplicity of intertextual threads in the diachronic plane, we can also multiply the intertextual threads in the synchronic plane (following a similar argument by Orlikowski and Yates [1994] with their "genre repertoire"): the uptake by the voters may be complicated by the topical issues, the economic situation, the voters' party affiliations, accessibility of the voting locations, and many other factors.

This formulation of uptake is consistent with Freadman's (2012) position that neither can an individual's skill control nor can genre predict the outcome of a discursive event (559). The individual's skill can be foiled by an opposing participant; genre cannot account for all the variables—all the participants, all the intertextual threads in both diachronic and synchronic planes, the material conditions, the political and cultural contexts, and so forth—at this particular node in the intertextual network.

As Freadman's (2012) case study of a political interview shows, this complexity and uncertainty are more pronounced in an adversarial setting in which each side presents and emphasizes one particular intertextual thread over others. As the following analysis of a case of public discourse shows, this uptake analysis of multiple expectations can help us understand why certain rhetorical expectations are influential for uptake while others are not or are less so, particularly in public deliberations.

CASE STUDY: THE SOPHONOW INQUIRY

The Sophonow case began in 1981 with the murder of a young woman in Winnipeg, Canada. The police investigation led in 1983 to the arrest of Thomas Sophonow, who was convicted through, among other things, multiple faulty police lineups, unreliable witnesses, coercive interrogation techniques, jailhouse informants, suppression of exculpatory evidence, the police's tunnel vision, and an apparently malicious prosecution. Although he was eventually acquitted through appeals, he had to spend four years in prison, and he came out with long-term psychological damage and a marred reputation as somebody who got away with murder on technicalities. The horror of incarceration persisted even after his release while Sophonow sought to clear his name. It was not until 2000, when the Manitoba government acknowledged its mistake and released an official apology in their official newsletter, that Sophonow was finally exonerated. The apology was followed by an Order-in-Council, a legislative action (though its authority derives, nominally, from the Crown) to create a commission to investigate the causes for Sophonow's wrongful arrest, conviction, and incarceration as well as to suggest ways of preventing future miscarriages of justice.

But what is important for our purpose in this chapter is that the inquiry served as a catalyst for certain judicial reforms based primarily on psychology research originally published in scientific journal articles. As I argue elsewhere (Tachino 2012), this inquiry functioned as an "intermediary genre"—facilitating the uptake of one genre by another, thus serving as a crucial uptake point in knowledge mobilization. The intertextual network model I described previously is used here to reveal the ways in which different discursive events and genres interact in a complex genre ecology to influence uptakes.

PUBLIC INQUIRY

A public inquiry is a government-initiated ad hoc commission in Canada with a vague triggering condition: it responds to "any matter connected with the good government of Canada or the conduct of any part of the public business thereof" (Inquiry Act, R.S.C., ch. 1–11 1985).[1] The commission is granted the authority to summon and subpoena witnesses to a trial-like preliminary hearing in which witnesses are examined and cross-examined by counsels representing different parties to the event under inquiry. The commissioner presides at the preliminary hearing like a trial judge and uses the inquiry as the official fact-gathering venue. The commission produces a report, which typically contains policy recommendations,[2] but these recommendations are not legally binding. Many public inquiries use expert witnesses, but they are not required.

The specific mandates of the Sophonow Inquiry were to discover the causes that led to the wrongful conviction of Thomas Sophonow and to suggest ways of preventing future miscarriages of justice. The Order-in-Council appointed a former Supreme Court of Canada judge, Peter Cory, as the commissioner to hear the Sophonow Inquiry. The commission invited researchers from various disciplines (psychology, law, forensic psychiatry) to the preliminary hearing, and the recommendations in the commission report (the Cory Report) had a wide impact on law enforcement policies across Canada.

To examine the uptake paths in the genre ecology surrounding the Sophonow Inquiry, especially as they relate to knowledge mobilization, I took the commission report as the starting point and traced its sources through explicit citations and other textual clues. I also examined all the transcripts from the expert portions of the preliminary hearing and read enough of the relevant literature in psychology so I could identify the original studies by the descriptions alone (as the report and transcript usually lacked full citations). I also looked for citations of the Sophonow Inquiry to evaluate its impact in policy papers, law journals, and newspapers, among others. Furthermore, I conducted interviews with the commissioner, the lead counsel, and two of the expert witnesses, and I conducted a detailed citation analysis of the commission report to capture the nature of uptake at the microtextual level in a systematic manner (Tachino 2008; 2012).

Most of my full analysis of the case does not relate to the specific theoretical discussion of this chapter. Therefore, I will be selective in presenting the data, primarily to illustrate the mechanisms of agency in uptake through the strength of intertextual threads, changes in the configuration of the intertextual network, and rechanneling through an intermediary genre.

INTERTEXTUAL MAP AND MULTIPLE INTERTEXTUAL THREADS OF THE COMMISSION REPORT

Figure 9.2 presents a schematic representation of the genre ecology of the commission report. The left-most column lists a number of sources cited by the texts in the Sophonow Inquiry, and the arrows indicate the direction of citation. For example, US government publications are cited by the preliminary hearing, which in turn was cited by the commission

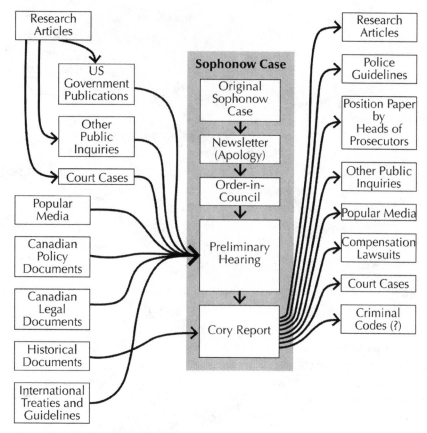

Figure 9.2. Intertextual network of the Cory Report.

report. Although the content and the text from some US government publications were repeated in the commission report—sometimes (near) verbatim—the report never attributes them to those publications (except once to make an entirely different point). They are, instead, attributed to the transcript from the preliminary hearing or the experts themselves at the hearing (see Tachino 2012). For this reason, there is no direct arrow from the US government publications to the commission report. The right-most column, on the other hand, lists some of the texts that cite the Sophonow Inquiry. Some of the items in this column are repeated from the left-most column, indicating the recursive nature of uptake.[3] For example, research articles are cited by the preliminary hearing and the commission report, and the commission report is cited by other research articles that postdate the commission report.

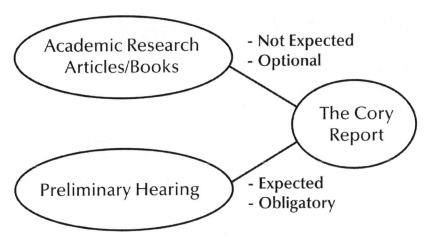

Figure 9.3. Rhetorical expectations in the Cory Report.

RELATIVE STRENGTHS OF INTERTEXTUAL THREADS AND EXPECTED UPTAKE

Figure 9.3 is a simplified schematic representation in that it does not account for every single connection, but it is still meant to emphasize the complexity and multiplicity of the intertextual network among diverse genres—academic, professional, public, and popular—across many traditional boundaries. Also important is that all these texts and genres do not neatly line up on a single thread to provide a unified uptake perspective. For example, the linear vertical thread in the center column is the official legal thread of the Sophonow case; using this thread, one could recount the official version of the Sophonow case as a public inquiry righting a previous miscarriage of justice in the judicial system (police-lineup wrongdoing affirmed in a court). But this is not the only intertextual thread. One could also focus on the thread that links the Sophonow Inquiry with other public inquiries to say this inquiry was simply another rhetorical instantiation of the genre (of public inquiries). The thread that links the commission report to similar policy documents in the United States might even allow us to say that the Sophonow case illustrates what policy analysts call a "policy transfer" (Stone 2001), taking a public policy in one context (usually in one country) and applying it to another. The connection with international treaties and guidelines enables others to say that the recommendations in the commission report were simply a logical deduction of the existing principles outlined in those international treaties.

While all these multiple uptakes along any of the intertextual threads are possible, the strength of each thread is not equal: some contribute to a greater likelihood of uptake while others contribute little or may even work against the uptake. In discussing this relative strength of intertextual threads, I find it useful to turn to Orlikowski and Yates's (1994) idea that only certain genres are most frequently invoked in any rhetorical situation (thus constituting the repertoire) while other genres remain dormant or are rejected from the genre system. A similar argument can be made for rhetorical expectations and uptake, but a more complex one. At any intertextual node with competing rhetorical expectations, uptake of the rhetorical expectation from a given source or a genre cannot only be more or less frequent but can also vary on a range of degrees of expectation: from obligatory, to routine, to expected, to not expected but not unusual, to not expected, to unusual, to forbidden.

In the Sophonow case, the commissioner was legally required to take up the Order-in-Council, its terms of reference, and the preliminary hearing; therefore, it is not surprising to see various linguistic and rhetorical elements cross the generic and textual boundaries and enter the commission report through repetitions of various kinds. On the other hand, the direct link between research articles and the commission report is considerably weaker because citation of the research articles is neither required nor expected in a public, quasi-judicial inquiry like this one (see Fig. 9.3).

Reflecting this relative strength of the intertextual thread, the commission report cites[4] the preliminary hearing much more often (109[5] out of 413 citations) than academic articles (9 out of 413). Such observation allows us to imagine and evaluate various solutions to the knowledge-mobilization problem: How do we strengthen the intertextual thread between research genres and policy genres so more policies may be informed by research (or policies may be more strongly informed)? How can we use the already strong link between policy genres and other genres to facilitate knowledge mobilization?

One radical, if not obvious, solution is to reform the legal procedure to formally make research more influential. Such changes in the metagenres—genres that explicitly regulate genres, such as statutes and procedural rules in this case—would certainly change the configuration of the network. The prescriptive force from the metagenre would strengthen the uptake path between research genres and policy genres, even if the formerly strong uptake path might persist for a long time. However, such proposals are likely to incur the wrath of the legal community and thus have little hope of succeeding. As legal and policy scholars point out, the current legal processes embody certain assumptions of basic human rights and protection of these rights: an attempt to privilege expert discourse and knowledge disrupts and undermines some of the fundamental beliefs of the legal system. For example, historical attempts to create a special science tribunal with legal status (of various kinds) have encountered stiff resistance and successful legal challenges (Golan 2004).

If such changes to the fundamental configuration of the intertextual network are unlikely, uptake of research genres will always remain optional (at least legally). But given this constraint, a multiple-genre-uptake analysis might suggest avenues where academic researchers trying to influence public policy can still find some ways of changing the level of expectations to make uptake more likely. The following section outlines two such factors.

FACTOR 1: UNEXPECTED UPTAKE IN THE CONTEXT OF THE EXPECTED

While it is true that the level of expected uptake—that is, expected *uptake enactment* (Dryer, chapter 3, this volume)—is partly determined by the existing intertextual network, it is still possible for a rhetor to modify the relative strength of each rhetorical expectation, which exists in Dryer's *uptake affordances*. In other words, a rhetor may weaken a strong rhetorical expectation or strengthen a weak rhetorical expectation, potentially changing the outcome of the uptake in unexpected ways. I will illustrate this process through issues that arose from the compensation amount for Sophonow's four-year wrongful incarceration and the resulting long-term psychological damage. Although the compensation payment may not seem like an issue of research knowledge, the compensation scheme was drafted by an academic law professor who testified at the preliminary hearing and introduced a variety of scholarly books and journal articles. Furthermore, this issue is particularly revealing about the process of reframing expectations.

From the outset, the government agreed that Sophonow was entitled to compensation for the government's miscarriage of justice and all the pain he had endured and still suffered. The Order-in-Council specified in its terms of reference that the compensation amount was to be determined by the public inquiry. Following this mandate, the commission determined $2.6 million was the appropriate amount (an unprecedented amount awarded to an individual on the basis of a public inquiry) and allocated specific amounts among the federal government, the provincial government, and the city of Winnipeg. Although the commissioner's recommendations were legally nonbinding, the

Table 9.1. Formal intertextual thread

Before the Cory Report			After the Cory Report		
Manitoba Government News Release	Order-in-Council	Preliminary Hearing	**Cory Report**	Lawsuits against province	Lawsuits against city

configuration of the intertextual network and the genre history of the public inquiries placed strong rhetorical expectations on these government bodies to accept the recommendations. As seen in Table 9.1 (see also Fig. 9.2), the official thread began with an apology by the attorney general, and the commission was legislatively invoked with specific references to the Manitoba Evidence Act. Given the legal nature of these intertextual threads and the government-initiated nature of the inquiry, we would expect the commission's recommendations to be taken up without problems.

As anticipated by this intertextual thread, the federal government and the provincial government complied with the recommendations. However, the city of Winnipeg refused to pay on the grounds that a compensation payment of this nature was usually the responsibility of the provincial government, not of the city; therefore, the city argued, the provincial government should bear the amount that had been assigned to the city. By saying so, the city was invoking an entirely different intertextual thread (a history of compensation payments), the expectation of which competed with that of the commission report. The city's invocation of this intertextual thread was motivated by the policy of the city's insurance company, which refused to pay the city for that reason.

In response to this refusal (and after some failed negotiations), Sophonow launched a lawsuit against the province to obtain the amount the city had refused to pay. In the end, the province agreed to pay the amount for the city and reimburse itself by launching a lawsuit against the city. On the surface, this alternative series of events may look the same: Sophonow was paid $2.6 million; the federal government, the province, and the city each paid the amounts recommended by the commission. However, this time the city's insurance policy covered the compensation amount because there was a precedent for a payment as a result of a lawsuit (though it was the province's lawsuit, not Sophonow's).

The struggle over the compensation payment illustrates three theoretical points. First, the existing intertextual network and expected uptake do not guarantee the actual uptake. In this case, the existing intertextual network and rhetorical expectations predisposed the three

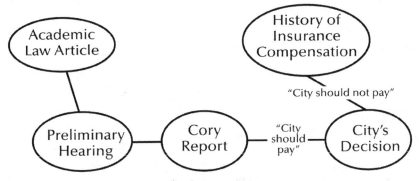

Figure 9.4. Competing intertextual threads on compensation payment.

government entities for unproblematic uptakes. But this uptake did not happen for the city.

Second, the intertextual network can be expanded like Bruno Latour's (2005) "actor-networks" or what Spinuzzi and Zachry (2000) call an "open system." The history of the insurance policy was not part of the intertextual network but was added (or "enlisted," to use Latour's term) when the city refused the payment and used it as a reason. But new texts don't merely extend the network; they shift the relative positions of every text in the entire network, changing the significance of each text. In short, adding a text to the intertextual network is not additive but transformative (see Spinuzzi 2008 for a similar argument developing Latour's framework in relation to RGS.)

This transformative aspect of the intertextual network is more clearly seen in Sophonow's lawsuit against the province and the province's lawsuit against the city. By this time, the commission report was no longer the direct force that prompted the city to pay. Rather, the shift in the entire network and the commission report's relative position in the intertextual network made it so that it now served as evidence for the claim (see Table 9.2). Because uptake affects not only the *uptake artifact* (Dryer, chapter 3, this volume) but also the source artifact through its shifted position in the network, uptake is, as Freadman (2002; 2012) argues, bidirectional and necessarily destabilizing. Similarly, the expert evidence for the commission report may have become less salient or perhaps dropped out of the discursive "memory" (Freadman 2002). But even then, it would be quite wrong to assume that the expert left no influence in the process. On the contrary, the expert's testimony was crucial in setting up the shape of the intertextual network at one point in the process so the influence would continue to live in the shape of

Table 9.2. Shift in the configuration of intertextual network

After the Cory Report	After the Lawsuits
Claim	**Claim**
(Cory Report)	(Court Ruling)
Evidence	**Evidence**
(Expert Evidence)	(Cory Report)
	(Expert Evidence)

the subsequent intertextual networks no matter how unpredictable the forms might be.

This potential of a discursive event to change the likelihood of uptake is the point I made with my proposal of the concept "intermediary genre" (Tachino 2012). An intermediary genre may facilitate the uptake by design (primary intermediary genre) or by accident (secondary intermediary genre). The archetypical example of the former is the press release, a genre with the explicit purpose of mediating corporate genres and news genres. An example of the latter is news genres when they (unintentionally) serve to facilitate the uptake of political speeches by late-night comedians who want to make fun of them.

Intermediary genres relate to our current discussion of uptake because intermediary genres may be parts of a routine uptake path. Routine uptake may preserve the local structure, but it may be blind to the structures beyond the immediate uptake. In other words, ordinary and routine uptakes may be setting up some highly unusual uptakes in the future. In the compensation example, the routine uptake was the payment as a result of the lawsuit, which had the effect of the unprecedented payment in response to the recommendation from a public inquiry. The lawsuit in this case served as the intermediary genre that facilitated the uptake of the commission report by the city.

Elsewhere in the Sophonow Inquiry, the preliminary hearing served as the intermediary genre to facilitate the uptake of research genres in experimental psychology (e.g., police-lineup procedures) by the commission report. The commission report, in turn, became an intermediary discursive event and facilitated further uptake by various Canadian legal and policy genres.

It is worth pointing out in this context that genres have multiple functions, the point Freadman (2012) makes when she argues that the abstract genre cannot a priori predict the function of a discursive event said to belong to that genre. In the above examples, the preliminary hearing was the primary intermediary genre, the primary function of which was to facilitate uptake. The primary purpose of the commission report, on the other hand, was to investigate the specific circumstances that led to the wrongful conviction of Thomas Sophonow and to prevent similar miscarriages of justice in the future. So its function as an intermediary genre was secondary. Yet the uptake, or "appropriation," to use Bakhtin's (1981) term, by the commission report changed the status of the relevant psychology knowledge in the eyes of the Canadian legal and policy communities, and the knowledge that had been available for twenty-five years in the psychology research communities was now legitimate Canadian legal knowledge. This change in the knowledge status was crucial in its further uptake by various policy genres across the country.

So far, the compensation issue has illustrated that the existing network is not deterministic and that the network is scalable. The combination of these two points leads to the third theoretical point. This framework allows us to accommodate Anthony Giddens's (1984) "duality of structure," the stabilizing force that constrains individual improvisations and the rhetorical agency that enables individuals to change the structure (a persistent problem in genre theory). One theoretical contribution of this multiple-uptake analysis of the intertextual network lies in its ability to explain how these contradictory forces exert their power and how individuals may leverage agency in the network. In the context of knowledge mobilization, researchers are not powerless bystanders whose work only serves as a post hoc justification for an already decided policy, as some political scientists suggest (Piven 2004). Researchers do wield some degree of agency—even though, as Freadman (2012) points out, this agency for change is not (only) about shaping one's own rhetoric to some immutable standard of excellence but about recognizing the existing intertextual network and other participants' positions and then "returning the serve" strategically. The analysis in this section has accounted for the stabilizing force in the form of the existing network and the rhetorical expectations, and some participants may want to preserve and work toward preserving the existing network. Agency for change, on the other hand, is accounted for by the scalability of the network, which allows the rhetor to add texts to the existing network. In this case, it was the city's enlisting of the insurance policy that afforded the city the ability to resist the rhetorical expectation and change the configuration of the intertextual network; it was Sophonow and the province's enlisting of legal precedents that further changed the configuration of the network and successfully challenged the city's rhetorical move.

FACTOR 2: RHETORICAL EXPECTATIONS
AND RHETORICAL RESISTANCES

The previous section discussed the role of rhetorical expectations and the scalability of the intertextual network only in relation to the diachronic, official legal intertextual links. This section, by comparison, examines both synchronic and diachronic intertextual threads of the public-inquiry genre. Through this analysis I will develop the notion of rhetorical expectation to include rhetorical resistance as well as its mediational capacity.

By the time the Sophonow Inquiry took place, Canada already had a long history of public inquiries, so all the participants and the public had some sense of what to expect from a public inquiry. In particular, the genre expectations from other similar public inquiries had important impacts on the Sophonow Inquiry, with significant consequences.

For example, the rules of practice and procedure for the Sophonow Inquiry were modeled after the one approved for the Krever Inquiry (1993) and the one adopted for use in the Morin Inquiry (1996).[6] This means that the existing intertextual thread of the genre exerted a stabilizing force on the Sophonow Inquiry by determining how the evidence was to be gathered and what would count as evidence.

Equally important are the previous public inquiries that made it common for experts to appear in the hearings. In particular, the Morin Inquiry made use of expert witnesses from several areas (e.g., jailhouse informants, contamination of forensic evidence) relevant to wrongful convictions. Thus, although it was still optional, there was nothing uncommon about inviting expert witnesses in the Sophonow Inquiry. If the formal intertextual thread did nothing to require or expect expert witnesses, it also did not prevent or discourage their appearance. The intertextual thread of the genre of public inquiries, on the other hand, made such appearances a common occurrence.

This observation points to another aspect of rhetorical expectation: rhetorical resistance, the force that compels a lapse in the discursive memory. In a mundane example, we routinely fail to take up junk mail (assuming we even pick it up). We recognize the genre, the intertextual network, and other participant's positions, and we exercise our agency and move on with our lives as if we hadn't been addressed at all. In knowledge mobilization, many research studies fail to be taken up for one reason or another, but in some policy genres, research does not play a role and is not expected to play a role at all. In those cases it takes greater efforts among the participants or more unusual circumstances for successful knowledge mobilization. In the Ryan case discussed by Freadman (2002), the norm in Australia at the time was for the state premier *not* to take up death sentences as executions. Despite this expectation from the intertextual thread and the unwillingness of other participants, the premier overcame the resistance with great effort—and had Ryan executed. The presence or absence of such rhetorical resistance is just as important as that of rhetorical expectation because they both contribute to the likelihood of uptake.

But the influence of genre in the Sophonow case was not limited to its lack of rhetorical resistance to expert testimony. At least in one case, the selection of experts was influenced by other inquiries. This was the case with Sheila Martin, the expert on compensation, whose opinion was also solicited in the Milgaard Inquiry (2004), which was taking place concurrently. Her status in the Milgaard Inquiry made her visible among commission counsels, and one of the counsels invited her to be consulted in the Sophonow Inquiry as well.

When thinking about factors that facilitate uptake, we should not forget the factors that impede uptake that could be present. Absence of such rhetorical resistance may be important in a particular uptake. To take up Dryer's (2008) call quoted in the beginning of this chapter, I would suggest that we identify factors that facilitate and impede uptake and analyze (or formulate) resistance strategies.

CONCLUSION

This chapter has extended Freadman's (2002) theory of uptake by framing it in a complex (both synchronically and diachronically) intertextual network with multiple intertextual threads. The proposed framework accounts for both the stabilizing forces of uptake (in the form of the existing intertextual network) and rhetorical agency (in the rhetor's ability to manipulate the strengths of the intertextual threads and add to the network to transform its configuration and influence its functioning and effects).

As I illustrate through the case study, a theory of uptake can suggest possibilities both for maintaining stability and for effecting changes in those most complex and consequential matters that public genres treat. We must pursue those possibilities to understand how rhetors disrupt (or preserve) existing intertextual networks and the routine uptakes of which public discourse is constituted.

Acknowledgments

I would like to thank the editors and Natasha Artemeva for their constructive comments on an earlier version of the chapter. A special thanks goes to David R. Russell for his helpful feedback and support throughout.

Notes

1. Perhaps as a result of this broad triggering condition, L. Graham Smith (1982) observes that public inquiry is "a favorite instrument of government in Canada" (565), and it is estimated that 1,200 to 1,600 major public inquiries took place since 1867 (Salter 1981).

2. Some public inquiries are policy inquiries, which are established for the explicit purpose of policy change. However, investigative inquiries (like the Sophonow Inquiry) still typically contain policy recommendations.

3. I have avoided the bidirectional arrow to preserve the temporal dimension of uptake.

4. *Citation* is defined here as any of the following: (1) when the text is accompanied by citation information, such as "(Inquiry, Vol. 10, page 986)"; (2) when the text is inside quotation marks; (3) when the text is in a blocked quote to indicate a direct quote (easily distinguishable from blocked quotes for other purposes); (4) when the text is accompanied by an expression of attribution (e.g., *state, testify, in his opinion, by her*). The Inquiry Report contained other textual and ideational borrowings, but these instances could not be identified reliably. Therefore, these unmarked instances were excluded for the purpose of counting.

5. There were 109 explicit citations in the transcript of the preliminary hearing. However, there were an additional 183 references to the oral testimonies themselves, many but not all of which took place in the preliminary hearing. Therefore, the actual number of references to the preliminary hearing is somewhere between 109 (26.41 percent) and 292 (70.71 percent). But even the most conservative estimate (26.41 percent) makes it clear that the preliminary hearing was the most important source.

6. The Krever Inquiry investigated the contamination of the Canadian blood bank with HIV and hepatitis C; the Morin Inquiry, like the Sophonow Inquiry, investigated another wrongful conviction case.

References

Artemeva, Natasha, and Aviva Freedman, eds. 2006. *Rhetorical Genre Studies and Beyond.* Winnipeg, MB: Inkshed.

Bakhtin, M. M. 1981. *The Dialogic Imagination: Four Essays.* Edited by M. Holquist, translated by C. Emerson and M. Holquist. Austin: University of Texas Press.

Bakhtin, M. M. 1986. "The Problem of Speech Genres." In *Speech Genres and Other Late Essays,* translated by Vernon W. McGee, 60–102. Austin: University of Texas Press.

Bawarshi, Anis, and Mary Jo Reiff. 2010. *Genre: An Introduction to History, Theory, Research, and Pedagogy.* West Lafayette, IN: Parlor.

Bazerman, Charles. 1994. "Systems of Genres and the Enactment of Social Intentions." In *Genre and the New Rhetoric,* edited by Aviva Freadman and Peter Medway, 79–101. London: Taylor & Francis.

Bitzer, Lloyd. 1968. "The Rhetorical Situation." *Philosophy & Rhetoric* 1:1–14.

Burke, Kenneth. 1945. *A Grammar of Motives.* New York: Prentice Hall.

Caplan, Nathan. 1979. "The Two-Communities Theory and Knowledge Utilization." *American Behavioral Scientist* 22 (3): 459–70. http://dx.doi.org/10.1177/00027642 7902200308.

Carden, Fred. 2005. "Making the Most of Research: The Influence of IDRC-supported Research on Policy Processes." Paper presented at the International Conference on African Economic Research Institutions and Policy Development: Opportunities and Challenges, Dakar, Senegal. http://www.academia.edu/2226660/Making_the_ most_of_research_The_influence_of_IDRC-supported_research_on_policy _processes.

Coe, Richard M., Lorelei Lingard, and Tatiana Teslenko, eds. 2002. *The Rhetoric and Ideology of Genre.* Cresskill, NJ: Hampton.

Court, Julius, Ingie Hovland, and John Young, eds. 2005. *Bringing Research and Policy in Development: Evidence and the Change Process.* Warwickshire, UK: ITDG. http://dx.doi .org/10.3362/9781780444598.

Crewe, Emma, and John Young. 2002. "Bringing Research and Policy: Context Evidence and Links." ODI Working Paper No. 173. http://www.odi.org.uk/publications /working_papers/WP173.pdf.

Devitt, Amy J. 1991. "Intertextuality in Tax Accounting: Generic, Referential, and Functional." In *Textual Dynamics of the Profession: Historical and Contemporary Studies of Writing in Professional Communities,* edited by Charles Bazerman and James Paradis, 335–57. Madison: University of Wisconsin Press.

Dryer, Dylan B. 2008. "Taking up Space: On Genre Systems as Geographies of the Possible." *JAC* 28:503–34.

Emmons, Kimberly K. 2009. "Uptake and the Biomedical Subject." In *Genre in a Changing World,* edited by Charles Bazerman, Adair Bonini, and Debora Figueiredo, 134–57. Fort Collins, CO: WAC Clearinghouse.

Figueroa, Maria Elena, D. Lawrence Kincaid, Manju Rani, and Gary Lewis. 2002. *Communication for Social Change: An Integrated Model for Measuring the Process and its Outcomes.* New York: Rockefeller Foundation. http://www.communicationforsocialcha nge.org/pdf/socialchange.pdf.

Freadman, Anne. 1994. "Anyone for Tennis?" In *Genre and the New Rhetoric,* edited by Aviva Freadman and Peter Medway, 43–66. London: Taylor & Francis.

Freadman, Anne. 2002. "Uptake." In *The Rhetoric and Ideology of Genre: Strategies for Stability and Change,* edited by Richard Coe, Lorelie Lingard, and Tatiana Teslenko, 39–53. Cresskill, NJ: Hampton.

Freadman, Anne. 2012. "The Traps and Trappings of Genre Theory." *Applied Linguistics* 33 (5): 544–63. http://dx.doi.org/10.1093/applin/ams050.

Freedman, Aviva, and Peter Medway, eds. 1994. *Genre and the New Rhetoric.* London: Taylor & Francis.

Giddens, Anthony. 1984. *The Constitution of Society: Outline of the Theory of Structure.* Berkeley: University of California Press.

Giltrow, Janet. 2002. "Meta-Genre." In *The Rhetoric and Ideology of Genre,* edited by Richard Coe, Lorelei Lingard, and Tatiana Teslenko, 187–205. Cresskill, NJ: Hampton.

Golan, Tal. 2004. *Laws of Men and Laws of Nature: The History of Scientific Expert Testimony in England and America.* Cambridge, MA: Harvard University Press.

Grindle, Merilee S., and John W. Thomas. 1991. *Public Choices and Policy Change: The Political Economy of Reform in Developing Countries.* Baltimore, MD: John Hopkins University Press.

Haas, Ernst B. 1991. *When Knowledge Is Power: Three Models of Change in International Organizations.* Berkeley: University of California Press.

Kingdon, John. 1984. *Agendas, Alternatives and Public Policies.* Boston: Little, Brown.

Latour, Bruno. 2005. *Reassembling the Social: An Introduction to Actor-Network-Theory.* Oxford: Oxford University Press.

Miller, Carolyn R. 1984. "Genre as Social Action." *Quarterly Journal of Speech* 70 (2): 151–67. http://dx.doi.org/10.1080/00335638409383686.

Orlikowski, Wanda J., and Joanne Yates. 1994. "The Structuring of Communicative Practices in Organization." *Administrative Science Quarterly* 39 (4): 541–74. http://dx.doi.org/10.2307/2393771.

Piven, Frances Fox. 2004. "The Politics of Policy Science." In *Problems and Method in the Study of Politics,* edited by Ian Shapiro, Rogers M. Smith, and Tarek Sasoud, 83–105. Cambridge: Cambridge University Press. http://dx.doi.org/10.1017/CBO97805 11492174.005.

Salter, Liora. 1981. *Public Inquiries in Canada.* Ottawa: Science Council of Canada.

Smith, L. Graham. 1982. "Mechanisms for Public Participation at a Normative Planning Level in Canada." *Canadian Public Policy* 8 (4): 561–72. http://dx.doi.org/10.2307/3549306.

Spinuzzi, Clay. 2003. *Tracing Genres through Organizations: A Sociocultural Approach to Information Design.* Cambridge: MIT Press.

Spinuzzi, Clay. 2008. *Network: Theorizing Knowledge Work in Telecommunications.* Cambridge: Cambridge University Press. http://dx.doi.org/10.1017/CBO9780511509605.

Spinuzzi, Clay, and Mark Zachry. 2000. "Genre Ecologies: An Open-System Approach to Understanding and Constructing Documentation." *ACM Journal of Computer Documentation* 24 (3): 169–81. http://dx.doi.org/10.1145/344599.344646.

Stone, Diane. 2001. "The 'Policy Research' Knowledge Elite and Global Policy Processes." In *Non-State Actors in World Politics,* edited by Daphné Josselin and William Wallace, 113–32. London: Macmillan.

Tachino, Tosh. 2008. "Academic Research and Public Policy: Rhetorical Lessons from the Sophonow Inquiry." PhD diss., Iowa State University, Ames.

Tachino, Tosh. 2010. "Genre, Ideology, and Knowledge in Academic Research and Public Policy." *Linguagem em (Dis)curso* 10 (3): 595–618. http://dx.doi.org/10.1590/S15 18-76322010000300008.

Tachino, Tosh. 2012. "Theorizing Uptake in Knowledge Mobilization: A Case for Intermediary Genre." *Written Communication* 29 (4): 455–76. http://dx.doi.org/10.1177/0741088312457908.

Weiss, Carol H. 1977. "Research for Policy's Sake: The Enlightenment Function of Social Research." *Policy Analysis* 3:531–47.

PART IV

Digital Public Genres

*Mediating Public Engagement and Expanding
Public Participation*

10
APPROPRIATING GENRE, "TAKING ACTION" AGAINST OBESITY
The Rhetorical Work of Digital Genre Systems in Public Discourse

Monica M. Brown

INTRODUCTION

In 2013, the American Medical Association (2013) (AMA) announced the decision to classify obesity as a disease rather than as a condition or risk factor for other diseases (e.g., type II diabetes, cardiovascular disease). In a widely cited press release, an AMA board member praised the new obesity policy as having the power to "change the way the community tackles this complex issue that affects approximately one in three Americans." Indeed, some commentators speculated that the policy change might motivate US doctors to be more proactive in addressing weight issues in their patients. The move to classify obesity as a disease, others reasoned, might also improve funding and insurance coverage for medical treatment. Opponents, however, argued that by declaring the condition a disease, the AMA medicalized obesity, expanding the number of people classified as diseased and narrowing care and treatment options.

The AMA's decision represents only a recent development in the ongoing debate about the status of obesity as a medical condition, an epidemiological trend, and a pressing public health concern. In recent years, myriad experts—among them physicians, public health experts, epidemiologists, and policymakers—have sought to define and influence attitudes toward the relationship between weight and health. In spite of persisting lack of agreement about pathology, obesity has within these debates frequently been characterized as an "epidemic" that must be monitored, contained, and guarded against. Often used to foster a sense of urgency, the metaphor of obesity as an epidemic has been described at length by a number of scholars. Of those scholars who write critically about obesity, many tend to regard the epidemic metaphor

DOI: 10.7330/9781607324430.c010

as central to the moral panic that surrounds obesity—increasingly, on a global level.[1] The epidemic metaphor is also seen as crucial to the framing of obesity as a matter of personal responsibility, a threat against which each and every one of us must take action.

A vital means through which various health agencies disseminate information about obesity amidst claims of a global epidemic is the web-based public health campaign. In addition to adopting many of the user-centered features of Web 2.0—for example, surveys, slide-shows, social media buttons and feeds, and interactive games—web-based campaigns often incorporate digitized versions of traditionally print-based public health genres such as posters and brochures. In his writing on the topic, Charles Bazerman defines the genre system as a "set of interrelated genres that interact with each other in particular settings" (Bazerman 1994, 97). Indeed, because web-based public health campaigns typically incorporate traditional, print-based public health genres into interactive websites aimed at inducing user engagement, these campaigns might be regarded as digital genre systems. This chapter extends the scholarship on obesity rhetoric by examining the effects of digital genre systems on public perceptions of obesity as well as on public engagement.

As I examine the rhetorical work of web-based obesity campaigns, I focus mainly on the problem of genre appropriation. According to Walter H. Beale (1987), genre appropriations resolve situations of rhetorical indeterminacy by using genre "as a 'vehicle' for the communication of uncharacteristic or unexpected fields of meaning" (49). In novels, for example, the appropriation of the epistolary form has long been a persuasive method of representing consciousness. Amidst uncertainty about the status of obesity, however, corporations have turned to genre appropriation as a strategy for manufacturing rhetorical ethos (credibility). That is, increasingly, private interests use the web-based public health campaign as a vehicle for shaping public perceptions and influencing public engagement in response to the issue of obesity. Specifically, I consider the implications of the appropriation of features of the US Centers for Disease Control and Prevention's (CDC's) web-based obesity campaign on The Weight of the Nation, a promotional website and public-private initiative of Home Box Office (HBO).

In this example, genre appropriation illustrates the centrality of form to digital genre systems. More important, an analysis of genre appropriation highlights the potential pitfalls of mediating public engagement via the web. Specifically, I hypothesize connections between genre appropriation and "slacktivism," the trend of performing online actions on behalf of an issue or cause that have little to no impact on its advancement. Slacktivists usually commit these token acts of support through social media—for example, by joining a Facebook group, liking a social media post, or signing an online petition. Recent studies have shown, however, that slacktivists tend to be less likely to support these same causes through direct action (e.g., giving, volunteering). Many critics have written off slacktivism as largely an effect of technological advancement, just one of the many ways we can now engage with one another online. Conversely, I propose that slacktivism might be examined quite productively from the perspective of genre theory, and I argue that genre theorists have much to offer to debates about the ethics of online public engagement.

MANUFACTURING ETHOS THROUGH GENRE APPROPRIATION

I define genre appropriation as the incorporation of rhetorical, discursive, and formal features of an established genre into situations in which these features bestow legitimacy on a communicative act. Although a change in situation usually indicates the production of a new genre, genre appropriation entails the effort to maintain the appearance that no such transformation has taken place. Corporations may, for instance, in producing appeals similar in form and function to web-based campaigns developed by federal health agencies, imply that they share the credibility and motivations of the public health establishment. Genre is thus a resource for manufacturing rhetorical ethos on the web.[2] Such an observation about the goals of genre appropriation aligns with Barbara Warnick's (2004) comments about how users perceive and assess what she calls "online ethos." In assessing a web source's authority or credibility, Warnick explains, users "tend to rely on appearances" rather than on "traditional models of credibility," and they do not "make credibility judgments in the way they say they do" (257). When surveyed, for example, web users ranked site authorship as indicative of a web source's credibility yet reported being guided more by formal features, or visual cues, in their assessments of the quality of the information provided therein.[3] Warnick's findings indicate that genre appropriation may be an important rhetorical strategy on the "authorless" space of the web, where traditional measures of credibility have been displaced by a different set of standards. Web users in the studies cited by Warnick, for example, frequently assessed website credibility on the basis not of authorship but of usability and quality of appearance, features that can quite easily be transported from one web source into another.

An early use of the term *appropriation* to describe this rhetorical strategy appears in Beale's "pragmatic theory" of rhetoric, which is concerned with *"what human beings do with discourse,* rather than with the linguistic or cognitive conditions that underlie the doing" (Beale 1987, 1; emphasis in original). What Beale terms "generic strategy" involves the appropriation of "the strategies and formal operations familiar to one set of purposes and circumstances for use with another set of purposes and circumstances" (49). A strategy used often in poetry and fiction, generic appropriation tends to be most advantageous, according to Beale, in situations of rhetorical indeterminacy in which the appropriated genre "specifies a form of modal stance and contact" that may otherwise be unavailable (51). Generic strategy thus tends to be adopted when the introduction of new media brings about a change of situation that poses challenges for the rhetor or writer. The web genre frequently asked questions, or FAQ, provides a relevant example. Developed in response to the introduction of the e-mail list, when network storage space tended to be costly, FAQs limit the flow of messages to a mailing list by anticipating and addressing possible user queries. To do so persuasively, FAQs appropriate the form of question and answer, a textual tradition that dates as far back as the thirteenth century and a genre of moral instruction (see, e.g., Wesselhoeft 2010). In adopting and adapting the genre of question and answer, FAQs supply site administrators tasked with enforcing propriety the "voice," or authority, to direct communicative exchanges on networked mailing lists. Perhaps because of its effectiveness in fulfilling this need, the FAQ web genre continues to play a role in the enforcement of netiquette, the social conventions that facilitate networked interactions.

FAQs persuasively demonstrate the appropriation of genre for practical purposes. In this example, an appropriation serves both to enforce authority and to accommodate technological constraints on the authorless space of the web. However, genre appropriation, particularly in the sense I describe—as a strategy for manufacturing rhetorical ethos—might more effectively be likened to "astroturfing." A metaphor for political acts undertaken mainly by corporate or private interests, astroturfing refers to any appeal fabricated to have the appearance of a grassroots response to a political and social issue. Jennifer Lee (*New York Times,* January 27, 2003) recounts the use by political organizations of web technology that sends preprogrammed letters to the editor on behalf of web users. Groups such as the Republican National Committee and Planned Parenthood have used social media and e-mail lists to circulate to users form letters intended to seem as if they had been written and submitted directly by concerned citizens rather than by lobby organizations. Astroturfing via digital media may make it easier for lay people to participate in political activism, as proponents have argued. Still, the strategy also frustrates those tasked with vetting the authenticity of these appeals and, further, raises concerns about transparency and accountability in online public debate. Even when they agree wholeheartedly with the sentiments expressed therein, the citizens who actually sign and submit these preformulated letters and circulate them to news outlets pose a challenge to perceptions of their sincerity. Organizations engage in astroturfing in order to give the impression of widespread public support for a cause and to advance a cause in the absence of the degree of public engagement such an aim typically requires. As with genre appropriation, astroturfing works on perceptions of ethos, remediating the web user as activist and the corporation as advocacy organization.

Just as public commentators have been critical of astroturfing, genre scholars have been more circumspect about the motives behind certain kinds of genre appropriation. Perhaps the most relevant example is Vijay Bhatia's (2004) discussion of the appropriation of generic "resources [that] may be lexico-grammatical, rhetorical, discoursal or other generic conventions" (87; see also chapter 1, this volume). Bhatia is particularly critical of the use of genre appropriation to incorporate promotional strategies into otherwise nonpromotional genres, which compromises the integrity of the latter. "Although appropriation of generic resources is often a natural socio-rhetorical option available to most genre writers," Bhatia concludes, "it will be inappropriate to assume that such appropriations are always legitimate. They often have a potential to create conflicts in genre construction and interpretation" (95). Concern about the legitimacy of genre appropriation—and, in particular, with the ability of web users to *interpret* the authority, motives, and aims of appropriations—has similarly been a feature of debate about "public health 2.0."[4] Some critics argue, for example, that corporate health sites, particularly those developed to approximate the form and functions of web campaigns sanctioned by federal and government agencies, undermine trust in public health authority.

In an analysis of a personal blog created and maintained by Walmart, Cornelius Puschmann (2009) also echoes concerns about genre appropriation for corporate purposes. For Puschmann, genre appropriation, or "(ab)usability," is similarly a means of manufacturing ethos that affects the ability of audiences to interpret credibility and motive. As Puschmann demonstrates, the *Life at Wal-Mart* blog incorporates features of the personal blog into its corporate blog in order to cloak a public-relations exercise in the prosocial ethos of the blog genre. A persuasive example is the company's uses of categories—a technical, or formal feature of personal blogs—not to classify entries but rather to shape perceptions of Walmart's contributions to community issues such as healthcare. In other words, the strategic appropriation of a formal feature of an established web genre potentially raises the company's profile significantly in terms of its community involvement.

Interestingly, Puschmann posits "(ab)usability as an indicator of genre," arguing that, in the dynamic space of the web, genre appropriations can be an indicator of "genre salience." That is, within a web-based instance of genre appropriation, "the exploiter must assume that his audience will recognize the genre he is imitating based on formal criteria if he wants his manipulation to succeed" (Puschmann 2009, 51). In his comments on form, Puschmann responds to genre theorist Amy Devitt's observation that "in action-based theories of genre . . . form combines with substance to create meaningful generic action" (2009, 28). Especially on the web, formal features lead to "calculable assumptions on the part of the reader regarding the communicative goals and authorship of a text," which "can be exploited by genre users with covert goals" (Puschmann 2009, 50–51). Puschmann's critique of corporate appropriations as an "abuse" or "exploitation" of genre sets an important precedent for my own examination of the effects of genre appropriation in the context of obesity debates. Just as Puschmann reveals Walmart's use of the blog genre to elevate its brand, I show how corporations have adapted the perceived communicative goals of the web-based public health campaign. And whereas Puschmann details the use of genre appropriation to advance private interests, I reveal its use to redefine what it means to take action in response to a public health issue of ongoing debate.

WEB-MEDIATED "STRATEGIES TO COMBAT OBESITY"

Prior to my own examination of genre appropriation, which appears in the section that follows, in this section I introduce some of the rhetorical work of CDC.gov/obesity. A prominent web-based obesity campaign, this site exemplifies many of the features—rhetorical, discursive, visual, and formal—that have served as vehicles for redirecting, and redefining, public engagement in response to obesity.[5] Familiarity with some of these features, then, is necessary to understand the appropriation of this digital genre system by a major corporation. CDC.gov/obesity comprises the web-based component of the agency's broader campaign to encourage members of the inarguably diverse US public to take "take action" against obesity. As noted on the campaign's main page, this effort to address obesity is headed by the CDC's Division of Nutrition, Physical Activity, and Obesity (DNPAO). Users can gain access to the CDC's obesity campaign via CDC.gov, the hub of the agency's web portal, via a hyperlink index of health topics, listed alphabetically, that appears at the top of every page on the site. To put into perspective the website's significance as a source of health information—and, in particular, as the host of a web-based obesity campaign—the CDC reported over 650 million page views in 2012, a number that has steadily risen from 200 million page views in 2004.[6]

Although as of January 2013 the most common internal search term used to navigate the site was *flu*, the most popular topics included "BMI: Child and Teen Calculator" and "BMI: Adult BMI Calculator," both of which have been hyperlinked to CDC.gov/obesity.[7] The pages that compose CDC.gov tend to be informational, although it is important to note that not every health topic indexed on the site merits an interactive web campaign composed of multiple, interacting genres and opportunities for user engagement. For example, while CDC.gov/obesity spans multiple hyperlinked and cross-referenced pages, on which textual information has been segmented for ease of usability, most topics have been limited to the span of a single, static informational page. Further, while some health topics, such as "Kawasaki Syndrome," include little to no room for user engagement or interaction, CDC.gov/obesity incorporates multiple instances of web 2.0 technology, such as a Twitter feed and online BMI calculator.

The incorporation of multiple, interrelated genres into the CDC's obesity campaign—in contrast to static information pages accorded to other topics—forms the basis for my characterization of the web-based public health campaign as a digital genre system. Many of the technical and presentational features of CDC.gov/obesity signal to users that the topic comprises the subject of a coordinated effort to address the topic and instruct and inform a broad public audience on a range of issues related to obesity. Not only has the main page's textual information been segmented into boxes labeled primarily with instructional headings (e.g., "Strategies to Combat Obesity," "Learn About Obesity"), but a news slider also provides links to current news about the topic. (As of December 2013, one of the links on the news slider advertises the site for the public-private initiative, The Weight of the Nation.) These aspects of the web campaign distinguish "overweight and obesity," in scope and severity, from other health topics addressed on CDC.gov and structure the campaign around the set of standards that, according to Warnick (2004), users associate with online ethos—in particular, ease of navigation and quality of appearance. Of course, CDC.gov/obesity is not entirely distinct from every other topic addressed on the site. Nevertheless, in terms of technical and presentational features, the agency's obesity campaign shares more in common with other, more comprehensive CDC campaigns, such as CDC.gov/flu. In contrast to static information pages, these more comprehensive campaigns incorporate multiple genres—for example, information videos, fact sheets, posters, and brochures—both to emphasize obesity's urgency and complexity and to reach a potentially broader audience. In other words, in web-based public health campaigns, appearances alone may thus shape users' perceptions of the scope, severity, and seriousness of a public health issue.

On CDC.gov/obesity, certain discursive features, such as pronoun use, also work to specify an intended audience and bolster user identification with campaign aims. For example, a series of hyperlinks on the main page of the web campaign uses the first-person-singular pronoun to appeal to users as individual citizens. These links, which direct individual users to different pages of the campaign, imply multiple, overlapping views of obesity: as a personal issue ("For Me"), a family concern ("For My Family"), and a community crisis ("For My Community"). On the pages to which these hyperlinks redirect users, the mode of address switches. On the pages "Strategies to Take Action for Me" and "Strategies to Take Action For My Community," for example, the user is addressed in the second person. In sentences such as "Learn what you can do in your community to make the healthy choice the easy choice," the pronoun *you* refers to a generic third person, as in *one*. Conversely, on the page "Strategies to Take Action for My Family," most pronouns have been replaced by nominal references to "parents" and "children." Shifts in mode of address—in some instances, from individual ("me") to member of a collective (either "you" or "parents")—appear to parallel the aims of the CDC's web-based obesity campaign. Such aims include, perhaps most saliently, the recruitment of US citizens as activists in the campaign against obesity.

Shifts in address also reflect broader tensions about the status of obesity. Most noticeable is the tension between obesity as at once a possible medical condition, to be addressed at a personal level, and an epidemic, to be forestalled through major societal change. At a time of disagreement among experts about the pathology of obesity, such shifts in pronoun use, however, potentially do meaningful rhetorical work as they reflect the CDC's targeting (in the first person) of the individual as potentially a body at risk of obesity. At the same time, the agency can appeal to users (in the second person) as agents of change and members of a broader social movement. It is interesting to note that the main page of the obesity campaign includes a clarification of the CDC's responsibility for the "obesity epidemic," which explains that the "CDC's Division of Nutrition, Physical Activity, and Obesity (DNPAO) is working to implement policy and environmental strategies to make healthy eating and active living accessible and affordable to everyone." A departure from other CDC web campaigns, many of which foreground the individual, this comment appears to anticipate objections to the agency's injunctions to web users to assume personal responsibility for obesity.

Finally, visual features stress the complexity of obesity by positioning this issue as the subject of ongoing epidemiological investigation. The most prominent visual cue is the image of the US map, a visual metaphor both for epidemiological investigation and, more specifically, for the "obesity epidemic."[8] On the main page, the map appears twice, once on "Data and Statistics" as a signifier of the "epidemic" and of the professional expertise that has been recruited to track trends in weight size. The map also appears in "State and Community Programs," a box that links visitors to information about CDC-funded programs that prevent obesity. Here, the map features images of citizens engaged in activities of "civic fitness"—for example, parents embracing children, people playing sports, families walking together, and individuals engaged in other forms of "healthy living," such as eating together. Increasingly a feature of web-based public health campaigns, epidemiological maps and real-time surveillance systems satisfy the imperative of public health 2.0 to incorporate into public health campaigns dynamic, web 2.0 content.

On the surface, mapping tools and other highly visual features appear primarily to be informational: as Michael Hardey (2008) explains, maps give users the ability to track epidemics in real time and, perhaps, to make decisions about their health on the basis of map data. Yet, when incorporated into web-based public health campaigns, epidemiological maps and surveillance systems have rhetorical effects, among them the corroboration of claims of an "epidemic" of obesity. Indeed, in the context of international law, Christine Leuenberger (2013) argues that "with the democratization of mapping practices"—a key feature of public health 2.0, according to Hardey (2008)—"individuals, organizations, and governments are increasingly using maps in order to put forth certain social and political claims" (73). Maps posted to CDC.gov/obesity serve as a tool not to display the spread of the condition but instead to mediate perceptions of the scope and scale of obesity.

The incorporation of interactive web genres, from real-time epidemiological surveillance maps to online quizzes, appears to bolster the goal of the web-based public health campaign, which is public engagement. After all, through interactive web genres, federal health agencies can elicit real-time engagement at the same time as they provide information, thus modeling what it might look like to take action against obesity. An important element of the rhetorical work of the web-based public health campaign, interactivity also features prominently in efforts to reshape the very meaning of social action in favor of private interests. These efforts I view as a kind of genre appropriation that derives its persuasive force from the digital genre system.

THE WEIGHT OF THE NATION: TAKING ACTION BY CONSUMING MEDIA

As I delve into an examination of The Weight of the Nation as an instance of genre appropriation, I want to acknowledge that this particular campaign has received endorsement from US federal health authorities: The Weight of the Nation is the result of a partnership between the CDC and Home Box Office (HBO), which is owned by American multinational media corporation Time Warner. This promotional campaign is also backed by the Institute of Medicine and the National Institutes of Health.[9] Thus, in contrast to corporate-sponsored obesity campaigns such as the Pfizer-sponsored Campaign to End Obesity, The Weight of the Nation has the support of the federal agencies responsible for issues of health and medicine.[10] HBO's campaign might best be described as a public-private initiative or public-private partnership, interchangeble terms for an ongoing collaboration between government agencies and for-profit enterprises.

Already a common feature of the US healthcare system, which is composed of public and private interests, the public-private initiative has in recent decades been identified as a vehicle (quite like public health 2.0) for expanding the reach of the public health establishment. As the world's second-largest media conglomerate, Time Warner has a powerful incentive to intervene in the discourses of empowerment and civic fitness that define public health in ways that advance the goals of marketing media. In keeping with Bhatia's (2004) observations, the goal of genre appropriation on The Weight of the Nation is to redirect the mostly nonpromotional aims of CDC.gov/obesity toward promotional ends.

Given that the campaign emerges out of a public-private initiative, the focus of The Weight of the Nation is not obesity, per se. Instead, the campaign advertises the television documentary series for which the campaign is named and which airs on HBO, although episodes and series trailers can also be viewed online. Further, CDC.gov/obesity, the web campaign most closely associated with The Weight of the Nation, primarily highlights the CDC's efforts "to make healthy eating and active living accessible and affordable for everyone" and encourages similar actions among US citizens. Conversely, although it appears to do the same, The Weight of the Nation encourages engagement mainly with traditional and social media in the form of the documentary series and the web campaign itself. In promoting the series *The Weight of the Nation*, the site includes many of the same features used on CDC.gov/obesity to engage users as citizens and activists in the context of an obesity epidemic. For example, adapting the visual rhetoric of the typical web-based public health campaign, the most prominent feature of the web campaign's main page is a US map emblazoned with the title "The Weight of the Nation."

Above the campaign's ostensible logo appears the slogan, "To win, we have to lose," and beneath the map, the phrase "Confronting America's obesity epidemic." The metaphoric shift from "combat" on CDC.gov/obesity to "confront" is significant, given that, as a promotional endeavor, The Weight of the Nation advances a view of media consumption—and social media participation—as means of taking action against obesity. Despite HBO's alignment with federal health agencies, then, The Weight of the Nation, in its emphasis on media consumption as an expression of civic fitness, clearly redefines social action along the lines of slacktivism. Indeed, many of the site's appropriations of the map, as the visual metaphor both of the "obesity epidemic" and of coordinated social action, incorporate web 2.0 features that permit web users to undertake token acts of support for the cause. For example, web users can take a Pledge for Progress on Facebook or Twitter and then have their pledge plotted on an interactive US map. The effect is an interactive display of web users' commitment to a social cause—and, in turn, a show of support for online and social media as viable arenas for engagement and activism.

Although sleeker in appearance than its government-funded counterpart, The Weight of the Nation also appropriates many of the technical and presentational features used on CDC.gov/obesity to engage users as citizens and activists in a campaign against obesity. Yet these appropriations also constrain perceptions of what it means to take action against obesity. For example, the campaign logo appears at first glance to be a news slider not unlike the one that appears on the main page of CDC.gov/obesity, but in fact it only links web users to the campaign's two main pages, Watch the Films and Take Action. Another slider displays "facts" related to issues of weight, body size, nutrition, and physical activity—for example, "The obese workforce costs American business an estimated $73.1 billion per year" and "Children consume more than 7.5 hours of media a day, 7 days a week." Visual cues (e.g., a red arrow labeled *fact*; a shaded, rectangular box) give this slider prominence on the page, but the slider, and the content it displays, may be regarded as an attempt to exploit the association between news sliders and the informational aim of most web-based public health campaigns. Puschmann observes a similar strategy on *Life at Wal-Mart*, which appropriates the categories and tags associated with personal blogs in order to "harvest the positive associations of the blog prototype" (Puschmann 2009, 62). However, in many instances, these elements of The Weight of the Nation do not significantly expand user navigation but instead limit engagement with the issue of obesity either to viewing trailers and episodes of *The Weight of the Nation* or to visiting the campaign's social media pages.

Further, the visual display of "facts" on The Weight of the Nation exploits the informational aim of the web-based public health campaign by encouraging web users as slacktivists who can, for example, share each fact via social media with the mere click of a button. It is not that social media is absent from CDC.gov/obesity but rather that this aspect of The Weight of the Nation has been made much more prominent on the promotional campaign and streamlined for ease of use. According to Warnick's (2004) theory of online ethos, the usability of features of The Weight of the Nation has implications for the perceived credibility of information presented on the site. Ease of information sharing on The Weight of the Nation enhances HBO's profile as an authority on the "obesity epidemic," as more clicks mean more coverage of the corporation's efforts to advance a social cause.

The navigational hyperlinks that follow the "facts" slider—which, in pairing text and image, approximate the visual rhetoric of the links on CDC.gov/obesity—also direct attention not to obesity but to media consumption as a form of public engagement. Two of four links invite users to learn about the series ("About the project") and screen it in their communities ("Host a screening"), while two other links connect users to Facebook applications ("apps") on which they can show their support for The Weight of the Nation. Frequently, these hyperlinks mimic the links that appear on CDC.gov/obesity, which provide users with information on how to "take action" against obesity. On The Weight of the Nation, however, the links constrain the action taken to the space of the web, on which "confronting" obesity entails watching and promoting the documentary series and displaying support for the campaign via social media. Kirk Kristofferson, Kathryn White, and John Peloza call these actions "token support," explaining that token acts of support "allow consumers to affiliate with a cause in ways that show their support to themselves or others, with little associated effort or cost" (Kristofferson, White, and Peloza 2014, 1150). While HBO has clearly been engaged as a partner in this effort to expand the reach of public health, the reality, according to Kristofferson, White, and Peloza (2014), is that individuals who display token support for a cause tend to be less likely to make more tangible contributions. By contributing to the sense that, in addressing obesity online, HBO shares the motivations of the CDC, presentational and technical features of The Weight of the Nation contribute significantly to the campaign's slacktivist slant.

In contrast to the CDC.gov/obesity site, on which certain discursive features such as pronouns afford a means of interpellating users as citizens and activists, the main page of The Weight of the Nation uses relatively few pronominal references. The most prominent pronominal address appears in the campaign slogan "To Win, *We* Have to Lose" (emphasis added). A rhetorical move, the invocation of a collective *we* can be regarded as not merely an effort to interpellate web users as members of the audience for The Weight of the Nation but also an attempt to signify HBO's involvement in the "obesity epidemic" as a public health issue and social cause. Otherwise, a subject is addressed on The Weight of the Nation mainly through hyperlinked headings in which that subject is issued an imperative, as in Watch, Learn, and Take Action. The use of imperatives engages the web user as active citizen while maintaining the impression of both a flexible subject and an equally open-ended sense of what it means to "take action" against obesity. Indeed, according to one of the three imperatives issued on The Weight of the Nation, the web user can mobilize against obesity, both as an epidemic and as a medical condition, by *watching* HBO documentary films. So important is this measure that the main page contains two such links—at the top of the page and another beneath the site's news slider and corporate logo. In both instances, the imperative *watch* is juxtaposed with *take action*. The character of web interactivity may influence how users perceive these imperatives, as clicking either link will accomplish the very same end— users will navigate to another page of the site. Interactive symmetry may lend to the impression of some degree of equality between *watch* and *take action* as rhetorical imperatives.

Ellipsis—especially of personal pronouns—also leaves open to interpretation the public health subject constituted on The Weight of the Nation. The *you* invoked in HBO's campaign is broader and, as a result, not as stable as the subject of CDC.gov/obesity, on which shifts in mode of address lend nuance to subjectivity and, further, acknowledge contested definitions of obesity (i.e., as disease, as "epidemic," as social cause). Information design enhances the impression of a flattened subject. Every page of the CDC's site is framed on all sides by formal features (e.g., the CDC logo, Contact Us information) that make it easier for users to engage with the site on the basis of authorship, which is typical of web campaigns sanctioned by government agencies. In contrast, The Weight of the Nation makes far fewer gestures at authorship—for example, in the campaign banner, which features a relatively small, white HBO logo against a black backdrop. The Weight of the Nation has been designed to foreground user engagement with the product of this public-private partnership, the documentary series, and with social media interactions instead of with the site author. Although on The Weight of the Nation, HBO appropriates many of the features of the web-based public health campaign, some of these features have been adapted in ways that elide the corporation's responsibility for the issue at hand.

Clicking the site link to Take Action takes users to a page where, in order to proceed, they must log into their Facebook account. By doing so, users will be able to "see how our nation's problem impacts you and exactly what you can do about it." In many such instances on The Weight of the Nation, the informational aim of the web-based public health campaign is recruited in support of the goals of increasing media consumption and social media interaction. The use of form to assert a relationship between individual citizen and public health agency—particularly in the framing of web campaigns—has largely been displaced by the incorporation of formal features that instead individuate users on the basis of online presence.

Users may quickly realize that, in order to gain more access to information about obesity via The Weight of the Nation, they must either participate in social media or exchange campaign information for information about themselves. For example, users who cannot log into social media can click Not a Facebook user? and fill out a survey that asks questions about age, gender, and parental and relationship status. They must also select some very broad topics "within the obesity epidemic" of interest to them (e.g., Physical Activity; Media, TV, and Technology). Users may be unsure of the purpose of the survey, which only purports to "Make It Relevant For You." Presumably, this means that by answering more questions, users will be given information about the so-called obesity epidemic that has been tailored to their own interests and concerns. Yet having been given the impression that participation in the site constitutes taking action against obesity—and this is, in fact, the goal of this appropriation of genre—users may be even likelier to engage in information exchange. Token support for a cause thus *does* often come at a cost to users, but that cost may be obfuscated by the effort that goes into giving appropriations of the web-based public health campaign the appearance of credibility. That effort depends, to an extent, on the stability of formal, rhetorical, and discursive features of the web-based public health campaign. In other words, as Puschmann argues, the salience of this digital genre is "indicated by genre *abusability*" (Puschmann 2009, 51, emphasis in original), and genre abusability, in turn, has implications for the direction of public engagement via the web.

CONCLUSION: GENRE APPROPRIATION, SLACKTIVISM, AND TOKEN SUPPORT IN THE ERA OF PUBLIC HEALTH 2.0

In December 2013, Facebook announced the addition of a new feature to the site, a Donate button, which would allow users to give directly to various causes that maintain a presence on the social network rather than to simply Like their pages. Although many credited the technical change as a move in the right direction, the addition of the "Donate" button was also an acknowledgment that online and social media had radically altered the character of public engagement in the twenty-first century. In public debates, web 2.0 technology has been seen as the primary vehicle through which slacktivism takes hold. Yet the analysis presented here suggests that slacktivism also results from much more deliberate efforts to manufacture ethos, efforts undertaken to harness public engagement online and redirect this activity in certain ways.

In this chapter I have argued that the appropriation of features of an emerging digital genre system, the web-based public health campaign, lends private interest the authority to direct public engagement and social activism in the context of the "obesity epidemic." The Weight of the Nation has also been a platform for promoting token support as a legitimate strategy for "confronting America's obesity epidemic," positioning HBO as a stakeholder in public health and at the same time redefining media consumption as an expression of public engagement and perhaps even a form of social agency. To have influenced what it means to take action against obesity in this way potentially generates more resources, and more revenue, for media corporations such as Time Warner's HBO. Recent studies suggest, however, that such a redefinition of activism is unlikely to yield any direct benefits for federal health agencies, despite the fact that The Weight of the Nation emerges directly out of a public-private partnership. The primary result of this strategy is an engrossing web campaign that in fact rivals—and perhaps even undermines—the efforts of the CDC to cultivate civic fitness.

In advancing a view of public-private and corporate-sponsored web campaigns as, in effect, appropriations of genre, my goal is mainly to suggest that, methodologically speaking, genre theorists have much to offer to debates about the ethics of public engagement via the web. Public debates about slacktivism have tended to portray this trend in reductionist terms as a consequence of technological determinism, according to which technical features inherent to web and social media simply drive people to engage in only token rather than meaningful acts of support on behalf of important social causes. Period. Without denying the impact of web design on digitally mediated public engagement, I believe more could be said about the influence of genre appropriation on public engagement—that is, of the subversion of discursive, rhetorical, and formal features of emerging digital genre systems such as web-based public health campaigns. My study indicates that, in the effort to direct public engagement via the web, genre appropriation serves as an important rhetorical strategy. On the one hand, this strategy potentially resolves issues of indeterminacy that may arise from the transition of public engagement to the web. On the other hand, genre appropriation may also secure legitimacy for organizations, such as corporations, that seek to harness that engagement to serve certain purposes. Of the many criticisms that might be leveled at public-private partnerships such as The Weight of the Nation, perhaps the most important is that, by approximating the appearance of authority on issues of public health, corporations gain the license not simply to dictate what it means to take action but also, increasingly, to alter what it means to be healthy. To do so through appropriation of the voice of another is to seek to obscure that influence in ways that come at the expense of the web's credibility as a site of public engagement.

Notes

1. In *Folk Devils and Moral Panics*, sociologist Stanley Cohen describes a moral panic as a "condition, episode, person or group of persons [that] emerges to become defined as a threat to societal values and interests" (Cohen 2011, 1). Scholars who critique obesity as a moral panic include Natalie Boero (2012), Paul Campos, et al. (2006), and Kathleen LeBesco (2010).

2. By characterizing genre appropriation as a strategy for manufacturing ethos, I imply parallels between this approach and manufactured controversy, a strategy for creating public confusion, typically about issues of health, science, and technology. See, for example, Leah Ceccarelli (2011) for a discussion of manufactured science controversies.

3. Warnick (2004) derives these findings from a meta-analysis of the results of three separate studies of how users assess credibility on the web, which were conducted between 2000 and 2002.

4. While the term has been defined variously, here I invoke *public health 2.0* as referring to the use of web 2.0 technology in health education and promotion, such as dynamic and user-generated content and social media.

5. My analysis discusses the CDC's website as it appeared between 2013 and 2015. Since then, some of the features I discuss have been modified, in some cases to lessen the emphasis on personal responsibility.

6. During the 2009 H1N1 influenza pandemic, CDC.gov witnessed a sharp increase in user activity. That year, the site hosted eight hundred million page views. In the years since, the number of page views has steadily climbed and appears poised to hit H1N1 levels by 2014.

7. The CDC provides updated information about site use at CDC.gov/metrics.

8. The visual metaphor of the map also has political entailments that may have implications for user impressions of both the CDC's obesity campaign and, more generally, the status of obesity as a public health concern. During the 2012 US presidential elections, for example, the shaded electoral map became a metaphor for a nation divided. Epidemiological maps used in obesity campaigns and their corporate appropriations delineate trends in weight and body size according to geographic location—but also, in keeping with the rhetoric of the electoral map, imply the need for a coordinated effort to address these trends.

9. The initiative boasts two additional partners: Kaiser Permanente, a nonprofit healthcare consortium, and the Michael and Susan Dell Foundation, a nonprofit foundation.

10. HBO nevertheless indicates on The Weight of the Nation that the "content of this site, and related materials, are presented exclusively by HBO, which has sole editorial responsibility for the content of The Weight of the Nation®. The content does not reflect the official position of the Institute of Medicine, Centers for Disease Control and Prevention, National Institutes of Health, Kaiser Permanente, and the Michael & Susan Dell Foundation ('the partners'), their agencies or assigns." The fine print on The Weight of the Nation may be the only indication web users get that the campaign's contents have not been fully sanctioned by participating federal health authorities.

References

American Medical Association. 2013. "AMA Adopts New Policies on Second Day of Voting at Annual Meeting." http://www.ama-assn.org/ama/pub/news/news/2013/2013-06-18-new-ama-policies-annual-meeting.page.

Bazerman, Charles. 1994. "Systems of Genres and the Enactment of Social Intentions." In *Genre and the New Rhetoric*, edited by Aviva Freadman and Peter Medway, 79–101. London: Taylor & Francis.

Beale, Walter H. 1987. *A Pragmatic Theory of Rhetoric.* Carbondale: Southern Illinois University Press.

Bhatia, Vijay K. 2004. *Worlds of Written Discourse: A Genre-Based View.* London: Continuum.

Boero, Natalie. 2012. *Killer Fat: Media, Medicine, and Morals in the American "Obesity Epidemic."* New Brunswick, NJ: Rutgers University Press.

Campos, Paul, Abigail Saguy, Paul Ernsberger, Eric Oliver, and Glenn Gaesser. 2006. "The Epidemiology of Overweight and Obesity: Public Health Crisis or Moral Panic?" *International Journal of Epidemiology* 35 (1): 55–60. http://dx.doi.org/10.1093/ije /dyi254.

Ceccarelli, Leah. 2011. "Manufactured Scientific Controversy: Science, Rhetoric, and Public Debate." *Rhetoric & Public Affairs* 14 (2): 195–228. http://dx.doi.org/10.1353 /rap.2010.0222.

Cohen, Stanley. (1972) 2011. *Folk Devils and Moral Panics.* London: Routledge Classics.

Devitt, Amy. 2009. "Re-fusing Form in Genre Study." In *Genres in the Internet*, edited by Janet Giltrow and Dieter Stein, 27–48. Amsterdam: John Benjamins. http://dx.doi .org/10.1075/pbns.188.02dev.

Hardey, Michael. 2008. "Public Health and Web 2.0." *Journal of the Royal Society for the Promotion of Health* 128 (4): 181–89. http://dx.doi.org/10.1177/1466424008092228.

Kristofferson, Kirk, Katherine White, and John Peloza. 2014. "The Nature of Slacktivism: How the Social Observability of an Initial Act of Token Support Affects Subsequent Prosocial Action." *Journal of Consumer Research* 40 (6): 1149–66. http://dx.doi.org /10.1086/674137.

LeBesco, Kathleen. 2010. "Fat Panic and the New Morality." In *Against Health: How Health Became the New Morality*, edited by Anna Kirkland and Jonathan Metzl, 72–83. New York: New York University Press.

Leuenberger, Christine. 2013. "The Rhetoric of Maps: International Law as a Discursive Tool in Visual Arguments." *Law & Ethics of Human Rights* 7 (1): 73–107. http:// dx.doi.org/10.1515/lehr-2013-0002.

Puschmann, Cornelius. 2009. "Lies at Wal-Mart: Style and the Subversion of Genre in the *Life at Wal-Mart* Blog." In *Genres in the Internet*, edited by Janet Giltrow and Dieter Stein, 49–84. Amsterdam: John Benjamins. http://dx.doi.org/10.1075 /pbns.188.03pus.

Warnick, Barbara. 2004. "Online Ethos: Source Credibility in an 'Authorless' Environment." *American Behavioral Scientist* 48 (2): 256–65. http://dx.doi.org /10.1177/0002764204267273.

Wesselhoeft, Kirsten. 2010. "Making Muslim Minds: Question and Answer as a Genre of Moral Reasoning in an Urban French Mosque." *Journal of the American Academy of Religion* 78 (3): 790–823. http://dx.doi.org/10.1093/jaarel/lfq051.

11

EXIGENCIES, ECOLOGIES, AND INTERNET STREET SCIENCE
Genre Emergence in the Context of Fukushima Radiation-Risk Discourse

Jaclyn Rea and Michelle Riedlinger

In March 2011, a nuclear facility in Fukushima, Japan, was hit by an earthquake-induced tsunami, causing damage to three of the plant's nuclear reactors. The Fukushima nuclear incident was the most serious nuclear incident since Chenobyl in 1986 and a concern for Canadians who watched videos of "radiation plumes," carried by prevailing winds, reach them on the west coast of Canada. In late 2011 and early 2012, Health Canada and the Canadian Nuclear Safety Commission (CNSC) ordered reviews of their agencies' public communication responses to the Fukushima nuclear incident (Health Canada 2011; Knox, Patry, and Wright 2012). The reviewers found that government communication efforts relied on communication via traditional mainstream news media rather than new media. The reviewers also indicated that these agencies were not doing enough to coordinate the public release of radiation-level measurements or to engage the public in radiation-risk education when the opportunity presented itself (Knox, Patry, and Wright 2012).

Prompted by the findings of these reports, we conducted an examination of the Canadian Internet-based discourses that informed public discussions about the risks of radiation from the Fukushima nuclear incident (Rea and Riedlinger 2012; Riedlinger and Rea 2015). As part of this study, we identified a number of conditions that led to public knowledge-making activities, that is, the public's independent assessment and communication of radiation risk. These conditions included a lack of publicly interpretable data produced by credible research sources in the context of government and scientific reassurances that there were no radiation risks, a history of government deception or misinformation on similar issues, and the ability of some members of the public to independently create and distribute their own radiation-risk

DOI: 10.7330/9781607324430.c011

assessment information. This last condition became a fascination for us because, as we traced evidence of the public's active engagement in risk assessment, we stumbled upon what appeared to us to be a rather odd little genre: the YouTube Geiger-counter video. Originating in Tokyo and around the Fukushima precinct within the first few weeks after the Fukushima nuclear accident and posted on YouTube by members of the public, these videos quickly spread on the Internet. They are striking in their dry, dull regularity. Yet despite their dullness, they have managed to garner a respectful viewer following (notable in a platform where funny-cat and cute-baby videos hold sway).

In these videos, a camera focuses on a Geiger-counter screen that reads radiation levels. The Geiger counter is moved about an environment or over an item (e.g., a drain pipe, wet paper towel), and the counter's readings are interpreted by a narrator (the person holding the counter and producing the video, but whom we never really see). Figure 11.1 below provides an example of the introductory text and a transcription of the first thirty seconds of one video.[1]

The majority of the YouTube Geiger-counter videos we were able to access online measure radiation levels in Japan, the United States, and Canada, but some videos measure radiation levels in the Philippines, China, Korea, and Australia. Early videos tended to focus on radiation levels in rainwater; more recent videos show Geiger-counter measurements of radiation levels in food (canned and packaged fish, fruits, vegetables) and beverages (milk and juice). While many of the original videos posted after March 2011 are no longer available on YouTube, there currently exist over eight hundred Geiger-counter videos related to the Fukushima nuclear incident.

Its traction, however modest, made us curious about the genre's emergence and the exigencies that motivated its existence. More important, we wondered about this genre's emergence in relation to the public roles it offers its producers, roles that appear to redefine what it means to participate in risk assessment and, by implication, in scientific discourses of expertise. As others have indicated, new media platforms have been powerful in their ability to give agency to particular publics, making it possible for publics to legitimately participate in domains that, until recently, have been considered the domains of experts. In fact, new media platforms and related technologies have furnished members of the public not only with the means to assess radiation levels but also with new genres to communicate their assessments of risk. Public attention (how much something is "liked," forwarded, or Tweeted), in turn, legitimizes these genres in the public domain and

March 28th, 2012 rain check, HOT RAIN!

firebombclipper

Published on 28 Mar 2012

Well here we go again. More fukushima fallout on my lawn. Looks like 9–10 times background. All my tests are in micro-sieverts per hour. This is fallout. And for the raydon folks I checked my 130 year old stone basement. Normal... 0.12 – 0.13 micro-sieverts

Time	Video	Script/sound
0.00	Close-up shot. Indoor setting Black background. SOEKS Geiger counter on table showing screen with Green-colored reading of 0.17.	[Sound of Windows Operating System opening] Good morning from Eastern Ontario. We seem to be getting some rain today, so I... wiped my windshield.
0.21	Extreme close-up shot (zoom) of SOEKS Geiger counter showing screen with green colored reading 0.16	This is my regular background you're looking at. And....
0.30	Pan left to close-up sot of dish on table with paper towel inside.	... we'll carry it over here. I...wiped my windshield with a paper towel and folded it. And...

Figure 11.1. Example of transcript analysis of YouTube video.

leads to further attention and uptake, which often involves further production and circulation of these genres. In this way, boundaries between genre owners (government and scientific producers of risk-communication genres) and genre users (public consumers of risk-communication genres) are renegotiated.

Our analysis of Geiger-counter videos reveals that such boundary crossings or circumventions mark sites of redefinition where scientific discourses of expertise furnish occasions for members of the public to reimagine their roles as risk assessors. In fact, we found that online public participants in radiation-risk assessment activities harness scientific discourses of empiricism and objectivity to reimagine their roles as legitimate knowledge producers. This indicates that street-science genres, such as the YouTube Geiger-counter video, can be seen as niche responses to technological and discursive affordances made possible by the interactions and workings of scientific discourse itself. Thus, this chapter explores how boundary discourses (and related boundary genre performances) afford opportunities for new, competitive configurations of the public and, by implication, legitimate public involvement in risk assessment. In our analysis, we pay particular attention to the ways in which scientific discourses of expertise—unanchored by socioinstitutional boundaries but nonetheless ecologically crucial to the exigencies of public genres—act as text-external features that motivate generic activity.

We first present existing research on public involvement in radiation-risk assessment and risk assessment in general. We then explore a familiar metaphor in communication studies—the ecology metaphor—as a way to understand the complex intertextual and extratextual interactions that occur between multiple discourse communities and that give the Geiger-counter genre its motivational character. Central to our exploration is media niche theory, which we consider in light of rhetorical genre studies' accounts of exigence in online environments.

RISK-COMMUNICATION, PUBLIC-PARTICIPATION, AND PUBLIC-SCIENCE GENRES

Research on public engagement in science and risk assessment tends to focus on two configurations: (1) citizen science, which involves collaborations among lay persons and scientific experts, a result of the general push to engage public actors in research and engender support for research activity and (2) street science, produced by lay persons, often a result of public skepticism or mistrust of government and scientific expertise and/or a desire to include alternative community perspectives. Because citizen science highlights alliances between scientists and the public in the pursuit of new knowledge (Irwin 1995), the public's role in these alliances often accommodate the exigencies or motivations of researchers; that is, public involvement (e.g., conducting assessments or interviews within one's community) contributes to the production of scientific knowledge and thus to the production of "expert" rather than "lay" genres (e.g., a peer-reviewed article) or more traditional science and risk-communication genres that members of a public consume (e.g., Q&As, a public-event poster, an information leaflet). Street science, however, often works outside the domain of traditional knowledge-making activities and the knowledge-making roles these activities assume. Street scientists are motivated not so much by a need to contribute to existing scientific knowledge but to contribute to and/or change public policy, to offer localized public alternatives, or to augment the sort of expert knowledge that often informs policy decisions (see Corburn 2005). It would appear that publics who participate in street-science activities are defined not by any socioinstitutional role (e.g., biologist, chemist) but by their engagement in particular issues (e.g., fish toxicity). Hence, we often see street scientists recruit genres that are cheap to produce, easily untethered, and available to a wide variety of users, that is, not tied to particular contexts of use (e.g., public murals and public blogs).

To date, rhetorical genre studies has focused largely on socioinstitutional domains and on disciplined uptakes performed through disciplinary-sanctioned genres. But what happens to public productions of knowledge when there aren't officially sanctioned genres to enable legitimized or disciplined uptakes? How might street scientists recreate or repurpose disciplinary-sanctioned genres (rather than unsanctioned genres) and so perform the uptakes they need to legitimately participate in discussions around risk objects? To repurpose or transform official genres, public producers of these genres require, we imagine, the same conditions researchers have documented for members of other discourse communities engaged in these practices. In her study of engineering students' transformation of workplace genres, Natasha Artemeva (2009) finds that genre transformation requires "cultural capital, domain content expertise, and agency in the rhetor's ability to both seize and create kairotic moments in the chronological flux of time and respond to them in a proportional manner" (167). Our study supports the idea that rather than challenge official discourses in contexts where public actors do not have the required conditions to transform official genres, public producers work in their own domain, in new media environments where public production and uptake are paramount. Yet as we shall see below, public producers operating in public domains do not completely reject official risk-communication discourses and related genres; instead, they adopt the features of scientific discourse in their own genres, a move that both recognizes and challenges the power of scientific discourses of expertise.

As Carolyn Miller (2003) suggests, public engagements in risk assessment and related policy development can be hindered by a larger discourse of scientific expertise, one rooted in appeals to ethos rather than logos. In her analysis of the Atomic Energy Commission's *Reactor Safety Study* (1975), she notes that claims about radiation risks were based on the testimony of experts *as experts* (e.g., "in my expert opinion") rather than on findings from empirical studies, which, she points out, would have been difficult given the future-oriented, speculative nature of nuclear-risk assessment. More important for this chapter, Miller (2003) also raises questions about the ways this discourse of expertise shaped perceptions of public involvement in risk-assessment activities. While technical experts rely on ethical appeals for their claims about the risks associated with nuclear power, public opinions are often measured against the standard of empirical evidence. Falling short of this standard, public assessments are characterized, by risk researchers, as "risk perceptions"; expert opinions, on the other hand, are characterized as "risk analysis" (Miller 2003, 188). In other words, the public has perceptions and technical experts have analysis. Miller (2003) suggests that these characterizations may reflect and reinforce unequal power relations between scientific and nonscientific groups in ways that impede public involvement in risk-assessment and risk-communication efforts. Studies in other fields echo Miller's (2003) observations. For example, Brian Wynne's (1996) study of sheep farmers' assessments of nuclear risk in Cumbria after Chernobyl, and Gwen Ottinger's (2010) study of public assessments of air quality near a chemical plant in Louisiana, indicate that decision makers often disregard public contributions to decision-making processes, appealing, as they do, to the logic of "objective standards" to negate contestation of power by publics. This rhetorical strategy of setting impossible standards aims to keep nonexperts out of decision making and acts, as Miller (2003) implies, as a boundary discourse between experts and the public.

DISCURSIVE BOUNDARIES AND
INTERDISCURSIVE GENRE RELATIONS

In her research on public environmental debates on air-pollution risks in the United Kingdom, Anna Solin (2004) explores the overlap of text-based features in risk-related publicly available genres produced by government officials and scientific experts. She describes this intertextuality in terms of chains because, in her study, she found that the textual features she identified in scientist and government risk-communication genres were transferred to media and advocacy genres in a unidirectional process that did not acknowledge (e.g. in their citation practices) media or public contributions to the larger discourse on pollution risks.

While useful for demonstrating the media uptake of publicly available expert risk genres, Solin's (2004) use of the chain metaphor is problematic in a number of ways. First, this unidirectional framework neglects to acknowledge instances in which scientists and government agents draw on the textual and extratextual resources of media and advocacy groups. Second, the growing body of work on the "mediatization" of science indicates that mass-media discourses have transformed, to some extent, the practices of scientists. A number of scientists not only consider how their work will be reported in the media but also modify their scientific practices and the objects they study to accommodate the potential of media reporting (see, for example, Peters et al. 2008; Rödder 2011). Lastly, Solin (2004) acknowledges that government experts' and scientists' definitions of risk are contested by publics, but her work does not account for the ability of publics to create their own alternative definitions of risk or supplement official sources of information in publicly-generated genres that appeal to a wider public. A prominent example of this kind of alternative definition, and the generic creativity it implies, is captured by the publicly produced online mapping "mashups"[2] created from publicly collected and official data about radiation risk from Fukushima. According to Jean-Christophe Plantin (2011), these mapping "mashups" may have put pressure on the Japanese government to produce their own publicly interpretable radiation maps. This example suggests that new media platforms have made it possible for publics to cross or circumvent the expert/nonexpert boundaries that have, until recently, circumscribed participatory roles in risk discourses.

ECOLOGICAL METAPHORS

To account for more complex discursive interactions than the one implied in Solin's chain metaphor, we turn now to research that draws on ecology metaphors. Rhetorical genre theorists have also used the ecology metaphor to examine textual interactions. However, these scholars focus on the ways genres, in a given genre ecology, are situated and interact within one organization (see work by Spinuzzi and colleagues), one discourse community (see Sherlock 2009 on gaming communities) and, more recently, one physical location (see Schryer et al. [2011; 2012] on health professional-patient interactions). According to Spinuzzi and Zachry (2000), a genre ecology "includes an interrelated group of genres (artifact types and the interpretive habits that have developed around them) used jointly *to mediate the activities* that allow people to accomplish complex objectives" (172). In their exploration of the ways genres interact in open systems (or ecologies), Clay Spinuzzi and Mark Zachery's account of the opportunistic use of unofficial genres (e.g., the use of an unofficial genre, the Post-It note, with an official genre, the map used in a police officer's office) to mediate activities suggests that divergence and improvisation characterize genre ecologies (2000, 174). Indeed, drawing on Freedman and Smart's (1997) work on this topic, Spinuzzi describes genre ecologies in terms of their "dynamism and adaptability to exigencies" and in terms of their "opportunistic coordinations" (Spinuzzi 2004, 5).

Theresa Heyd (2009), however, uses the concept not to explore inter-actions among genres within a given space, time, or community, but to trace the antecedents of Internet genres to show how a genre can evolve out of a group of genres. These studies indicate that the ecology metaphor offers us a way to describe complex genre interactions and the selection pressures operating within particular environments and/ or over time that condition genre use or emergence. Yet rather than thinking about genres evolving out of other genres or interacting—opportunistically, collegially—within one socioinstitutional domain, we might think about the ways genre interaction and emergence are effects of a broader ecology, a discourse ecology in which official discourses and the participatory roles they afford are recognized, challenged, and transformed, then redistributed in and through emerging, alternative genres. In this chapter, we explore how far we can extend the ecology metaphor in order to better understand how scientific discourses of expertise might be challenged in a publicly produced, emerging risk-assessment genre. Doing so, however, requires understanding how ecol-ogies work, such as those drawn from niche theory.

ESTABLISHING NICHES

Initially developed in the field of ecology to explain the interaction between species and competition for resources (Leibold 1995), niche theory has also been used by media theorists to describe and predict the ways in which particular Internet-based mediums or platforms become outmoded and excluded or find a space to coexist with oth-ers (Dimmick, Feaster, and Ramirez 2011; Dimmick and Rothenbuhler 1984). In media studies, niche theory has mostly been used to account for patterns of media use by individuals. For example, John Dimmick et al. (2011) investigate the competing personal social-network channels of communication used by US college undergraduates in the context of their limited time and attention. They found that interpersonal chan-nels of communication (e.g., text messaging) can coexist as well as com-pete with each other because of three overlapping resource dimensions (or selection pressures) that create different user needs: type of relation-ship (e.g., family, close friend, or boss), time (e.g., amount available or time of day), and space (e.g., work, school, or home). Rather than ear-lier conceptions of niche work in which a medium was thought to always displace another medium (e.g., the replacement of the telegraph or the home telephone with online and mobile technology), these research-ers see a much more complex system of medium competition and coexistence operating within niches. In their genre analysis of blogs, Miller and Shepherd (2009) also refer to the resource dimensions of online mediums, but they describe these dimensions as "affordances" associated with online technology. These affordances include the inter-actional opportunities provided by the medium (the combination of the number of people producing online communication and the number of people viewing it), its inexpensive, speedy transmission and archiving abilities (see also Giltrow and Stein 2009), its multimodal components (verbal, written, and visual aspects), and the medium's fittingness or ability to satisfy participants (Miller and Shepherd 2009).[3] Miller and Shepherd (2009) suggest that the technological affordances themselves may provide rhetorical exigencies, that is, opportunities to act. Here, affordances depend on, but also define, a situation.

Considered from this perspective, Internet-based genres could be expected to remain unstable because they respond to ongoing changes in media technology as well as the changing needs and active work of what Axel Bruns (2006, 2008) has called "produsers." According to Bruns, produsers (rather than producers) "engage not in a traditional form of content production but are instead involved in produsage—the collaborative and continuous building and extending of existing content in pursuit of further improvement" (Bruns 2006, 2). Produsers make choices about the communication mediums they use based on the gratifications these mediums provide to users and other produsers. Genre scholars have referred to the uses and gratifications online medi-ums provide to produsers in a number of ways. Giltrow and Stein (2009) point to the push-pull aspects of online mediums, and, as we have seen, Carolyn Miller and Dawn Shepherd refer to the suasory (pleasing or satisfying) qualities of online technology to discuss rhetorical exigence in genre studies. The idea of a niche accounts for these affordances and accounts for the uses and gratifications these affordances permit or enable. Niche theory, with its focus on affordances and on competition, can help us better understand the exigencies that condition and define social actions, as exemplified within genres and, more broadly, mediums or platforms.

PUBLIC GENRES AS NICHE RESPONSES: THE CASE OF YOUTUBE GEIGER-COUNTER VIDEOS

As Michael Warner (2002) argues, publics can only really exist in and through discourse; that is, a discourse imagines a public, brings it into being by presupposing and anticipating its response (its "active uptake"), and requires for its existence "renewed attention" (419). Such attention provides discourse participants with opportunities to renew membership in the public or, in some cases, redefine or reimagine membership and thus the exigencies the discourse defines. For example, Grafton and Maurer (2007), in their exploration of blogs, argue that bloggers' discursive activities validate "the self as an integral part and perpetuator of discursive publics" (167). As "perpetuator[s] of discursive publics," bloggers (e.g., homeless bloggers writing about homelessness) reimagine or redefine the subject positions afforded members of a discursive public (e.g., homeless, yes, *and also* activist *and* citizen) (169). We suggest, then, that public genres of the sort Kathryn Grafton and Elizabeth Maurer examine could be considered niche responses to the *discursivity* of publics, that is, active uptakes marked, to some degree, by a competitive impulse. So we see, for example, competitive uptakes such as mapping mashups that intervene in official risk-assessment discourses and the public roles these discourses assume. The emergence of alternative public actions and roles following Fukushima suggests, in fact, that if publics are produced in and through discourse, then discourse, like online platforms, may very well be an *ecological exigence*, one that furnishes occasions not only for the competitive redefinition of publics but also for the exigencies these publics represent and that discourse defines.

As our earlier work on public risk-assessment practices in Canada (Riedlinger and Rea 2012, 2015) indicates, the public addressed in and through official radiation-risk discourse is, more specifically, an *affective* public, a public concerned and anxious about the dangers posed by the Fukushima nuclear incident. This affective public comes into being through official "expert" discourse characterized by its unidirectional communicative assumptions, its appeals to pathos (appeals to public concern and its alleviation) rather than ethos or logos, and an initial presumption that the matter was settled, closed (*there is no risk*). Marked by affect and certainty, official radiation-risk discourse defined an exigence (the need to stem public panic and possibly forestall larger questions about the safety of the Canadian nuclear-energy industry). However, our analysis of online comments posted to media sites revealed that members of the public (addressed in online news reports) were mistrustful of official discourse; questions about political machinations and histories of misinformation were posted alongside references to, among other things, Chenobyl, the Canadian government's handling of the H1N1 flu outbreak, and the Chalk River, Ontario, nuclear shutdown in 2009. In the context of discursive mistrust, members of the public found ways of shifting the discourse, opening it up, inviting epistemic involvements rather than simply affective ones. In turn, these public epistemic involvements, marked as they were by scientific uncertainty and appeals to logos, perpetuated a different sort of discursive public, one engaged in knowledge-making activities that afforded different subject positions for participants in the discourse (concerned citizen, yes, *and also* street scientist *and* public educator).

One of these niche responses to the certainty of official radiation-risk discourse is, of course, the production of the YouTube Geiger-counter video. It emerges in the context of other epistemic online activities that showcase public assessments of risk (e.g., radiation-monitoring sites such as the citizen-sourced SafeCast in Japan)[4] and highlights public imperatives to widen the niche available for these activities. Indeed, these epistemic responses arise out of and are responses to the limits of official discourse, in this case to the limits of untrustworthy information and a lack of ongoing, updated assessments of risk. So what we see in the Geiger-counter videos we examine is a discourse uptake, a competitive niche action that legitimates participation in a discourse of scientific expertise but that also affords opportunities for different instantiations of this discourse and the public it assumes.

Typically, YouTube Geiger-counter video produsers establish a niche for themselves to occupy in the online radiation-risk ecology by highlighting the need for independent public radiation-risk monitoring videos. This often involves invoking public expressions of need, such as the one TheLonewolfottawa invokes in the preamble to his video: "I figured I'd come out and take a reading for yous 'cause I was stopped in public actually by a guy on YouTube, headmaniac. And uh . . . he seemed quite upset that I wasn't doing videos anymore . . . so this is for you headmaniac." More often, though, establishing need involves identifying a gap in the larger discourse, a gap that media and government should be filling but are not: "Any local news or government website could have done video tests like this and dispelled a lot of fear that guys like Alex Jones have been hyping. . . . I hope to be able to do some more baseline tests as the reactors are still in full or partial melt and further explosion due to the molten fuel hitting water" (STEVEDIGIBOYtv). Produsers also position themselves as independent assessors of radiation risk working within a community of independent assessors; they do this by referring to the existing state of knowledge on radiation risk in Canada that has been produced by fellow citizen scientists and by providing links, in the written preamble to their videos, to public radiation-monitoring sites.

All of these moves (highlighting a community need, identifying a gap media or government should be filling, and demonstrating the wider independent radiation-risk-monitoring niche) contribute to niche work. These moves work in much the same way as the moves associated with niche making that John M. Swales (1990) identified in researchers' articles. Like researchers, produsers attempt to establish the necessity of the work they are doing and create a space for these videos to coexist with other forms of radiation monitoring in Canada. Moreover, the public comments linked to individual YouTube videos confirm the validity of these contributions as legitimate uptakes in a wider discourse ecology of radiation risk. In fact, in many, many instances, posters thank produsers for their efforts and in so doing often acknowledge the gap produsers attempt to address.

> thanxs, something your not going to hear about on mainstream (scared straight100, March 28, 2012).

> The government as usual tells us nothing (unless it's a lie) so we've got to educate ourselves. Thanks for the motivation! (SparkyMcBiff, August 14, 2011)

> Thanks man. You're doing a great thing here! I love that you did a few in one day. It helps with plotting decay when it rains. . . . Where is the Government / Health Canada / CBC? (Firebombclipper, August 14, 2011)

More important, posters confirm produsers' contributions as legitimate epistemic contributions, often referring to produsers' activities using the language of empirical study, of tests, measurements, evidence, and data.

> Great work bro. You take the time to do these videos and log the data etc (RadLevelsEngland, September 8, 2012).

> Can you run a test at the same spot after the rain is dried up so we have some sorta idea what normal is for that location. (connectingdots2, September 8, 2012)

> Proper methodology would involve collecting a sample and taking measurements at regular intervals over the course of several hours. (timsolrey, October 19, 2013)

In addition to establishing the wider niche that the videos themselves are meant to occupy, YouTube Geiger-counter video produsers make a number of standardized moves within their videos that are worth mentioning. These moves include establishing an initiating event (e.g., a change in weather), establishing a background or baseline reading, providing an intervention (e.g., soaking a paper towel with rainwater, moving the Geiger counter across a landscape), highlighting results, and interpreting the results. For example, after introducing an intervention, produsers, such as electrosyl, highlight results by pointing to changes (if any) to the baseline reading: "So . . . I would say this is 10 000 counts per minute . . . [6 sec pause] . . . or 10 milirenkins per hour" (August 24, 2011). In this case, the radiation reading has increased from 100 to 10,000 counts per minute. In all cases, produsers focus our attention, via close-ups, on the number on the Geiger counter and the movement of the counter's stripes, which represent, apparently, the objective evidence for the interpretation of results: "Lots of stripes in that little graph above the main window. [3 sec pause]. It does seem to be . . . staying high and . . . beeping lots, eh?" (firebombclipper, March 28, 2012). Produsers also emphasize their results through expressions of surprise, exclamations, or expletives: "Fuck. Do you see that there? It's point 66" (TheLoneWolfOttawa, September 3, 2013). This "surprise" may be an attempt to capture the distance between the produser and the resulting radiation reading. That is, the change in reading is as much a surprise to the produser as to their imagined viewers. While we see produsers working hard in these videos to distance themselves from the radiation measurements they make, mirroring the distancing moves in scientific genres, the "results move" particularly emphasizes this distancing.

We can consider the exigence of the moves mentioned above in light of Miller's (2003) work on expert scientific discourse and the public it addresses, a public with opinions rather than analyses. Given this official discursive context, video produsers' choices to focus on the scientific experimental process is not only understandable but essential. As risk-communication researchers have indicated, and as we point out above, one important rhetorical strategy to delimit active public uptakes in risk-assessment discourse is to set impossible measurement standards (Ottinger 2010; Wynne 1996). If, as Miller argues, risk-assessment discourse is a boundary discourse between decision makers and the public, it is not surprising that produsers not only adopt the boundary-marking language advocated by experts but use it to challenge expert claims associated with radiation risk and to fill perceived gaps in public information. Indeed, produsers, working within and in response to radiation-assessment discourse, recognize the authority embedded in the scientific method and make use of the features of scientific-communication genres to establish their own authority. In doing so, they also challenge the authority of experts as the only community able to make claims about radiation risk in Canada.

Most notably, produsers appeal to the scientific concepts and activities valued within research communities: to the value of random sampling, controls, reproducibility, correlations, and scientific objectivity. For example, STEVEDIGIBOY emphasizes random sampling as a significant factor in his videos: "Those are three . . . or . . . more than three random samples at each location here and we're not picking up any shocking numbers so that is good news" (June 29, 2011). Other produsers preempt viewers' criticisms of their methodology by claiming that they have controlled their radiation assessment for other forms of radiation: "Well here we go again. More fukushima fallout on my lawn. Looks like 9–10 times background. All my tests are in micro-sieverts per hour. This is fallout. And for the raydon [sic] folks I checked my 130 year old stone basement. Normal . . . 0.12–0.13 micro-sieverts" (firebombclipper, March 28, 2012). Some produsers measure radiation levels in the same spot and refer to the need for reproducible results or make statements related to the need for "objective" readings. Interestingly, it is this appeal to scientific standards that most captures the imagination and encourages the active uptake of viewers. In fact, in comments linked to these videos' sites, posters often engage, themselves, in discussions of methods. For example, indigruv points out that there might be a methodological problem with the results of the reading: "Putting your meter in a bag can give false readings, due to buildup of gases inside the bag" (September 8, 2012). And pcuimac asks, "Do you really measure mSv/h ? It should be micro not milli Siverts / hour. 10^–6 not 10^–3?" (June 29, 2011).

PUBLIC NICHE ROLES

As a boundary discourse between decision makers and the public, radiation-risk assessment and its associated genres are constructed to appeal to both expert and nonexpert viewers who make up the discourse community of an Internet-using public concerned about radiation risk from Fukushima. This creates a number of roles for produsers of YouTube Geiger-counter videos as they validate, to borrow Grafton and Maurer's words, "the self as an integral part and perpetuator of discursive publics" (Grafton and Maurer 2007, 167). They can be peers who are contributing to the collective knowledge of the community, educators who are giving explanations to others about the technical aspects of radiation risk, or concerned citizens raising the alarm on behalf of others as part of their civic duty. Produsers' roles as contributors of knowledge to radiation-risk discussions are clear not only in the "scientific" moves they make but in the way they highlight the contributions of their peers and emphasize the community focus of this genre. For example, some produsers encourage others to create their own YouTube Geiger-counter videos, assess radiation risk for themselves, and generate more knowledge for the community. Other produsers welcome criticism from the community to strengthen their own performances. For example, electrosyl writes in the preamble to their video, "Some of you have sent me really good info and I want to share it with all of you. . . . Thanks for all your comments, including the negative ones!" (August 24, 2011).

In addition to referring to viewers as though they are potential contributors to knowledge, produsers demonstrate attempts to "educate" viewers about the Geiger-counter videos and their use and therefore take on the role of public science educators. As JJ Gittes explains, "I mentioned before there's a graph on top that lets you know when it picks up the radiation . . . the other bar on the top is a twenty second countdown so basically you have to wait . . . at least . . . ah . . . for it to take five . . . uh measurements here . . . five twenty second measurements and that gives you . . . ah . . . the ah . . . Backgr . . . gives you the Background re . . . the proper readin . . . the accurate reading" (August 21, 2011).

Finally, produsers fulfill the role of concerned citizens in their videos, raising issues on behalf of others as part of their civic duty. This role is evident, for example, in the titles produsers choose for their videos: *Dangerous Radiation Levels Detected In Canada* (electrosyl, August 24, 2011) and *HOT RAIN!* (firebombclipper, March 28, 2012). These titles seem to combine elements from both newspaper-article titles and sensational YouTube-video titles. What is interesting about the role suggested in these titles is that it echoes the sort of public assumed in official online radiation-risk discourse: a concerned, anxious public (note the use of emotive language ["dangerous," "HOT"] and punctuation [!]). In the process, this role calls into being a concerned, anxious public of its own. This confirmation of affective rather than epistemic involvement might, however, be the result of the online media platform itself. YouTube videos, to garner attention or active uptake, seem to require such discursive addressees and the involvements they represent, just as some newspaper articles do. A quick scan of the top Canadian YouTube video titles show similar strategies: *Pretending to be Famous Experiment! Sorry, Zombie Panic in Quebec, Driver and Cyclist Fight in Downtown Vancouver Street* (February 1, 2014). As we have suggested, the visual content and narrator commentary appeal to epistemic discourses of expert risk assessment rather than affective fears, so the "neutrality" and "objectivity" of the videos themselves stand in stark contrast to the sensationalism of their titles. It makes sense, though, that as a genre in a media platform, the YouTube Geiger-counter video would take on, to some extent, the rhetorical conventions and stylistic predispositions of its platform, especially in a context in which produsers compete for viewers' attention.

As our brief account of YouTube titles indicates, it would be remiss to neglect the discursive role of the YouTube platform itself in helping to shape the genre of the YouTube Geiger-counter video. The visual nature of the YouTube platform means that produsers make choices about what to emphasize in their videos based on what they can film. The focus of these videos is primarily on the Geiger counter and its screen and on the object being measured. At no time in these videos is the produser or a human subject visible. The fact that produsers choose to focus on the Geiger counter and the measured object emphasizes the measurement rather than the measurer, the demonstration rather than the demonstrator. We could liken this to the use of agentless passive language (e.g., the data were obtained) or the ways agency is attributed to non-human agents in scientific research papers (e.g., the results show). In addition, produsers use the camera zoom and pan functions to emphasize particular niche-identifying or niche-filling moves in the videos. For example, all baseline readings and results require extreme close-ups of the Geiger-counter screen, and produsers often introduce interventions by panning or zooming out to encompass the object being measured. It is clear that instances of this genre would be impossible to produce without the technological affordances of the YouTube platform, without its visual emphasis, dissemination capability, and its community-engendering focus.

SOME CONCLUDING THOUGHTS

We have attempted in this chapter to explore the exigencies that motivate the emergence of public genres, paying particular attention to the YouTube Geiger-counter video genre. One of these exigencies, of course, is new media, which is often promoted as a public platform, or space, for public consumption and production. It is not a stretch, then, to speculate that changes in technological affordances will continue to influence public exigencies under conditions in which public produsers dominate and Internet-based genres become sites of even greater public activity. However, while we note that the participatory moves and roles exemplified in the YouTube Geiger-counter video are enabled by the technological affordances that have redefined recurring social action in online environments, we suggest that this genre's emergence can only really be accounted for by examining its operation, not only in relation to other genres and/or in the contexts of online platforms but in relation to and within a larger discourse ecology brought together around radiation risk (in this case, an ecology of scientific, government and public discourses of expertise). As we have attempted to show, street-science genres, such as the Geiger-counter YouTube video, are attempts to both engage in and compete with official discourses of radiation risk. Geiger-counter YouTube video produsers co-opt discourses of expertise, but in doing so they compete with these same discourses, offering, as they do, alternative discourses of radiation risk, alternative identities for those who participate in these discourses, and a genre that defines these alternatives and the need for their existence.

Our study, then, offers a way to understand how public genres emerge as predictable responses to official or dominant discourses—as definitional strategies that legitimatize public actions and reimagine public identities. We suspect that discourse ecologies—complex interactions of discourses interacting with other discourses—furnish opportunities for the identification and fulfillment of niches. That is, street science and other public genres can be seen as niche responses to the affordances made possible in the interactions and workings of discourses themselves. Other studies, of course, have examined the relation between genre and discourse, but these studies typically focus on the ways various discourses (academic, professional, or institutional) are represented and enacted in genres tied to specific socioinstitutional domains (e.g., hospitals, engineering firms, research labs). Yet discourses often reflect and reinforce larger, more widely dispersed exigencies, often of power and control. These, in turn, are enacted within particular situations through the genres that name these situations. For example, in analyses we have done on social-work language practices (Rea and Riedlinger 2013), we have observed, casually, that localized legal and medical discourses interact with widespread public discourses on the child, the family, and on gender. The specificity of these discourse interactions is enacted in the genre (social-work recording), which is shaped by and is a response to both the local exigencies (the work of social workers, hospital care for children) as well as the wider exigencies these discourse interactions define. Moreover, the fact that discourses have text-external features (see Bhatia 2010; chapter 1, this volume) that show up in multiple genres means that analyses of genre would benefit from further analyses of the ways larger discourse interactions act as important components of the local exigencies genres appear to name. For example, the value of scientific objectivity, a text-external feature of a larger scientific discourse of expertise, can be seen in any number of genres; its existence across genres and contexts suggests that there is something here that needs our attention.

Thus, closer analyses of the relationship between genre and discourse in online environments—more loosely configured domains—could provide rhetorical genre studies with further insights into the complex exigencies that motivate genre emergence and performance. As our study indicates, it is only by mapping the interactions of discourse, rather than mapping interaction exclusively at the level of genre, that a fuller picture of the exigencies that motivate genre emergence and performance becomes visible.

Notes

1. See http://www.youtube.com/watch?v=r9Af47MdoDA&list=TLnA4KX6M7GyQ.
2. While some of these visual representations of radiation levels were created in collaboration with paid scientific researchers, many mapping efforts were conducted by nonprofessionals, working outside of institutions, in order to provide alternative framings of the issue in public debate. See, for example, the Safecast Network website at http://blog.safecast.org/.
3. From a broader niche perspective, these affordances are similar to the environmental conditions available to an animal within its environmental niche.
4. See also the Japan Geigermap and the international Radiation Network hosted by Mineralab, a company that sells Geiger counters: http://japan.failedrobot.com/, http://www.radiationnetwork.com/.

References

Artemeva, Natasha. 2009. "Stories of Becoming: A Study of Novice Engineers Learning Genres of Their Profession." In *Genre in a Changing World*, edited by Charles Bazerman, Adair Bonini, and Debora Figueiredo, 158–78. West Lafayette, IN: Parlor.

Bhatia, Vijay. 2010. "Interdiscursivity in Professional Communication." *Discourse & Communication* 4 (1): 32–50.

Bruns, Axel. 2006. "Towards Produsage: Futures for User-Led Content Production." In *Cultural Attitudes towards Communication and Technology*, edited by Fay Sudweeks, Herbert Hrachovec, and Charles Ess, 1–10. June 28–July 1, Tartu, Estonia, June 28–July 1. http://eprints.qut.edu.au/4863/.

Bruns, Axel. 2008. *Blogs, Wikipedia, Second Life, and Beyond: From Production to Produsage*. New York: Peter Lang.

Corburn, Jason. 2005. *Street Science, Community Knowledge and Environmental Health Justice*. Cambridge: MIT Press.

Dimmick, John, John Christian Feaster, and Artemio Ramirez Jr. 2011. "The Niches of Interpersonal Media: Relationships in Time and Space." *New Media & Society* 13 (8): 1265–82. http://dx.doi.org/10.1177/1461444811403445.

Dimmick, John, and Eric Rothenbuhler. 1984. "The Theory of the Niche: Quantifying Competition among Media Industries." *Journal of Communication* 34 (1): 103–19. http://dx.doi.org/10.1111/j.1460-2466.1984.tb02988.x.

Freedman, Aviva, and Graham Smart. 1997. "Navigating the Current of Economic Policy: Written Genres and the Distribution of Cognitive Work at a Financial Institution." *Mind, Culture, and Activity* 4 (4): 238–55. http://dx.doi.org/10.1207/s15327 884mca0404_3.

Giltrow, Janet, and Deiter Stein. 2009. "Genres in the Internet: Innovation, Evolution, and Genre Theory." In *Genres in the Internet: Issues of the Theory of Genre,* edited by Janet Giltrow and Deiter Stein, 1–26. Philadelphia, PA: John Benjamins. http://dx.doi.org /10.1075/pbns.188.01gil.

Grafton, Kathryn, and Elizabeth Maurer. 2007. "Engaging with and Arranging for Publics in Blog Genres." *Linguistics and the Human Sciences* 3 (1): 47–66.

Health Canada. December 2011. *Lessons Learned Review, Declaration of Nuclear Emergency –Japan.* Ottawa: Health Canada.

Heyd, Theresa. 2009. "A Model for Describing 'New' and 'Old' Properties of CMC Genres: The Case of Digital Folklore." In *Genres in the Internet: Issues of the Theory of Genre,* edited by Janet Giltrow and Deiter Stein, 239–62. Philadelphia, PA: John Benjamins. http://dx.doi.org/10.1075/pbns.188.10hey.

Irwin, Alan. 1995. *Citizen Science: A Study of People, Expertise and Sustainable Development.* London: Psychology.

Knox, K., G. Patry, and H. Wright. 2012. "Report of the External Advisory Committee Examining the Response of the Canadian Nuclear Safety Commission to the 2011 Japanese Nuclear Event. Ottawa: Canadian Nuclear Safety Commission." http:// nuclearsafety.gc.ca/eng/commission/pdf/EAC-Final-Report-Apr2012-e.pdf.

Leibold, Matthew A. 1995. "The Niche Concept Revisited: Mechanistic Models and Community Context." *Ecology* 76 (5): 1371–82. http://dx.doi.org/10.2307/1938141.

Miller, Carolyn. 2003. "The Presumptions of Expertise: The Role of Ethos in Risk Analysis." *Configurations* 11 (2): 163–202. http://dx.doi.org/10.1353/con.2004.0022.

Miller, Carolyn, and Dawn Shepherd. 2009. "Questions for Genre Theory from the Blogosphere." In *Genres in the Internet: Issues of the Theory of Genre,* edited by Janet Giltrow and Dieter Stein, 263–90. Philadelphia, PA: John Benjamins. http://dx .doi.org/10.1075/pbns.188.11mil.

Ottinger, Gwen. 2010. "Buckets of Resistance: Standards and the Effectiveness of Citizen Science." *Science, Technology & Human Values* 35 (2): 244–70. http://dx.doi.org /10.1177/0162243909337121.

Peters, Hans Peter, Harald Heinrichs, Arlena Jung, Monika Kallfass, and Imme Petersen. 2008. "Medialization of Science as a Prerequisite of Its Legitimization and Political Relevance." In *Communicating Science in Social Contexts: New Models, New Practices,* edited by Donghong Cheng, Michel Claessens, Nicholas R.J. Gascoigne, Jennie Metcalfe, Bernard Schiele, and Shunke Shi, 71–92. New York: Springer. http://dx.doi.org /10.1007/978-1-4020-8598-7_5.

Plantin, Jean-Christophe. 2011. "The Map Is the Debate: Radiation Webmapping and Public Involvement during the Fukushima Issue." Paper presented at the Oxford Internet Institute, A Decade in Internet Time: Symposium on the Dynamics of the Internet and Society, Oxford, UK. http://papers.ssrn.com/sol3/papers.cfm? abstract_id=1926276. http://dx.doi.org/10.2139/ssrn.1926276.

Rea, Jaclyn, and Michelle E. Riedlinger. 2012. "Rhetorical Motives, Situations, and Genre Ecologies." Paper presented at Genre 2012: Rethinking Genre 20 Years Later, Ottawa, Canada. http://www3.carleton.ca/genre2012/pdf/genre-2012-program-full.pdf.

Rea, Jaclyn, and Michelle E. Riedlinger. 2013. "Managing Risk: Social Work Recordings and Situated Talk about Language Use." Paper presented at the annual conference of the Canadian Association for the Study of Discourse and Writing, Victoria, BC.

Riedlinger, Michelle E., and Jaclyn Rea. 2012. "Constitutive Contexts and Discourse Ecology: Communicating Risk in the Aftermath of the Fukushima Nuclear Incident." In *Proceedings from the 12th International Conference on Public Communication of Science and Technology: Quality, Honesty and Beauty in Science and Technology Communication,* edited by M. Buchi, 34–38. Florence, Italy. Retrieved from http://www.pcst2012.org/.

Riedlinger, Michelle E., and Jaclyn Rea. 2015. "Discourse Ecology and Knowledge Niches: Negotiating the Risks of Radiation in Online Canadian Forums, Post-

Fukushima." *Science, Technology & Human Values* 40 (4): 588–614. http://dx.doi.org /10.1177/0162243915571166.

Rödder, Simone. 2011. "Science and the Mass Media: 'Medialization' as a New Perspective on an Intricate Relationship." *Sociology Compass* 5 (9): 834–45. http:// dx.doi.org/10.1111/j.1751-9020.2011.00410.x.

Schryer, Catherine F., Stephanie Bell, Marcellina Mian, Marlee M. Spafford, and Lorelei Lingard. 2011. "Professional Citation Practices in Child Maltreatment Forensic Letters." *Written Communication* 28 (2): 147–71. http://dx.doi.org/10.1177 /0741088311399710.

Schryer, Catherine F., Allan McDougall, Glendon R. Tait, and Lorelei Lingard. 2012. "Creating Discursive Order at the End of Life: The Role of Genres in Palliative Care Settings." *Written Communication* 29 (2): 111–41. http://dx.doi.org/10.1177 /0741088312439877.

Sherlock, Lee. 2009. "Genre, Activity, and Collaborative Work and Play in World of Warcraft Places and Problems of Open Systems in Online Gaming." *Journal of Business and Technical Communication* 23 (3): 263–93. http://dx.doi.org/10.1177 /1050651909333150.

Solin, Anna. 2004. "Intertextuality as Mediation: On the Analysis of Intertextual Relations in Public Discourse." *Text* 24 (2): 267–96. http://dx.doi.org/10.1515 /text.2004.010.

Spinuzzi, Clay. 2004. "Describing Assemblages: Genre Sets, Systems, Repertoires, and Ecologies." Computer Writing and Research Lab White Paper Series #040505-2. Austin: University of Texas; https://static.aminer.org/pdf/PDF/000/592/399 /examining_the_use_case_as_genre_in_software_development_and.pdf.

Spinuzzi, Clay, and Mark Zachry. 2000. "Genre Ecologies: An Open-System Approach to Understanding and Constructing Documentation." *AMC Journal of Computer Documentation* 24 (3): 169–81. http://dx.doi.org/10.1145/344599.344646.

Swales, John M. 1990. *Genre Analysis: English in Academic and Research Settings.* Cambridge: Cambridge University Press.

Warner, Michael. 2002. "Publics and Counter Publics." *Quarterly Journal of Speech* 88 (4): 413–25. http://dx.doi.org/10.1080/00335630209384388.

Wynne, Brian. 1996. "Misunderstood Misunderstandings: Social Identities and Public Uptake of Science." In *Misunderstanding Science? The Public Reconstruction of Science and Technology,* edited by Alan Irwin and Brian Wynne, 19–46. Cambridge: Cambridge University Press. http://dx.doi.org/10.1017/CBO9780511563737.002.

12

SPREADABLE GENRES, MULTIPLE PUBLICS
The Pixel Project's Digital Campaigns to Stop Violence against Women

Jennifer Nish

Much research to date on digital or Internet genres has focused on blogs and website homepages (Askehave and Nielsen 2005; Dillon and Gushrowski 2000; Miller and Shepherd 2004, 2009; Rak 2005). While these were important early web genres, and they are fruitfully compared to their offline, antecedent genres (see Giltrow and Stein 2009), a great deal of complex, compelling digital rhetorical activity remains understudied by rhetorical genre theorists. A particularly compelling aspect of digital genres lies in their public nature. This publicity is partly enabled by some of the affordances of digital media, such as interactivity, reach, and mobility. Scholars have noted that the degree of textual, technical, and social interactivity of the Internet and mobile phones allows individuals more opportunities to respond (to other individuals, to companies) than, say, radio or television (Baym 2010, 7).[1] Since dialogue is a key component of public activity (cf. Fraser 1990; Hauser 1999; Warner 2002; Warnick and Heinemann 2012), this increased opportunity for interaction enhances the potential for digital media to be used for public discourse. Digital media also have the potential to reach a much larger and more geographically widespread audience than previous forms of media available for everyday use by individuals (Baym 2010, 10). Mobility is another important affordance of digital media that affects the publicity of digital genres. Whereas many older forms of media, such as the landline telephone or a face-to-face conversation, required participants to be in a particular place at a particular time, some digital media enable communication in a wider range of times and places (Baym 2010, 11). While this does not automatically facilitate public dialogue, the affordances of digital media offer greater potential for public activity. To use Dylan Dryer's terms (chapter 3, this volume),

DOI: 10.7330/9781607324430.c012

publicity is an *uptake affordance* of many digital genres. Multiple forms of public activity are included in this concept of public *uptake affordances*, and digital genres often facilitate multiple and diffuse *uptake enactments*, or actions taken in response to digital genres and their affordances.

For many activist communities, engaging with genres involves a public performance; genres offer a way for a rhetor to (publicly) demonstrate membership within a public or connection to a public. One way for participants to demonstrate this public connection is by sharing materials related to that public. Digital communication can both increase the reach of public-activist genres and make the practice of spreading material more visible than some print-based forms of activist communication—for example, the spread of a digital text through social media and the web can often be tracked in ways that the spread of a pamphlet or flyer cannot. Many current digital activist campaigns create discursive materials intended to spread among a variety of communities and audiences as a part of their participants' everyday interactions with social media. Studying the processes of how genres spread offers important insight into the social and public actions performed through genres. In this chapter, I explore the ways in which what I call *spreadable genres* perform specific rhetorical functions: helping to form and coordinate publics centered around activist issues.

DIGITAL AND SPREADABLE GENRES

In *Spreadable Media: Creating Value and Meaning in a Networked Culture*, Henry Jenkins, Sam Ford, and Joshua Green describe the ways in which social media and other digital platforms provide a means for individuals to interact by sharing material with one another. The authors describe the facilitation of sharing as an aspect of media's "spreadability," defining spreadability as "the technical resources that make it easier to circulate some kinds of content than others, the economic structures that support or restrict circulation, the attributes of a media text that might appeal to a community's motivation for sharing material, and the social networks that link people through the exchange of meaningful bytes" (Jenkins, Ford, and Green 2013, 4). The concept of spreadability offers rhetorical genre theorists a useful lens for examining cultural and technological factors that influence the development, circulation, and use of genres. In particular, spreadability is involved in the creation of recurrence. As Carolyn Miller notes, recurrence is socially constructed, and the social and cultural contexts in which we interpret rhetorical situations as recurrent are key to understanding how genres work (Miller 1984, 156).

Spreadability offers rhetorical genre theorists a way to understand how digital communication contributes to recurrence by shaping and distributing rhetorical situations and generic resources across media and contexts. Examining how genres spread within and among specific publics offers an important perspective on the everyday social actions many people perform in their encounters with digital genres. These actions often involve navigating the complex forms of publicity enabled by the combination of technological affordances and social actions enabled by everyday communication through genres.

The publicity and growing popularity of spreadable genres coincide with the widespread adoption of social media. Many readers will be familiar with a variety of spreadable genres, even if the term is new. For example, Internet memes offer many well-known examples of spreadable genres, including LOLcats, Epic FAIL, Grumpy Cat, and Doge. Sites like Know Your Meme (knowyourmeme.com) provide overviews, examples, and histories of these genres, functioning as metagenres, or "situated language about situated language" for different memes (Giltrow 2002, 190). Instagram photos are another example of spreadable genres. The genre of a square-cropped mobile phone photo with a filter applied might represent a broad genre, developed through a combination of cultural influences (an upsurge in popularity of the "look" of film photography—including both the use of old film cameras and the use of postprocessing to mimic film effects in digital photos—as well as the cultural influence of social media and the desire to share moments of everyday life with others who are not physically copresent) and technological affordances (such as the interactivity and mobility provided by mobile phones and smartphones with cameras, photo-editing applications, and Internet access, along with the reach of the World Wide Web and social media). Filters offer opportunities to stylize photos, making "phoneography" more presentable for sharing. Within this broad genre are more specific genres such as food/drink photos, "what I'm doing" photos, "where I stand" photos, pet photos, and selfies. The above examples show the usefulness of Theresa Heyd's (2009) model of genre ecologies in which digitally mediated genres participate in relation to both a functionally defined supergenre and as one among several formally distinct subgenres.

Of course, collecting and sharing content is not a brand-new practice, but new technological connectivity has increased the speed and scope of travel for many texts. Jenkins, Ford, and Green explain that "an array of online communication tools has arisen to facilitate informal and instantaneous sharing" (2013, 2). These tools include digital technologies and platforms for sharing and hosting communicative content, such as social-networking websites (Jenkins, Ford, and Green 2013, 30). While Jenkins, Ford, and Green focus on "media"—by which they mean both the specific means of transmitting communication as well as the social practices that occur around these communication technologies— spreadability can also offer useful insights to rhetorical genre studies. Individual texts or even sets of genre conventions can spread through various communities and have a rhetorical impact through their circulation. One of these impacts is to help the formation and coordination of publics centered around activist issues. While the use of genres to coordinate social activity is well established within rhetorical genre studies, spreadable genres support the formation and coordination of more diffuse publics by allowing for a wider distribution of uptakes than institutional genre systems and sets allow.

Thus, the concept of spreadable genres offers useful insights into digital activists' rhetorical practices and is a helpful framework for understanding the public genres of the Pixel Project, which are the focus of this chapter. In the following case study, I examine the Pixel Project's use of spreadable genres in order to facilitate awareness and public dialogue about violence against women. In particular, I discuss two different genres used by the group, examining their construction as *spreadable* genres and their purpose to coordinate relations and carry out social actions for the group. Participants who take up the Pixel Project's spreadable genres help the organization accomplish its goals in one way or another. By passing the genre along to someone who needs it, sharing a genre more generally to spread awareness, or using the genre themselves, they participate in the public activity of the Pixel Project. Spreadable genres can help members identify with one another and with the Pixel Project, spread messages of support, offer information to those who need help, educate nonparticipants, and gain participants or support for the Pixel Project's cause.

SPREADABILITY AS UPTAKE

Rhetorical genre theory can extend the concept of spreadability by helping us understand more specifically how individual agency and social purposes play a role in spreading material: creators of a text make specific rhetorical choices to facilitate the spread of that text, and individuals who encounter a text also make choices about whether, how, and with whom to share that text. Jenkins, Ford, and Green's approach focuses on communication systems, cultural norms, and other patterns and processes that facilitate spreadability. However, they also reinforce the importance of the agency and choice of participants in this process: "Different technological choices, then, can shape the uses the public makes of media content, facilitating some while constraining others, but technologies can never be designed to absolutely control how material gets deployed within a given social and cultural context. Indeed, both popular and niche uses of technology always emerge far outside anything foreseen by the designer" (Jenkins, Ford, and Green 2013, 38). The individual rhetors who engage in creating and spreading texts are central to the processes of spreading material. Moreover, a focus on spreadable *genres* allows for attention to the social actions enabled through this process of spreading. In order to focus on its implications for rhetorical genre studies, it is useful to consider the relationship between spreadability and the concept of uptake.

Rhetorical genre theorists often discuss uptake as the interaction between texts and as the relationship between text and action. Anne Freadman, in her discussion of uptake, explains that uptake "selects, defines, or represents its object"; she posits uptake as an act of translation with specific intentions for the outcome, which is informed by the genres and uptakes preceding it (Freadman 2002, 48). Uptake, as a specific choice from a set of possible choices, includes an interpretation on the part of the person engaging in that uptake. Kimberly Emmons describes uptake as a "performative and interpretive [act]" (Emmons 2009, 140), and Heather Bastian sees uptake as "a performance that occurs within everyday life" (Bastian 2010, 55). In a public context, selecting and sharing material can be a way for individuals and groups to perform cultural and political identification. Jenkins, Ford, and Green articulate the ways in which the spreading of texts (broadly defined) shapes our "cultural and political landscape" (Jenkins, Ford, and Green 2013, 45). Spreading genres, as a form of uptake, shapes individuals' public identities and social relationships and often does so as a part of individuals' everyday rhetorical activity. It is important to distinguish between two aspects of spreadability here. Spreading a genre enactment is one form of uptake; it is not a brand-new uptake process. But the visibility of this practice has been amplified by the technological affordances and social contexts that facilitate this uptake. Alongside the increased visibility of spreading as an uptake process is an increase in genres designed with this uptake in mind. That is, as this uptake process has become more visible, genres designed for spreadability have also become more widespread across diffuse publics and social contexts. Spreadable genres invite both kinds of uptake: they invite people to spread a genre enactment (i.e., an individual text), and they invite the creation of new texts designed to spread.

To illustrate the ways spreading a genre enactment works as uptake, consider the spread of a genre via Facebook. Spreading a genre—by posting a link or clicking a Share button—involves an interpretation of that material as interesting or relevant to the sharer and some part of their network. This is partially conditioned by familiarity with social-networking genres and with Facebook's features: the profile is expected to inform audience members about its creator, and the genres of wall posts and comments are expected to be a public or semipublic performance of connection among the person who posts the content, the profile owner, and other "friends" or followers on the site. These expectations condition rhetors' choices: sharing on one's own page or posting a genre to someone else's page can be actions that carry different meanings. Furthermore, sharing a genre can distribute possibilities for a wide range of further uptakes. Members of the publics to whom a shared genre is visible might engage in a number of uptakes in response: reading or viewing the genre, sharing the genre themselves, clicking Like or commenting on the genre, responding to the genre by taking another type of action (e.g., initiating conversation with the person sitting next to them), or creating a new genre enactment (a new enactment of the shared genre or a different genre).

Drawing attention to the ways in which uptake can work collectively and individually within social systems, Emmons notes that "in most scholarship on uptake, analysis focuses on sequences of texts at the expense of attending to individual, embodied subjectivities" (Emmons 2009, 136). To extend Emmons's theorization of uptake's individual and collective functions, I propose that one important function of uptake with spreadable genres is to mediate between the individual and the collective. Individuals who take up an activist genre by spreading it—by sharing a blog post or retweeting a message, for example—are also making themselves visible to the activist public and performing their identity as an activist. When individuals share a genre that demonstrates their relationship to an activist public, they engage in an uptake that asserts their individual agency by positioning themselves in relation to a collective.

Likewise, knowledge of genres and previous uptakes influences a person's decision to choose a specific uptake in relation to their needs and desires within a particular context. Anis Bawarshi discusses this relationship between genre, uptake, and agency, describing how individual actors within genre systems become "double agents"; a writer is "both an agent of his or her desires and actions and an agent on behalf of already existing desires and actions" (Bawarshi 2003, 50). As individuals encounter digital activist genres, their interaction with those genres is shaped by their previous experiences: experiences with digital communication, experiences as participants in advocacy and activist campaigns, experiences with the cause addressed in the genre. These experiences will influence the ways in which different individuals "take up" a genre in this context. The range of possible uptakes may expand as the genre spreads to new situations. Brian Ray's (2013) analysis of *Downfall* parody videos on YouTube offers an example of a genre designed for spreadability, both in the sense that the genre enactments are intended to be shared and in the sense that the parodies invite other parodies. The parodies literally and figuratively remake the original *Downfall* movie: by adding captions to alter the meaning of the film's scenes, by altering perceptions of the original source for parody viewers, and by inserting specific political, public commentary into the parodies. In addition, the spread of multiple enactments of this genre invites participants to create their own versions; the parodies also inspire other uptakes, including news articles and comments on the YouTube videos (187–89). One can imagine a particularly spreadable parody being posted to multiple social networking sites, where it inspires commentary by the person posting it as well as that person's digital social network. Heyd points to a similar phenomenon in which the spread of digital folklore "exploits existing social networks," which both helps the genre spread and helps participants maintain contact with one another (Heyd 2009, 251). As individuals choose to spread genres, their identities are also remade—or, perhaps more accurately, simply continue to be made in the never-finished process of identity making. Individuals who choose to take up a genre by spreading it perform acts of interpretation and meaning making.

Similarly, there are multiple ways in which creating or spreading genres for an activist public are techniques for individuals' negotiation of their identities in relation to that public and its cause. Thus, *spreadability* is a fruitful term for considering the public performances of genres and their uptakes in digital contexts. In the next section, I propose that certain online activist genres are designed with spreadability in mind and that this spreadability is an integral part of building activist publics through digital media. In order to do this, I examine two digital genres used by the Pixel Project, an organization devoted to transnational digital campaigns that oppose violence against women. Each genre has a unique purpose, is composed using the affordances of a particular online platform, and reaches out to a specific audience or set of audiences. Together, the genres show how the Pixel Project brings multiple publics together and coordinates multiple uptakes in support of their cause.

THE PIXEL PROJECT: ORGANIZATIONAL
AND RHETORICAL CONTEXT

The Pixel Project describes itself as "a global, virtual, 501 (c)(3) registered nonprofit organisation which works to [take] fund-and-awareness raising for the cause to end violence against women (VAW) into the 21st Century by delivering innovative, powerful viral campaigns across various online and virtual channels including social media" (Pixel Project 2014b). The organization's purpose is to unite a public in order to end violence against women, as expressed in the campaign's tagline: "It's time to stop violence against women. Together" (Pixel Project 2014a). By situating itself as global and virtual, and by describing its campaigns as "viral," the Pixel Project aligns itself with spreadable media. Although the Pixel Project uses the more commonplace term *viral* instead of *spreadable*, its intended meaning seems to be that its campaigns are spread among many individuals and communities. In order to emphasize the agency of the people who pass these materials along, I will use the term *spreadable* instead of *viral*.[2]

The Pixel Project's main website features a variety of links to information as well as awareness- and fund-raising campaigns. In addition to its webpage and blog, the Pixel Project has a LinkedIn group with 208 members, a Twitter account with 16,900 followers, a Facebook page with 13,000 "likes," and a YouTube channel. Through these different avenues, the Pixel Project uses interconnected genres in order to target different groups of people for different purposes. There are lists of ways for men to help stop violence against women. There are fact sheets about different forms of violence and checklists for victims or their friends and family that offer suggestions for leaving and getting help. On Twitter, tweets regularly point to resources for individuals in different regions. Together, these might be considered a genre set, or even several interconnected sets. Amy Devitt notes that "a group usually operates through a set of genres to achieve the group's purposes, but the nature of that genre set varies in different types of groups" (Devitt 2004, 58). In particular, Devitt notes the connection between the type of group (i.e., how the people in a group are connected) and the ways in which the genres they use relate to one another (58). The Pixel Project uses genres likely to have meaning to individuals involved in activist pursuits as well as those struggling with experiences with violence. The variety and range of genres used by the organization indicate their understanding that different genres resonate with different people, in different contexts; therefore, producing a range of genres is a strategy that will likely reach a variety of populations and produce a variety of effects.

In what follows, I analyze two of the Pixel Project's spreadable genres in order to determine how they serve the Pixel Project publicly and rhetorically. The Pixel Project has a variety of online campaigns, some of which run at certain times of the year (e.g., during the month of June), and some of which are ongoing, year-round projects. In selecting the genres for analysis, I considered various features, such as the platform and modes used to produce and disseminate the genres as well as the intended audience and purpose of the genres. These spreadable genres are used to build a public; in choosing two genres, I intend to indicate that the Pixel Project accomplishes this public building in multiple ways.

ANALYZING THE PIXEL PROJECT'S SPREADABLE GENRES

Jenkins, Ford, and Green note that as material is spread, it can become remade. In this way, spreadable genres facilitate multiple and diffuse uptakes. As genres are spread in particular contexts by particular individuals, they "become meaningful because they are played within [and across] certain rules and boundaries" (Bawarshi and Reiff, 2010, 84). Retweeting a Pixel Project tweet about resources for victims of domestic violence might function to identify someone as a supporter of the Pixel Project or as an ally to women who need help with a domestic-violence situation. Visiting the link might educate another participant on the kinds of resources available to women who need help. Calling a phone number might be an important step for a woman who is trying to escape a situation in which she faces domestic violence. These are several ways a genre might be taken up differently by various participants, all of which are important social actions for the Pixel Project. Through this use of multiple, spreadable genres to reach a variety of individuals, the Pixel Project attempts to construct a diverse public around the issue of violence against women and to organize and coordinate social actions that help their cause. As genres spread among different publics, a variety of people encounter the issue and the organization. Through different social networks and genres, supporters from multiple publics can engage with the Pixel Project.

HELPLINE TWEETS

The first spreadable genre I examine is a *helpline tweet*. I created this label for the genre based on the language commonly used to refer to communication on Twitter (as *tweets*) as well as the Pixel Project's own rhetoric, in which a series of tweets are referred to as a "daily Violence

Against Women Helpline Re-Tweet session" (@PixelProject February 22, 2014). The helpline tweet is one of several Twitter genres used by the Pixel Project. Other Twitter-based genres include promotional tweets for current campaigns, tweets about other domestic-violence-related organizations and projects, and tweets that direct followers toward domestic-violence resources in various regions and languages via links (@PixelProject). These genres are mixed in various ways in the Twitter feed for the campaign. Often, a series of tweets in the same genre will be posted sequentially; tweets relating to a region (e.g., Israel or Brazil) may also be grouped together.

In order to analyze the genre of the helpline tweet, I collected all tweets from the Pixel Project's twitter account for a one-week period (February 1–7, 2014), which resulted in a selection of 565 tweets. I then gathered the helpline tweets that occurred within this selection. For my sample, I defined the helpline tweet as a tweet that included contact information (usually a phone number) in the tweet itself. The tweet typically identifies the audience of the organization to which it refers (e.g., women in a particular region) and the purpose of the helpline (e.g., "for help with domestic violence"). Helpline tweets made up 65 percent of the sample (364 tweets), making this genre a substantial portion of the Pixel Project's Twitter activity. The helpline tweet is primarily circulated via Twitter and is one of several spreadable genres used by the Pixel Project to point victims of violence toward help. The genre is posted daily by the campaign's Twitter Tag Team members, who are volunteers charged with regularly sending out tweets for the organization.

The helpline tweet in Figure 12.1, for example, is intended to spread, via Twitter, to women in India: "#INDIA: For women facing sexual abuse & domestic violence, call 8793088814 /15 /16 (This is a 24/7 helpline) #VAW" (@PixelProject February 21, 2014). This style of Twitter message is a regular occurrence in the Pixel Project's Twitter feed. These tweets can often be identified with a hashtag for the country and possibly also a #VAW hashtag, which identifies the tweet as relevant to that country and to those interested in the topic of violence against women (VAW), respectively. Because hashtags can both gather and generate conversation, their use in this genre serves important social functions for the Pixel Project's public. Scholars have noted that hashtags are a part of Twitter users' folksonomy (Gleason 2013, 967; Gruzd, Wellman, and Takhteyev 2011, 1301) and serve conversational functions, helping individuals to find and contribute to conversations on Twitter (Huang, Thornton, and Efthimiadis 2010, 3, 5). Zizi Papacharissi and Maria de Fatima Oliveira contend that "hashtags present a user-generated

The Pixel Project
@PixelProject

#INDIA: For women facing sexual abuse & domestic violence, call 8793088814 /15 /16 (This is a 24/7 helpline) #VAW

↩ Reply   ⇄ Retweet   ★ Favorite   ••• More

RETWEETS
2

11:06 PM - 5 Feb 2014

Figure 12.1. Helpline tweet for victims of sexual abuse and domestic violence in India.

collaborative argument on what is news" (Papacharissi and de Fatima Oliveira 2012, 268). While the audience for the helpline tweet above seems to be people in India (or who know people in India) who need help with domestic violence (and read English), there may also be a larger audience. Some audience members will see this tweet and form an impression of who the Pixel Project is as an organization and what its purpose is; others might retweet the information as a way of identifying with the Pixel Project or the public discourse about violence against women, thus using this genre as a way of performing this public identity. Through the retweet and the various publics who see it, rhetors can make themselves visible to the Pixel Project's existing public and make the Pixel Project visible to other members of their network.

Users of the helpline tweet are interacting around the Pixel Project's general theme of violence against women but also around a specific aspect of that topic. Whereas some genres promote awareness raising, political activism, or fundraising, this particular genre appears to offer a kind of immediate assistance to victims of domestic violence. The reappearance of the tweets (the Twitter Tag Team cycles through them regularly) may work to reinforce the helpline resources (the name and/or number of the organization or helpline for people in a particular region). These tweets almost always include the name of the country to which they apply, often at the beginning of the tweet (sometimes marked as a hashtag, as in the #INDIA example in Fig. 12.1) and a telephone number. Other common elements of the genre include the name of the organization with which the phone number will connect callers, a description of the organization's area of concern or focus (e.g., domestic violence, missing persons, trafficking, rape), and, as mentioned earlier, the hashtag #VAW. Occasionally, the tweets are preceded by a request that followers share the information, such as "Pls RT" (please retweet) or "please share." This explicit request for followers to retweet the message shows that spreadability is a key goal of this particular genre; beyond simply using a genre and platform that offer this possibility, the campaign representatives specify retweeting as a desirable uptake for other members of this public. Through the retweet, the Pixel Project can reach a wider audience with this information while also expanding the public engaged in stopping violence against women. In addition, the retweet can expand the range of the genre, opening up the possibility for further uptakes: as more people see the genre, more people encounter the possible uptakes of retweeting or calling the phone number provided. Further, the spread of the genre might expand the range of uptakes; audience members might take up the genre by engaging the Pixel Project's cause in ways that relate to their own experience or expertise. A person who works at a shelter might see the genre and contact the Pixel Project about including their organization. Other audience members might take up the genre by offering to participate on the Twitter Tag Team or to translate a tweet into another language. An activist might reshape the genre for use with their own organization's cause. The spread of the genre, then, offers the possibility for multiple and distributive uptakes.

"30 FOR 30" FATHER'S DAY CAMPAIGN INTERVIEWS

Although women who are victims or survivors of violence are central to the Pixel Project's rhetorical activity, they are not the only public addressed through the organization's spreadable genres. The second genre I've chosen to examine is the "'30 for 30' Father's Day Campaign Interview" (hereafter, the "30 for 30" interview), a genre that specifically engages men. This genre uses a different platform (the Pixel Project's blog) and also varies in its purpose, which might be said to work toward *preventing* violence from occurring. According to the Pixel Project's description (see Fig. 12.2) of the "'30 for 30' Father's Day Campaign," the "30 for 30" interviews are meant to "acknowledge the vital role Dads play in families, cultures and communities worldwide" and to "provide men who are fabulous non-violent male role models with a space to publicly share their ideas, thoughts and feelings about how Dads can actively help prevent and stop violence against women" (*The Pixel Project* 2012a). The strategy of specifically addressing men and highlighting their role

"30 For 30" Father's Day Campaign 2012 Interview 1: Asohan Aryadyray, 49, Malaysia

Welcome to <u>The Pixel Project's "30 For 30" Father's Day Campaign 2012</u>! In honour of Father's Day, we created this campaign:

- To acknowledge the vital rold Dads play in families, cultures and communities worldwide.
- To showcase good men from different walks of life who are fabulous positive non-violent male role models.

Through this campaign, we will be publishing a short interview with a different Dad on each day of the month of June.

Our first "30 For 30" Dad is Asohan Aryaduray from Malaysia.

Figure 12.2. Example of the "30 for 30" interview title and introduction.

in violence against women is important. This genre attempts to spread in a way that will address a *cause* of violence against women rather than its effects.

The "30 for 30" interviews appear on the Pixel Project's blog, which is on a section of the main website. The genres are also shared via the Pixel Project's Facebook and Twitter accounts. The genre is distributed during the month of June, in honor of Father's Day. Each blog post's title includes the campaign name, the interview number, and the name, age, and location of the father interviewed. Each post also includes a brief overview of the campaign and the justification for it. This choice is appropriate for a genre intended to spread. Readers who click on a link that takes them directly to this blog post (e.g., from their Facebook news feed or a friend's tweet) will understand the context and purpose of this interview and its relationship to an organization dedicated to stopping violence against women.

The blog post then includes a short "Dad Bio (In His Own Words)," and answers to three questions:

1. What is the best thing about being a Dad?
2. A dad is usually the first male role model in a person's life and fathers do have a significant impact on their sons' attitude toward women and

girls. How has your father influenced the way you see and treat women and girls?

3. Communities and activists worldwide are starting to recognize that violence against women is not a "women's issue" but a human rights issue and that men play a role in stopping the violence. How do you think fathers and other male role models can help get young men and boys to take an interest in and step up to help prevent and stop violence against women? (*The Pixel Project* 2012b)

Through responses to these questions and the accompanying photos, fathers share their diverse experiences as sons, grandsons, and brothers as well as fathers, explaining how the men in their lives modeled the right or wrong ways to treat women and relating different experiences with fatherhood and family to the Pixel Project's work. In focusing on men and their role in stopping violence against women, these interviews send an important ideological message: violence against women is an issue that concerns men. This genre, then, works to integrate men into the public discourse of the Pixel Project.

Members of the Pixel Project's public might take up this genre in several ways. By sharing the blog posts with others (e.g., by sharing the link on social media), individuals can perform an important social action by highlighting men's relationship to this issue. Through this particular uptake (spreading the genre), participants might promote the idea that men have a responsibility to both speak out against violence against women and to model appropriate behavior for others, especially younger men. A woman who shares a "30 for 30" interview might be calling on the men she knows to take up this responsibility, thus creating new exigencies or calling for new uptakes through her act of spreading. A man sharing the "30 for 30" interview might be identifying himself as a member of this public and suggesting that he supports other men who do the same. These uptakes are enabled by the features of this blog, which includes a Share This Post! button at the bottom of each blog post (see Fig. 12.3). When readers place their cursor over the button, a menu of sharing options appears. Clicking on one of nine square logos in the menu puts the blog post's information into a post format appropriate for that website (the website options are Twitter, Digg, Facebook, Del.icio.us, StumbleUpon, Google Bookmarks, LinkedIn, Yahoo Buzz, and Technorati).

CONCLUSION

The two examples presented here offer just a glimpse of the ways in which spreadable genres allow activists to use the affordances of

Figure 12.3. Sharing options on "30 for 30" blog posts.

digital platforms in order to enact specific rhetorical strategies. Through spreadable genres that address multiple publics, the Pixel Project works to organize, coordinate, and perform public, social actions for participants. The genre of the helpline tweet reaches out to a public of victims with resources for help while also reminding other publics of important elements of the Pixel Project's mission: that violence against women is always, now, affecting women, that it is a problem across geographic boundaries, and that it is an issue for which sharing/spreading discourse is an uptake that might help (and might inspire other uptakes). The genre of the "30 for 30" interview reaches out to men as role models, fathers, and sons, emphasizing that men play a key role in stopping violence against women. This genre encourages men to enact, support, and reward healthy, nonviolent relationships with women, making men's uptakes of the genre not only multiple but central to the goals of the campaign. Women who read and share enactments of this genre can emphasize the importance of men to the work of the Pixel Project.

Arjun Appadurai has written about the increasing speed with which people, objects, and ideas flow across geographic and national boundaries, a growth in transnational traffic that includes activist discourses (Appadurai 2010, 4). "Likewise," Appadurai notes, "this current period—approximately from the nineteen seventies to the present—is characterized by the flows not just of cultural substances, but also of cultural forms, such as the novel, the ballet, the political constitution, and divorce, to pick just a few examples" (7).[3] Appadurai goes on to connect this "flow of forms" to transformations in historical and epistemological processes, noting that "the global is not merely the accidental site of the fusion or confusion of circulating global elements. It is the site of the mutual transformation of circulating forms, such as the nation and the novel. . . . The 'work of the imagination' and the circulation of forms produce localities not by the hybridization of contents, art, ideology, or technology, but by the negotiation and mutual tensions between each other. It is this negotiation which creates the complex containers which further shape the actual contents of local practice" (10–11). Appadurai speaks of broad, abstract cultural and material flows, yet his points may help us consider the implications of spreadability for the study of genres and their public performances. Spreadable genres provide rich material for rhetorical analysis and offer an especially compelling site for analyzing the complexities of transnational rhetoric. Scholars such as Rebecca Dingo (2012) and Mary Queen (2008) address the importance of understanding how rhetorics travel; rhetorical genre theorists might bring this discussion into conversation with the ways genres spread across geographic borders and cultural contexts. Perhaps, as Appadurai suggests, the spread of genres is linked to creative interventions: "Indeed, the circulation of forms produces new and distinct genre experiments, many of which are forced to coexist in uneven and uneasy combinations" (Appadurai 2010, 10). What can the idea of spreadability bring to our understanding of genre and the growing body of work theorizing uptake? We might use the idea of spreadability to consider how and why genre enactments, and genres themselves, spread across contexts and cultures, enabling distributive uptakes. Spreadability helps us understand how participants' social networks and genres operate in the formation of diffuse activist publics. Further, following Appadurai, we might consider how this spread interacts with cultural processes. As genres spread, they reach multiple publics; their uptakes coordinate activity and negotiate meaning. The genres outlined above are just two examples of many genres used by the Pixel Project. What I hope my analysis has shown is that the Pixel Project organizers, in their use of a variety of spreadable genres, use the affordances of digital media and the practice of spreading to work toward an activist public engaged in opposition to violence against women. By capitalizing on the affordances of digital media, spreadable genres and their uptakes offer ways for everyday, social actions to involve meaningful public engagement.

Notes

1. Though, of course, broadcast television as a medium doesn't allow users to respond, work on convergence shows us that new media is often employed by individuals or groups who want to "talk back" or simply interact around television or radio (cf. Jenkins 2008). Individuals and fan communities gather online and create wikis about their favorite shows, live tweet current episodes (conversations in which shows' actors, writers, and producers are often involved), write, edit and share fan fiction, and more.

2. Jenkins, Ford, and Green argue for using a concept like spreadable instead of viral, noting that although the biological metaphor viral has gained popularity in both

public and scholarly conversations, this metaphor (and others like it) neglects the ways that viewing and choosing to pass along the content involves active decision making: "Audiences play an active role 'spreading' content rather than serving as passive carriers of viral media: their choices, investments, agendas, and actions determine what gets valued" (Jenkins, Ford, and Green 2013, 29).

3. Appadurai is not a rhetorical genre theorist, so it is useful to clarify how he is using the term *form*. I offer his own explanation: "By 'forms' I mean to indicate a family of phenomena, including styles, techniques, or genres, which can be inhabited by specific voices, contents, messages, and materials. Unfortunately, the philosophical conundrum of separating form from content cannot be unraveled in this essay. In using the word 'form' I simply wish to temporarily place the issue of global circulation on a slightly more abstract level" (Appadurai 2010, 9).

References

Appadurai, Arjun. 2010. "How Histories Make Geographies." *Transcultural Studies* 0 (1): 4–13.

Askehave, Inger, and Anne Ellerup Nielsen. 2005. "Digital Genres: A Challenge to Traditional Genre Theory." *Information Technology & People* 18 (2): 120–41. http://dx.doi.org/10.1108/09593840510601504.

Bastian, Heather. 2010. "Disrupting Conventions: When and Why Writers Take Up Innovation." PhD Diss., University of Kansas.

Bawarshi, Anis S. 2003. *Genre and the Invention of the Writer: Reconsidering the Place of Invention in Composition.* Logan: Utah State University Press.

Bawarshi, Anis, and Mary Jo Reiff. 2010. *Genre: An Introduction to History, Theory, Research, and Pedagogy.* West Lafayette, IN: Parlor.

Baym, Nancy K. 2010. *Personal Connections in the Digital Age.* Malden, MA: Polity.

Devitt, Amy J. 2004. *Writing Genres.* Carbondale: Southern Illinois University Press.

Dillon, Andrew, and Barbara A. Gushrowski. 2000. "Genres and the Web: Is the Personal Home Page the First Uniquely Digital Genre?" *Journal of the American Society for Information Science* 51 (2): 202–5. http://dx.doi.org/10.1002/(SICI)1097-4571(2000)51:2<202::AID-ASI11>3.0.CO;2-R.

Dingo, Rebecca Ann. 2012. *Networking Arguments: Rhetoric, Transnational Feminism, and Public Policy Writing.* Pittsburgh, PA: University of Pittsburgh Press.

Emmons, Kimberly K. 2009. "Uptake and the Biomedical Subject." In *Genre in a Changing World,* edited by Charles Bazerman, Adair Bonini, and Débora Figueiredo, 134–57. Fort Collins, CO: WAC Clearinghouse and Parlor.

Fraser, Nancy. 1990. "Rethinking the Public Sphere: A Contribution to the Critique of Actually Existing Democracy." *Social Text* 25/26: 56–80. http://dx.doi.org/10.2307/466240.

Freadman, Anne. 2002. "Uptake." In *The Rhetoric and Ideology of Genre: Strategies for Stability and Change,* edited by Richard Coe, Lorelei Lingard, and Tatiana Teslenko, 39–53. Cresskill, NJ: Hampton.

Giltrow, Janet. 2002. "Meta-Genre." In *The Rhetoric and Ideology of Genre: Strategies for Stability and Change,* edited by Richard Coe, Lorelei Lingard, and Tatiana Teslenko, 187–205. Cresskill, NJ: Hampton.

Giltrow, Janet, and Dieter Stein, eds. 2009. *Genres in the Internet: Issues in the Theory of Genre.* Amsterdam: John Benjamins. http://dx.doi.org/10.1075/pbns.188.

Gleason, Benjamin. 2013. "#Occupy Wall Street Exploring Informal Learning About a Social Movement on Twitter." *American Behavioral Scientist* 57 (7): 966–82. http://dx.doi.org/10.1177/0002764213479372.

Gruzd, Anatoliy, Barry Wellman, and Yuri Takhteyev. 2011. "Imagining Twitter as an Imagined Community." *American Behavioral Scientist* 55 (10): 1294–318. http://dx.doi .org/10.1177/0002764211409378.

Hauser, Gerard A. 1999. *Vernacular Voices: The Rhetoric of Publics and Public Spheres.* Columbia: University of South Carolina Press.

Heyd, Theresa. 2009. "A Model for Describing 'New' and 'Old' Properties for CMC Genres." In *Genres in the Internet: Issues in the Theory of Genre,* edited by Janet Giltrow and Dieter Stein, 239–62. Amsterdam: John Benjamins. http://dx.doi.org/10.1075 /pbns.188.10hey.

Huang, Jeff, Katherine M. Thornton, and Efthimis N. Efthimiadis. 2010. "Conversational Tagging in Twitter." *Proceedings of the 21st ACM Conference on Hypertext and Hypermedia,* 173–78. New York: ACM Digital Library. http://dx.doi.org/10.1145/1810617.18 10647.

Jenkins, Henry. 2008. *Convergence Culture: Where Old and New Media Collide.* New York: New York University Press.

Jenkins, Henry, Sam Ford, and Joshua Green. 2013. *Spreadable Media: Creating Value and Meaning in a Networked Culture.* New York: New York University Press.

Miller, Carolyn. 1984. "Genre as Social Action." *Quarterly Journal of Speech* 70 (2): 151–67. http://dx.doi.org/10.1080/00335638409383686.

Miller, Carolyn R., and Dawn Shepherd. 2004. "Blogging as Social Action: A Genre Analysis of the Weblog." In *Into the Blogosphere: Rhetoric, Community, and Culture of Weblogs,* edited by Laura Gurak, Smiljana Antonijevic, Laurie A. Johnson, Clancy Ratliff, and Jessica Reyman. Minneapolis: University of Minnesota. http://hdl.handle .net/11299/172818.

Miller, Carolyn R., and Dawn Shepherd. 2009. "Questions for Genre Theory from the Blogosphere." In *Genres in the Internet: Issues in the Theory of Genre,* edited by Janet Giltrow and Dieter Stein, 263–86. Amsterdam: John Benjamins. http://dx.doi.org /10.1075/pbns.188.11mil.

Papacharissi, Zizi, and Maria de Fatima Oliveira. 2012. "Affective News and Networked Publics: The Rhythms of News Storytelling On #Egypt." *Journal of Communication* 62 (2): 266–82. http://dx.doi.org/10.1111/j.1460-2466.2012.01630.x.

Pixel Project. 2012a. "'30 For 30' Father's Day Campaign 2012 Interview 1: Asohan Aryaduray, 49, Malaysia." *The Pixel Project | It's Time to Stop Violence Against Women. Together,* June 1, 2012. Accessed March 24, 2014. http://www.thepixelproject.net /2012/06/01/asohan-aryaduray-malaysia/.

Pixel Project. 2012b. "Announcement: The Pixel Project's First Ever '30 For 30' Father's Day Campaign." *The Pixel Project | It's Time to Stop Violence Against Women. Together,* June 1, 2012. Accessed March 3, 2014. http://www.thepixelproject.net/2012/06/01 /announcement-the-pixel-projects-first-ever-30-for-30-fathers-day-campaign/.

Pixel Project. 2014a. "Home Page." *The Pixel Project | It's Time to Stop Violence Against Women. Together.* http://www.thepixelproject.net/.

Pixel Project. 2014b. "The Pixel Project—An Introduction." *The Pixel Project | It's Time to Stop Violence Against Women. Together.* http://www.thepixelproject.net/.

Queen, Mary. 2008. "Transnational Feminist Rhetorics in a Digital World." *College English* 70 (5): 471–89.

Rak, Julie. 2005. "The Digital Queer: Weblogs and Internet Identity." *Biography* 28 (1): 166–82. http://dx.doi.org/10.1353/bio.2005.0037.

Ray, Brian. 2013. "More than Just Remixing: Uptake and New Media Composition." *Computers and Composition* 30 (3): 183–96. http://dx.doi.org/10.1016/j.compcom.20 13.07.003.

Warner, Michael. 2002. *Publics and Counterpublics.* Boston: MIT Press.

Warnick, Barbara, and David S. Heinemann. 2012. *Rhetoric Online: The Politics of New Media.* New York: Peter Lang.

ABOUT THE AUTHORS

MARY JO REIFF is professor of English at the University of Kansas, where she teaches courses in rhetoric and composition theory, research, and pedagogy. She is co-managing editor of *Composition Forum* and serves on the editorial boards of the Reference Guides to Rhetoric and Composition and *Written Communication*. Her books include *Approaches to Audience: An Overview of the Major Perspectives; Genre: An Introduction to History, Theory, Research, and Pedagogy* (with Anis Bawarshi); *Ecologies of Writing Programs: Profiles of Writing Programs in Context* (with Anis Bawarshi, Christian Weisser, and Michelle Ballif); *Scenes of Writing: Strategies of Composing with Genres* (with Amy Devitt and Anis Bawarshi); and *Rhetoric of Inquiry* (with Kirsten Benson).

ANIS BAWARSHI is professor of English at the University of Washington, where he specializes in the study and teaching of writing, rhetorical genre theory, writing program administration, and research on knowledge transfer. He is co-managing editor of the journal *Composition Forum* and coeditor of the book series Reference Guides to Rhetoric and Composition. His publications include *Genre and the Invention of the Writer: Reconsidering the Place of Invention in Composition; Genre: An Introduction to History, Theory, Research, and Pedagogy* (with Mary Jo Reiff); *Scenes of Writing: Strategies for Composing with Genres* (with Amy Devitt and Mary Jo Reiff); and *Ecologies of Writing Programs: Profiles of Writing Programs in Context* (with Mary Jo Reiff, Christian Weisser, and Michelle Ballif).

* * *

RISA APPLEGARTH is associate professor of English and women's and gender studies at the University of North Carolina at Greensboro, where she teaches and conducts research in genre theory, the history of rhetoric, feminist theory, and spatial and material rhetoric. Her prior research includes the book *Rhetoric in American Anthropology: Gender, Genre, and Science* and articles in *College Composition and Communication, Rhetoric Society Quarterly,* and *College English.* Her current research investigates vocational genres and embodied rhetorical training for black and white professional women in the early twentieth century.

VIJAY K. BHATIA retired as professor from the Department of English, City University of Hong Kong. His research interests include critical genre analysis; academic and professional discourses in legal, business, newspaper, and promotional contexts; ESP and professional communication; simplification of legal and other public documents; and intercultural and cross-disciplinary variations in professional genres. Two of his books, *Analysing Genre: Language Use in Professional Settings* and *Worlds of Written Discourse: A Genre-Based View,* are widely used in genre theory and practice. He is working on his next book on genre theory, *Critical Genre Theory.*

MONICA M. BROWN, a PhD candidate in English at the University of British Columbia, studies the history and theory of rhetoric and specializes in rhetoric of health and medicine. Her research explores how different institutions, including public health agencies, communicate risk and assign responsibility for the maintenance of health and prevention of disease. In her dissertation, she examines the use of health education and promotion to engage individuals as citizens and encourage personal responsibility during infectious-disease outbreaks, from seasonal influenza to the crisis of antibiotic-resistant "superbugs." She has also written about the use of metaphor in media coverage of health research.

AMY J. DEVITT is professor of English and Chancellors Club Teaching Professor at the University of Kansas, where she teaches courses in composition, rhetoric, and English-language studies and has won numerous teaching awards. She previously served as director of Kansas's first-year writing program and as associate director of the writing-across-the-curriculum program. Her primary research specialty for over twenty years has been genre theory, with publications including the books *Writing Genres, Scenes of Writing: Strategies for Composing with Genres* (with Mary Jo Reiff and Anis Bawarshi) and *Standardizing Written English* and articles in several journals and edited collections.

DYLAN B. DRYER is associate professor of composition studies at the University of Maine. His work explores the capacities for and consequences of genre uptake, a topic with implications for teachers and students as well as for citizens and the persistence of social institutions generally. Articles addressing these topics have appeared in *CCC, JAC,* the *Community Literacy Journal, WPA, Written Communication,* and in chapters in *Naming What We Know: Threshold Concepts in Writing Studies* and *Keywords in Writing Studies.* He recently guest edited a special issue of *Composition Forum* on the past, present, and possible futures of rhetorical genre studies, now available at http://compositionforum.com/issue/31/.

JENNIFER NISH is assistant professor in the English department at the American University of Beirut, where she directs the university's writing program. She teaches undergraduate and graduate courses on digital rhetorics and academic writing. Her research interests include public rhetoric, transnational feminism, and critical media studies. Her most recent research projects explore women activists' uses of digitally mediated rhetoric to foster transnational public dialogue about feminist issues.

JACLYN REA is a senior instructor in arts studies in research and writing at the University of British Columbia, Vancouver, Canada, and chair of the UBC Vantage College Arts Program. Her areas of expertise include language ideologies, writing studies, rhetorical genre studies, and discourse analysis. Her current research investigates the interplay between epistemology and affect in a range of genres.

MICHELLE RIEDLINGER is assistant professor at the University of the Fraser Valley (UFV). Her current research focuses on discourses of environmental risk and genres of risk assessment. She is particularly interested in the boundary-communication practices of environmental science and community collaborations.

LINDSAY ROSE RUSSELL teaches at the University of Illinois at Urbana-Champaign, where she is also core faculty in the center for writing studies. Her primary research interests include rhetorical genre theory, histories and descriptions of the English language, and feminist historiography.

GRAHAM SMART is associate professor of applied linguistics and discourse studies at Carleton University in Ottawa, Canada. He has published research on writing in professional and academic settings, including his book, *Writing the Economy: Activity, Genre and Technology in the World of Banking,* an ethnographic study of the collaborative discursive knowledge-making practices of economists at Canada's central bank. His current research focuses on the discourses and argumentation of various social actors in the debate over global climate change.

TOSH TACHINO is an independent scholar whose research areas include rhetorical genre theory, academic writing, and legal genres. Recent work has appeared in *Written Communication* and *Linguagem em (Dis)curso.* His current interest is in the use of citation and reported speech in legal genres at the oral/written interface, and he is currently working on a project to analyze these features in multiple public inquiry reports. He teaches rhetorical grammar and informal logic and privately tutors academic writing, Japanese, and classical Latin.

INDEX